HOME WATERS

Jane Crosen ~ 1983

A LIFE IN BOATS

The Years
Before the War

A LIFE

IN BOATS

The Years
Before the War

by Waldo Howland

Mystic Seaport Museum, Inc.
Mystic, Connecticut   1984

To the memory of my father

Published by Mystic Seaport Museum, Inc.
Mystic, Connecticut

Design by Sherry Streeter
Typeset by WoodenBoat Publications
Printed by Casco Printing Company

Acknowledgments

The creation of this book has been in the happiest sense a collaborative effort, and my only regret about offering the acknowledgments that follow is that I cannot thank by name each and every institution and individual that helped the venture on its way.

I owe a debt to the authors of many books, especially Howard I. Chapelle (author of *The American Fishing Schooner*, New York, 1973, among other fine histories), Captain Arthur H. Clark (*The Clipper Ship Era*, New York, 1910), and Alfred F. Loomis (*Ocean Racing*, New York, 1936); as well as to contributors, known and unknown, to such boating magazines as *The Rudder*, *Yachting*, and *Yachting Monthly*, and such annuals as the *Yearbook* of the Cruising Club of America. Printed sources have not simply helped fill in the ever increasing gaps in my memory, but have often enough caused me to rethink and correct mistaken notions and assumptions.

I am deeply beholden to Margaret Gamble, for 30 years Concordia Company's bookkeeper, who dusted off her retired typewriter as my longhand chapters materialized and, with great patience and understanding, turned my secret scrawl into properly spelled and punctuated typescript.

My nephew Llewellyn Howland III (who edited these acknowledgments, as, indeed, he edited the rest of the book) bears some of the blame for launching me on my literary career. This is all Louie has allowed me to say about his part in the proceedings.

There is no way *A Life in Boats* would have seen print without the generous cooperation and sponsorship of Mystic Seaport Museum. Revell Carr, Director of the Seaport and a real friend, endorsed the project and offered a contract for it. Jerry Morris, who is head of Seaport Publications, as well as Librarian of G.W. Blunt White Library, said "Can do" and did. Anne Preuss, confronted with an impossible copyediting deadline, met that deadline with room to spare. Down at the Seaport shipyard, Don Robinson, shipyard supervisor, asked, "How can we help?" Don, Bob Allyn (marine architect), and Ginny Jones (the shipyard's woman of all works) demonstrated "how" they could help time and time again.

And that was not the end of it. With preplanned timing and top professional skill, the crew of *WoodenBoat* took on the layout, typesetting, and design work for the book. Jon Wilson, *WoodenBoat*'s publisher and editor, courageously assumed the responsibilities inherent in a project such as this. *WoodenBoat*'s technical editor, Maynard Bray, my benefactor always and project partner often during the past 15 years, suggested important corrections, additions, and alterations to text and illustrations, and was a continuing source of advice and wise counsel. Sherry Streeter, *WoodenBoat*'s brilliant art director, and Judy Robbins, production manager, transformed a heavily annotated typescript and a grab-bag of illustrations into the book you now hold in your hands.

My wife and family blessed me—and bless me still—with their unfailing support, forbearance, assistance, and love. To them, and to all who have contributed to *A Life in Boats*—to *my* life in boats—I can only say: this book is as much yours as it is mine, and thank you for all the pleasures we have shared.

Waldo Howland
Padanaram, June 1983

Preface

In *A Life in Boats* Waldo Howland recalls that astonishing period between World War I and World War II, when, despite (one might even say because of) Prohibition and the Great Depression, American yachting reached a peak of competitive excitement it seems never to have attained before or since. In craft of every dimension, from Brutal Beasts to J boats, from paint-sick prams to full-rigged ships, Americans who could afford to, and a lot more who couldn't, went about the serious business of sailing for pleasure.

Ocean racing as we know it today was a creation of the 1920s and 1930s. The International and Cruising Club rules became our dominant racing rules at this time. Some of our greatest yacht designers—John Alden, William Hand, Francis Herreshoff, Frank Paine, Starling Burgess—produced their finest work in these years. Many another designer, including Ray Hunt, Aage Nielsen, Phil Rhodes, and Olin Stephens, achieved their first fame even as the war clouds gathered and the shadow of Hitler darkened the land.

To come of age at such a time was, no matter what your ambitions or expectations might have been, a heady and uncertain proposition. But, at least, if your passion was sailing, you could count on doing a lot of it.

Of an old New Bedford whaling family, Waldo Howland was born in Boston in 1908. He spent his formative summers in Padanaram—a tight-knit, prosperous Yankee village on the shores of Buzzards Bay, where the prevailing summer breeze is a boisterous afternoon sou'wester, where catboats and gaff-rigged schooners are still highly regarded, and where, if you value your good name and reputation as a sailor, you eschew outboard motors in favor of well-varnished ash oars.

Because of Padanaram Harbor's favored location in one of the prime cruising grounds of the East Coast, and also because of the gusty conditions and daunting chop of Buzzards Bay, round-the-buoys racing has not had quite the appeal for Padanaram sailors that it has had for yachting enthusiasts on Long Island Sound or Massachusetts' North Shore. But the record compiled by Padanaram boats in offshore races and passage-making is a brilliant one.

A Life in Boats traces the various influences—geographic and philosophical, parental and practical—that entered into Waldo Howland's making as a sailor and as a lifelong student of sailing, small craft, and the sea. *A Life in Boats* is, however, only coincidentally autobiographical. Although Howland's particular interest lies with the boats he has sailed and raced on, or helped design or build, he writes with the same empathy and delight about the wide range of amateur and professional sailors, designers, builders, yard-owners, and watermen who dominated the history of yachting between the two world wars. That boats have an almost human personality is axiomatic. But Waldo Howland's ability to make us *care* about—to value and celebrate—the character of a good boat is a very special part, indeed, of the appeal and fascination of this book.

This is a book fully as much about the how and the why, as about the who, the when, and the where. It is a book that can and will be read with profit and pleasure by a very broad range of sailing enthusiasts, both in the United States and abroad.

Foreword

Over the years many people have contributed to the growth and development of what has become the Mystic Seaport of today. As the Seaport grew, its unique potential potential became apparent to a few, with special talents, who were a positive influence on the future of this institution. Waldo Howland was one of these people who shared his clarity of vision, special skills, and strong sense of purpose. Now, through the pages of this book, he will share his insights with thousands of others.

It took special vision and imagination to become interested in the Seaport's watercraft collection at the time Waldo did. In the mid-1950s the vessels at Mystic were in need of an enormous amount of work. There had been decades of well-intentioned, but inadequate attention by a pitifully small staff and a Board of Trustees working under severe financial constraints. By the end of the decade, however, there were several new arrivals on the Mystic scene and things began to change. With Waldo Johnston in place as Seaport Director, Maynard Bray as Shipyard Director, and, finally, Waldo Howland as Chairman of the Trustees' Ships Committee, the appropriate team was assembled and progress was instantly apparent.

The task was staggering. Shipyard buildings and a lift dock needed to be constructed; rare, hard-to-obtain equipment needed to be procured; and a staff of skilled craftsmen needed to be assembled. In one of our conversations together, Waldo said, "If ever I stopped to think about how I was going to pay for the education of my children, I would have worried and fretted and might never have done it; but if you just keep going, somehow it works out and the next thing you know, you've done it. That's the only way we can face our ship restoration problems here." Waldo was right, and with that positive attitude the job was begun, and subsequently earned for Mystic Seaport an international reputation.

During the last thirteen years Waldo's devoted service to Mystic Seaport has won him the respect of all who have been privileged to work with him. The Museum has benefited enormously from having Waldo Howland involved so intimately and we are now honored to be able to publish his first book. Through it he shares his wisdom, common sense, and spirit in a form that will preserve it for generations.

Those of us who know Waldo will savor these writings, while those who have not had the opportunity to know him personally have a rare treat ahead as they meet the man from Padanaram in the pages of this book. What will touch us all is Waldo's level-headed, no-nonsense approach, his grasp of what is right, and, finally, his integrity.

J. Revell Carr, Director
Mystic Seaport Museum

Table of Contents

Part I:

EARLY DAYS

New Bedford Yacht Club before World War I.

Right—Could Buzzards Bay already be casting its subtle charms?

Below—Here, by invitation, my sister Priscilla and I follow our kind hostess, Mrs. Prescott, out to her swimming float at Rockland Farm. This property, as well as the Ricketson dock of which I write, was a favorite place to pass the long summer days.

1
In the Beginning

i

Seafaring craft of one sort and another crept into my life early on. Even my high chair rocked a bit, and had quite a gang of rigging to it, if you counted the boarding step, the guardrails, and the folding tray the rails supported. The really nautical part, however, was the double-bottomed plate designed to keep my vittles warm. (You poured hot water into the space between bottoms and screwed a sporty little German silver cap onto the filler pipe to prevent bilge slopping.)

The scene depicted on this plate haunts me to this day. Its location is atop a friendly height of land that overlooks a peaceful ocean. (I've never stood on the White Cliffs of Dover, but my imagination has them appearing quite like this.) On the brow of the pictured cliff stands a small blue-gray table with several rosy apples set upon it. On either side of the table are two small ladder-back chairs with cane seats. In my mind's eye one chair is occupied by my little sister. I occupy the other. A sweet young lady wearing a Dutch bonnet is bringing us our supper. Our view is forever. Below us lie the village and the church. Several gaff-rigged work boats are reaching out to the westward. Farther offshore small sails are disappearing toward Europe. On the horizon a steamer with smoke rising heavenward is heading to the ends of the world. Overhead six gulls are enjoying the best of the evening in their own special and graceful way.

Now I realize full well that the joys of cruising vary with the individual, but for me the mood within this flower-bordered plate captures a delightful essence of them all. And when it came time for me to graduate from my high chair, the next seascape I encountered was scarcely less delightful, though very much more real.

While still a small child, I was given my first vessel—an important one. Its double bottom, when filled with hot water, kept my vittles warm, and its charming pictured deck steered my imagination seaward.

To my pleasure and benefit, Father often included me on his various boating trips, from short harbor passages in skiffs like this to the later (and longer) overnight cruises in Buzzards Bay.

All good East Coast sailors know the location of Padanaram Harbor and the village of Padanaram in the town of Dartmouth, Massachusetts. However, the charts of the U. S. Coast and Geodetic Survey make no mention of the place. The charts do identify Apponagansett Bay. They note a number of settlements within the Town of Dartmouth, such as Apponagansett at the head of the Bay and, on the west shore going south, the summer colonies of Bay View, Nonquitt, and finally Salters Point and Mishaum Point a bit beyond Dumpling Rocks. Why neither the charts nor the U. S. Postal Service will acknowledge the existence of my home village of Padanaram I fail to understand. But I am grateful that the charts do identify Ricketsons Point—the lovely saltwater farm at the tip of Padanaram Harbor's eastern arm.

The Point is appropriately named, in that various members of the Ricketson family have owned it, lived on it, and encouraged their friends to enjoy it for many generations. My first years of Point training took place on its South Beach. Transportation there was furnished by a baby carriage, pushed by Captain Butts's wife, Nanny. The route was over the oyster shells of Fremont Street, then left down a wide grass path bordered by stone walls and fragrant Rosa rugosa bushes. Next came the lawns of the grand John Ricketson summer house and a smaller grass path that led through a miniature woods of bayberry, yellow-blossomed broom, windswept cedars, sweet fern, and other delights for nose and eye. Finally we crossed a wooden footbridge spanning a tiny stream, which wound its way gently down from a small freshwater pond and marsh tucked in behind the outer beach. Here in the soft sand and under the shade of an old salt works cover, Nanny Butts moored my carriage alongside other neighbor-owned carriages.

On my first visits to South Beach I was sand-bound. As the weeks went by, however, Nanny moved me closer toward and at last into the wavelets at the water's edge. By my third or fourth summer, I began some actual boating operations in company with friends. After fashioning little ships from bits of driftwood we took them up to the pond and followed their tortuous passage downstream to the sea. When we added paper square sails we ran into trouble. In the pond the prevailing southwest winds blew our craft into the lily pads and well out of reach. If launched off the outer beach they were soon blown back ashore. But it was all fun just the same and it kept us usefully busy.

In due course I discovered a beach west of Ricketsons Point where grown-up boating activity took place. Reaching this harbor shore required walking with Father along the path between beach and pond, then behind Oliver Ricketson's big Point House and over to his boathouse—a shingled structure set partially on a ledge at the shoreward end of a stone dock. The boathouse was just large enough to contain several clothes-changing cubicles and room for two skiffs and boat gear. The dock itself was L-shaped, affording a perfect protective inside corner for the skiff float. The center of the dock was grass-covered. The grass was kept nicely mowed and made a surface just fine for bare feet.

In those days skiffs were useful, a joy to look at, and cooperative by nature. The one we used was a 12-footer, built, I think, by Mr. Asa Thomson. She had three laps to a side, was almost straight along the bottom, but carried a lot of rocker at the stern: she rowed easily and did not drag water. With good freeboard forward and aft and a fair amount of flare, she rowed well even with two or more passengers—and sometimes five or six, if one of them was a small boy who could sit on the stem head.

For our first voyages, Father made a stout fishing pole out of a boathook and hung from its outer end a harness made out of a sail stop. After we had rowed the 75 yards to the swimming float, Father inserted me into the harness and told me to jump overboard. This maneuver was frightening at first and I don't think I liked it, but I know it worked because I did not drown and I did learn to swim. Indeed, I came to love this swim routine with Father. Even now, I think about it, especially in the fall.

On good days in midsummer, Mr. Oliver Ricketson's float was a busy place, and the skiff shuttled back and forth with many bathers. I became a proud boatman and felt most important as soon as I got the hang of rowing. On one occasion when Mother and Miss Sally Ricketson were enjoying a dip, Father appeared with Mr. Harold Fitzgerald, an old schoolmate of his. I have good reason to remember how Mr. Fitzgerald stepped out of the skiff and on to the float to be introduced to Miss Sally. For it seems certain ladies have very light bones and in the water float deceptively high and without effort. Miss Sally was one of these. Seeing her standing on the bottom with her shoulders well exposed, Mr. Fitzgerald gallantly jumped off the float with the intention of shaking Miss Sally's hand. Only Miss Sally was not standing, she was floating, and Mr. Fitzgerald briefly disappeared beneath the surface.

I don't recall Mr. Oliver Ricketson swimming very much, but I do think of him sitting on the deck of his little black schooner *Dorothy B.* We would row over, Father and I, to visit with him for a spell after our swim. The *Dorothy B.*'s mooring was just a few yards farther offshore than the float; both were well protected from the open by the Padanaram breakwater that lay only a few hundred feet off the west side of the Point. It was all very peaceful of a late afternoon with the wind drying out and high tea of one sort or another available. I remember the schooner's decks, houses, and rails were all painted white, which kept them cool and gave them a lovely pinkish glow in a lowering sun. If Mr. Ricketson happened not to be aboard we would row once around his ship for the pure pleasure of it and then back to the skiff float. After we (at any rate, Father) had hauled the boat out, we would tie the painter to one of the mooring rings, stow the oars with blades forward, and unship the oarlocks. For good measure, we'd sponge the bottom clean and dry.

After I had achieved a modest ability as a swimmer, I was introduced to Captain Henry Hiller. This gentleman sported a big white mustache and operated a little white harbor ferry named *Ocie*, a dory type some 25 feet long, round-bottomed and smooth-planked. *Ocie* was of moderate to narrow beam— 6 feet 2 inches—and had a beautiful round stern. The cockpit was oval with seats running all around, and the engine sat amidships under a canvas-topped box. There was a small locker aft for spare lines and other equipment, and another one forward for cleaning gear. Under the seats was still more stowage space—this partly concealed by white canvas fringed in Bristol fashion on its lower edge. Although there was a steering wheel forward, Captain Hiller preferred to sit on his special raised seat amidships and to starboard. Here a second wheel was mounted fore and aft, on the coaming, and here he could steer, handle shore lines, work his controls, and collect my 30¢ fare without moving. Captain Hiller's boat was spotless, and her brass was always shined.

Ocie's regular run was from the float on the north side of South Wharf, out and across Padanaram Harbor to Bay View (which is just about opposite Ricketsons Point), then south along the shore to the Nonquitt Post Office dock, and return. Occasionally Captain Hiller had reason to proceed on inside Dumpling Rocks to Salters Point.

Ocie could comfortably accommodate eight to ten passengers, most of whom would be trippers like me, although one or two usually had serious business in

mind—perhaps shopping in Padanaram or visiting friends in Nonquitt. I always sat aft so that I could, without getting in the way of others, tow at the end of a piece of fishline my home-made ships. (The high narrow ones tended to sheer and capsize; the flattish blunt ones did a little better.) Captain Hiller kept an eye on me for my parents' peace of mind, but made no objection to my ship trials as long as my towlines and boats were out of the water for departures and arrivals. It is a shame that conditions nowadays just don't seem right for power dories and Captain Hillers.

Dorothy B., being moored near the swimming float, was the first boat of any size to seriously catch my attention. Originally a working schooner, modeled and built by Charles Morse, she had been converted to a yacht by her present owner, Mr. Oliver Ricketson.

My first real sailing, about 1918, was in Father's open dory, rigged with centerboard, rudder, and leg-o'-mutton sail.

Little by little some actual sailing came my way. The first ventures were with Father in his open dory. This modified Cape Ann dory had a leg-o'-mutton sail, and like others of her kind she was a bit cranky, especially when light. She heeled easily and in a breeze was apt to take on water, no matter how well handled. Father was a good, a very, very good boat handler, but I wouldn't say he was a very sympathetic skipper. When you went with Father you took things as they came. If it was on the rough side for you, then at the next invitation you said you had other plans. I'm afraid Mother and many of Father's friends soon learned to have other plans, and I don't blame them in the least. It just happened that I liked it all, and therefore Father could count on me, and I learned early on to have respect as well as love for the water.

One great dory trip took us on a long but easy beat out toward Cuttyhunk some eight miles south and by west from Padanaram. To a small boy three hours of beating in a little open boat in a thick fog can be quite an adventure. The sound of unseen horns, and bells, and the weird mews of sea gulls, and all such, can add to his natural fear of the unknown. Even Father seemed amazed to see, looming suddenly through the fog, a great lighthouse set atop a high bluff, for there is no such light for miles around. Father's consternation must have been short-lived, but I surely felt the thrill of his brief astonishment. We luffed along into quieter water, and magically the lighthouse transformed itself into an old-fashioned white enamel coffeepot with the handle missing. At this same moment the cliff became a rectangular boulder on wave-washed Gull Island.

By the time Father bought the sloop *Alert*, I was 12 or 13, and he was in the oil business. The business was, I gathered, a risky but exciting one. Heavy debts one day, promises of great riches the next. At the refinery in Fall River one week a great number of small tankers were tied up at the New England Oil Company docks. They wouldn't leave until they were paid off, and, there was no money available for this purpose. One of Father's associates,

The knockabout sloop *Alert* came next in 1921. She was a good sailer, but by 1983 standards she had rather modest accommodations for cruising.

nothing daunted, ordered up a small plane to take pictures of the vessels. These pictures would show how busy the company was. Some days later an employee, Major William Smyth, wired from Venezuela that if Father would send him a Masonic sword and a barrel of apples and a few more such things, he thought the New England Oil Company could get control of most of the oil rights on Lake Maracaibo.

A heady business, this, to put it mildly, and it was no wonder that Father wanted to unwind when he came home of a summer evening. His idea of relaxing was not conventional, but for him it worked. Mother would give us a fine supper, and then Father and I would walk down to the harbor and, provisioned with a small basket of food, row out to *Alert*. *Alert* was a low-sided gaff-rigged sloop with a waterline length of about 20 feet, but an overall length nearer 30. She had a shallow watertight cockpit and a small cuddy cabin. Like so many of the little pleasure boats of those days, she was a good sailer—but not what we now think of as a cruising boat. It was usually dark before we got underway, but Father judged the conditions well; we always anchored in a good lee in time for a few hours of shut-eye. Then we were underway again before dawn in order to get home for breakfast. I usually went to bed after breakfast. But Father immediately drove back to work. He claimed that there was no secondhand oil to compete against, and that this made the oil business a good business.

One night cruise that I remember with particular clarity was in fact a dismally foggy one. From the moment we dropped our mooring in Padanaram Harbor I could see nothing on land or sea. At first there was gray fog and then just blackness. Only the dim reflection of our running lights and a little glow from the kerosene binnacle lantern broke the shroud of blackness around us. We had no charts out: we were headed for Hadley Harbor, and Father well knew the course there. With a moderate southwesterly breeze it is not a long trip out to the bell off Mosher's Ledge and then across Buzzards Bay to Naushon. But it was a relief to hear at last the outer bell off Woods Hole and to sharpen up into calmer water.

With no visibility, a strong current, and a fair number of outlying rocks, the approach to our special cove on Nonamesset could present a problem to some sailors. Father, however, had his own methods of navigation. All in good time he said: "Now, Waldo, you go forward, stand by the jib halyard, and when you can smell horses, let me know." It wasn't long before I could report: "I can smell 'em now, Father." Father thereupon told me to lower away and eased *Alert* up into the wind. As she lost headway, he brought the anchor forward and "let 'er go." By that time I was aft and hauling in the slack of the main sheet, and Father was dropping the main. We had arrived. We were in a snug, albeit invisible anchorage. After munching on a pilot biscuit and a generous piece of

Baker's German Sweet Chocolate, we were ready to stretch out for a night's sleep on our beds of pine boards, with rolled-up life jackets for pillows.

Awakened by the first glimmer of daylight and the sweet song of a meadowlark, I followed Father into the cockpit, and we made preparations to get underway forthwith. A stone's throw ahead and a point off our starboard bow I could see the mist-shrouded outline of the little height of land that extends out from the northwesterly end of Nonamesset. Here Mr. Malcolm Forbes's horses spent their idle summer hours chomping the sweet meadow grass and watching the boats that passed in and out through the narrow channel to Hadley Harbor.

ii

When he felt that the time was right Father issued a few constructive nautical rules and gave me his blessing to try it alone. The Padanaram Station of the New Bedford Yacht Club was to be my starting point, Padanaram Harbor and approaches were to be my sailing world, and Mother Experience was to do what she could for me.

Sailing seasons began at Cleveland's Boat Yard. This operation sprawled on a marshy piece of land north of South Wharf, which in turn was just north of

Padanaram (known to non-seagoing folk and mapmakers only as South Dartmouth) has long been a center for Buzzards Bay yachtsmen. The New Bedford Yacht Club dock is at left in this 1920 photo, and South Wharf, later to become the site for Concordia Company, is at far right. The A. Cary Smith-designed schooner *Palestine* lies at the end of the yacht club dock.

the yacht club. On this lot old Captain Al Cleveland had a light railway that could handle small boats with less than four feet of draft. The hauling line was manila, and the winch was hand-operated. For storage, boats in their cradles were skidded sideways on greased timbers away from the hauling track. The first boats hauled were the last ones launched. At the head of the railway and on slightly higher ground stood the shop, a shingled shed about 30 feet long in which there was a workbench, a big chest for rigging, overhead storage for sails, racks for oars and spars, shelves for paint, drawers for tools, and almost room enough for all those other interesting and salt-scented things needed for the care of boats. In addition there was an old chair, an upturned box, and a nail keg for sitting on. In the winter Al kept the big west double doors shut and came in through a small side door on the south, after which he would light his coal stove and putter about. Usually his long-time helper Tony Anderson would be present, working on mooring lines.

My first visit to Cleveland's had been with Father. It was May 30—Memorial Day—and our catboat was scheduled for launching that weekend. As it turned out, she was still hidden under her winter cover at the far end of the line. Father's face became real stormy-like, but when he located Al, he was only able to squeeze in the first few words of what was brewing up to be a long scorcher. Al took over immediately and held the floor for the remainder of the day. Neither the pipe that he held precariously between his teeth nor the rhythmic slap-slap of his paintbrush seemed in any way to interrupt the steady flow of information that issued forth. Father and I heard all about the hard winter, about everyone who had lived through it, and some who hadn't. We learned about the virtues and failings of each boat in the yard and the same about their owners. And we got a full blast about Al's landlord, Mr. Henry Tiffany, who had raised the rent again, but still refused to grant more than a one-year lease. When it was time for us to go home, Al gave us his parting shot of wisdom. "In weather like this," he said, "only a damned fool would want his boat in the water."

Needless to say Father didn't get the use of his boat for several weeks, but I know he secretly felt that Al's company and his endless yarns were almost as good as a sail. As for me, I had witnessed a valuable preview of boatyard operation. After this first encounter, I never again expected to have our boat in commission at any certain time. I just went to the yard each day that I could, and happily did all the listening and working and watching I wanted to.

As the seasons passed, Captain Cleveland gradually turned the management of his yard over to his son Harold. This entailed few if any changes. Harold had inherited his father's ability to face problems in a thoroughly straightforward way. At the end of one particular spring in the mid-twenties, he had launched all his boats—and again Mr. Tiffany had raised the rent. This was once too often. Harold held several private conferences with certain friends and relatives. One dark night soon thereafter, he mounted a quiet but busy operation. It commenced at the boatyard itself, proceeded on half a mile up Elm Street, then turned down to the shore again. Next morning, to the surprise of Mr. Tiffany and other early risers on their way to Lawrence's Store, the Cleveland boatyard had disappeared. Railway, cradles, winch, equipment...everything had vanished. Only an empty lot and an empty shed remained. Nor was this Tiffany lot ever rented again, or used for that matter, until my brother acquired it for our own boatyard many years later from Mr. Tiffany's estate.

The site to which Harold moved had, before the days of the Padanaram bridge, been a real shipyard. Work schooners and whaleships had been built there and then been floated on their sides, with the help of many barrels, down to deep water. It was a good location. And there Harold continued to store and commission Padanaram's small craft for two decades more.

When I joined the boating life just after World War I, everyone owned a dinghy or skiff. You had to. There was no yacht club launch service in Padanaram in those days. You learned to row, and if you had a good boat you soon found that you enjoyed rowing. A few lucky boat owners had their own docks, but most of us helped each other haul out on a yacht club float. My first dinghy was a big pine skiff painted green. Mother bought it for me. Father called it a freshwater boat. Nonetheless, he showed me how to make up marline lanyards for the oarlocks, and he helped me splice in a good manila painter. We found a galvanized bucket for bailing and clamming, and, from Father's bathtub, I acquired a big natural sponge for wiping off the thwarts and keeping the bottom free of water. Father organized a light grappling hook for an anchor. (He spliced the anchor line around the base or crown of the five flukes, then seized it with sail twine to the outside of the ring at the top.) This ground tackle was a menace, but a boat without an anchor is like a man without a leg.

Oars were a bit of a problem. My size called for short, light oars. The beam and freeboard of the skiff called for long, heavier oars. Father compromised by shaving down a pair of seven-footers so that they were lighter, but still long enough to reach the water at a good angle and shaped to balance comfortably in rowing position. A smaller boat would in many ways have been better for me. Nonetheless, the boat was mine, and I was some proud of her. Together we covered the harborfront in good shape.

During these early years it seemed that more than half the sailboats in Padanaram were Cape Cod type catboats. Most of them were only 15- or 16-footers. Even at this length, however, they represented a lot of boat. For general harbor work they were, and still are, "finest kind." Being centerboarders, they could be moored in shoal protected areas and near their owners' docks. They could be grounded out for cleaning or painting, or nudged up to the beach for picnicking. They were beamy and stable, and with their long, wide cockpits and tillers way aft, they had room and comfort for the whole family, young and old. The single gaff-headed sail with three sets of reef points was usually on the big side, but this was a necessary feature for boats without motors. The big main eliminated the need for light sails and all the gear light sails require. Several retired sea captains and a few commercial fishermen owned larger catboats with motors and cabins. These took a bit more understanding and experience to handle.

I have good reason to remember my first solo sail aboard Father's small cat. The incident involved the Padanaram bridge, and it turned out to be a major lesson for me, as well as a disaster. Knowing full sail could be too much for a small boy, Father had advised me to reef down before setting forth. Our mooring was well up the harbor on the west side of the channel, and to row across from the yacht club I had to hold to the south to counter the incoming tide. The wind was light, very light to none at all, but I reefed as directed and cast off. Back and forth I tacked against a fitful southerly air. On each tack I lost ground.

I had an anchor. I should have used it. I didn't. Old-timers on the bridge could easily see what the current was doing to me. They stopped whatever they were at (fishing for scup, mostly) and waited for the inevitable. This came soon enough. My mast and sail became tangled in the bridge girders, and there I was, pinned in ignominy. Advice good and bad poured down aplenty from above, but it had no effect except to make me lose all reason. The boat was saved from serious damage when a friendly motor boat towed me off. But my pride had received a serious blow. Ever since then, when I am preparing to get underway, a vision of the Padanaram bridge flashes before my eyes, and I pause to double-check my plans before casting off.

Another Padanaram catboat owner was Mr. Dwight W. Tryon. In New York and the international art world, his fame was as a painter. (He was a member of the National Academy, and the art gallery at Smith College is named after him.) In Padanaram, however, Mr. Tryon was celebrated for his ability to catch fish. He and his 20-foot cat made one beautiful team to behold. He had an ingenious swivel seat at the aft end of the cockpit. From this point of vantage he could control rudder, main sheet, and fishing tackle. He had a bowsprit with sheave from which to hang and to handle his light anchor. His sail was large in order to bring him home in time for supper, but he also had deep reefs and a topping lift, which he used as needed.

Every suitable morning Mr. Tryon could be seen reaching out of the harbor, destination unknown. We seldom saw him in the act of catching fish, but when he came ashore in the evening, his fish bucket was invariably full. I tried to bribe him with sweet melons from Mother's garden, in the hope he would tell me more about fishing. In this effort I was partially successful. Being young and inexperienced, I didn't present any great threat to his secrets. Besides, I promised not to tell, and I always said "thank you."

First of all, Mr. Tryon explained, sailing cats make fine fishing boats. They are shoal, quiet, very handy. They don't worry or spook the fish or the gulls. Second, he noted that wind and tide are important to boat and fish alike. Then he noted that, even if the fish don't happen to be biting, a good sail is still enjoyable. Finally, he spoke about the scup and flounder to be found west of Mishaum Point and near the sand flats in the lee of Barneys Joy Point.

Fishing was always good sport, but some folks were better at it than others. Artist Dwight Tryon was one of the best. Every suitable morning he'd set out in his catboat to return in the evening with a full bucket of scup and flounder. *Anna*, the catboat shown leaving the yacht club in this 1920 photo, was owned by ex-square-rigger seaman Captain Frank Stone.

Captain Stone (straw hat at right) supervised the spring launching of the Rockland fleet behind the private breakwater there. Waterfront activities like this were all of great interest and taught me that fun can be had with but the simplest of boats and equipment.

The success of a few short fishing trips lured me on to longer ones in Mr. Tryon's favored fishing grounds. But while Mr. Tryon had told me about the scup and flounder to be found there, I had to learn my own hard way about sand sharks. Sand sharks pulled hard and gave me some real thrills. But what a mess their blood made in the boat! I learned, too, why sharkskin could be used for sandpaper. On these voyages out past Dumpling Rocks to Mishaum Point and Barneys Joy, getting home was all too often a race against the dinner gong. So I would cut inside every ledge and rock possible to save distance, and often adverse tide as well. My course wasn't always free of bumps or groundings.

Captain Taylor was not so lucky a fisherman as Dwight Tryon. Like

16

Captain Taylor himself, his catboat was getting old. The boat was some 26 feet long and had a cabin that served as its owner's only home. Some years before, the boat had developed serious leaks, which Captain Taylor had only partially corrected by use of the cement remedy. Indeed, this solution to the problem is usually of a temporary nature in an old vessel, and by the time I came to know the Captain, conditions were again getting bad. By now, too, the boat was more or less permanently tied to the yacht club dock because sailing was not an essential activity, and it tended to loosen things up too much and aggravate the leaking.

Captain Taylor told me that he had worked out a pumping schedule that took care of the water the old cat took on during the day. But he noted that the night situation was more complicated and that oversleeping could result in placing the boat in a sinking condition. However, seagoing folks are generally ingenious as well as practical. Captain Taylor worked out a simple, inexpensive solution for the problem. He arranged his bedding in such a way that one bare leg hung out over the side of the bunk and could not work its way back in again without some wakeful rearranging. When the water in the bilge rose to a dangerous level, Captain Taylor would automatically be awakened and would arise and give the pump the needed number of strokes to insure his safe sleep for a few more hours.

iii

There wasn't much regular or formal yacht racing in my early days at Padanaram, and what there was didn't actively involve me. Had I been a few years older I would happily have joined those few convivial enthusiasts who had organized the Apponagansett Boat Club above the bridge. For headquarters, they perched six little boathouses out over the water on pilings at the foot of Hill Street. For boats they sailed flat-bottomed centerboarders with plenty of sail in their big jib and gaff main; just right for a bit of evening competition among friends. For organization they had a set time for a sip before supper.

If I had been one of the summer folks across the harbor at Bay View or Nonquitt, I probably would at one time have raced on a small keel submarine known as a Wee Scot. Later I might have competed in the Alden Fifteens, also known as O boats, or with the Twelve-Footers. This latter class included not only the famous Herreshoff Twelves, but also a few of the Alden Twelves. Although these two designs raced together, the former seemed to be faster in very light airs or in a strong breeze, while the latter, with their slightly larger sail area, had the advantage in moderate weather. I've often thought about this, for it really does seem that a good design starts to show its stuff when conditions get tough or when the breeze drops off to a breath. The better the shape the more easily it goes through the water.

My brother, Louie, in due course did join the Twelve-Footer competition in his *Cutty Sark*. Mother bought this boat for $850. She did so direct from Herreshoff Manufacturing Company, and thus had her name listed in the company trade publication along with other important customers such as Vincent Astor, A. S. Cochran, J. P. Morgan, and Harold S. Vanderbilt.

Why at this time my parents gave me a sailing dory built by the Cape Cod Power Dory Company I don't really know, although she was a nice little boat and, being no longer part of an active racing class, probably inexpensive. Perhaps the idea was to give us boys a chance to experience the many differences between handling a displacement keel boat and a light, lapstrake centerboarder. Both boats were certainly fun in their own way. Louie could beat me to windward in a strong or very light breeze, and I slipped along in good shape with started sheets, especially when it blew. Picking up the mooring required an entirely different approach with the two boats. Louie could take an easy turn up into the wind, and *Cutty Sark* would shoot quite a distance. He could also come straight downwind, put the helm hard down, and spin her to an almost immediate stop. For me, making a good mooring meant approaching the pennant from the side. My dory wouldn't turn quickly or carry her way dead into the wind.

It was while I owned this dory that Father told me never to sail close to leeward of a moored boat, a rowboat underway, or a person swimming. I gave this warning some thought. But not quite enough. One puffy day, with a northerly wind, I was beating unconcernedly up the harbor. Not being quite able to fetch Mr. Ricketson's *Dorothy B.*, I swung off at the last moment to sail under her stern. Of course right then a couple of those blue devils sent along an especially hard puff. With her main sheet fast, the dory wouldn't pay off. She just lunged up to windward. The result was a small telltale dent in *Dorothy B.*'s stern rail cap and a big one in my mind. Old Mother Experience was chalking up lessons right fast, and Old Father Howland's words were beginning to carry more weight with each passing day.

As chance chose it, my first taste of formal racing didn't occur in Padanaram at all, but on the North Shore of Massachusetts Bay. My long-time schoolmate John Noble, Jr., and a very attractive sister of his summered there with their parents at Prides Crossing. Johnny kept his boat just to the east in Manchester, but did his serious racing just to the west in Marblehead. His boat was a Manchester Fifteen, a dory type similar in some ways to my own, but a bit beamier and more of a boat all around. Of course over in Marblehead we were just one of the many smaller classes that "also ran." But while we were jogging back and forth awaiting our start, we had a front row seat from which to watch the Big Leagues in action.

Our own Marblehead Race Week routine, Johnny's and mine, was not of

My first real boat was a sailing dory like this. She sailed at her best with started sheets in a good breeze.

notable importance to American yachting. Just the same it was a great stepping stone for me. In our jointly owned, bright green late '23 Model T Ford, Johnny and I would drive over each morning from Prides Crossing to the Manchester Yacht Club. There our Fifteen joined a tow astern of the club launch run by Henry Hall. On the way over to Marblehead we would eat our sandwiches and study over our race circulars. Then Hall would cast us off the tow, and we would drift about on the sail-dotted waters waiting for the breeze to make in.

The big boats started first. Only after an astonishing number of guns had gone off for classes from all over Massachusetts Bay were we too on our way, trying to pick the elusive puffs before our competition did. All this while big cumulus clouds could be seen building up over the land and then crowding in on top of us. The light puffs suddenly became heavy gusts. Soon we were in the usual Race Week thunder squall. We scrabbled around to get sails down, while Henry in his launch darted back and forth in the blinding rain trying to see if any of his chickens had capsized. I remember the excitement of these daily storms far more clearly than I do our actual racing. But without realizing it, I did pick up a fair amount of general knowledge about racing rules, tactics, and tricks. Johnny was a good skipper. He had had good indoctrination crewing for his uncle Caleb Loring.

The racing fever did not spare Padanaram for long. By the mid-twenties a fleet of Herreshoff S boats was building up in home waters. John Stedman owned the first one—like most of the others, designed and built by Herreshoff. Lawrence Grinnell, Jr., acquired one of the few S boats built by George Lawley. Many of these Buzzards Bay S boats were equipped with watertight cockpits—a safety feature in rough weather, but a weight disadvantage otherwise. Nevertheless, we all raced boat for boat. No handicaps. I never owned an S boat myself, but I had plenty of chances to race as crew—usually with Johnny Stedman or Larry Grinnell. In the beginning we were quite consistently beaten by one of our experienced elders. We tried hard, though, and gradually worked our way up in the standings. For several seasons I soaked up half of Buzzards Bay, lying up on the windward rail of an S boat in that narrow wedge of deck between shrouds and cabin house. But one summer I had the loan of an S boat for the entire season, and on occasion Johnny Stedman and Larry Grinnell had to take their orders from me. You can be sure that they each took their rightful turns soaking up the other half of Buzzards Bay.

Along toward the end of our S boat racing days we decided to try our skill at a Marblehead Race Week. The experiment was not dull. The evening that Johnny Stedman and I were to go aboard his boat in Marion, I made the mistake of kicking what I thought in the dusk to be a black-and-white cat. It wasn't. Worse, I was decked out in my blue yachting trousers at the time. We successfully overcame that emergency by tying the offending garment to the end of a spare line and lowering it to the mud bottom beneath us.

Our next hazard came the following morning in the form of the Cape Cod Canal, which we hoped to sail our way through, despite the regulations prohibiting such transit without power. Our fair current turned foul, though our wind became strong fair and we made the Sandwich end of the canal by mid-afternoon. Here we thought to tie up to the wharf for the night. John quite rightly worried about his topsides; I pretended a confidence I did not feel. We stowed the jib. I was steering, and John handed me the main halyard. He stood by amidships with a spring line and fender. By lowering the mainsail to the point where our speed over the bottom was nil, we were able to use the head tide, and our steerageway through the water, to ease into the dock without damage. How I blessed *Fleetwing* as a beautiful boat to handle.

Next morning a fair tide and a light breeze took us out into Massachusetts Bay and into a blanket of fog. A chorus of horns surrounded us and called for some action. But what sort of action? Although we couldn't see the water 50 yards away, it was still strangely light overhead. We figured correctly that the

For many summers Padanaram enjoyed good boat-for-boat racing in a class that included both the Herreshoff Twelves and the Alden Twelves. The Alden boats (sail no. 11), less striking in appearance, were at their best in moderate winds, the more famous Herreshoff Twelves having the best of it in a breeze or very light air.

fog must be low. After climbing to a comfortable position aloft on the spreaders, I could clearly see the mast or upper structure of each and every nearby vessel.

The fog burned off in Massachusetts Bay, and we made fair progress with a hot and light westerly breeze. By mid-afternoon we were off Boston Harbor, nervously eyeing a mass of dark clouds that approached us from the north. The wind grew fitful, and an ominous greenish-yellow glow developed on the horizon in the center of the black clouds. It came at us fast. John had just got the mainsail off and was heading below for our oilskins when the wind struck cold and furious. I lacked even a shirt. When marble-sized hail stones started pelting me, I grabbed the galvanized bucket to put it over my head. What a rat-a-tat-tat this created! It almost drowned out the ominous horn blasts of a freighter coming out of Boston. *Fleetwing* was nearly flat in the water. But even under jib alone she remained responsive to her helm. A wonderful boat!

Like most horrors, the squall did pass, my teeth did stop chattering, and Johnny did get the main on once again. Once more I hopefully hung out my blue yachting pants, odorless now, to dry. At midnight we groped our way into Marblehead Harbor (despite confusion caused by an old chart we were using that showed Marblehead Light the wrong color). Next morning Larry Grinnell arrived by car. Our cruising gear was off-loaded into the dinghy. We were all set for our first big race.

During the next four days the local sailors showed us how little we actually knew about racing. On the fifth day, however, a Massachusetts Bay thunderstorm came to our rescue. We lowered all sail. While the wind squalled and the lightning flashed, we remained below and ate pilot biscuits and guava jelly. When the storm passed we set sail again, only to find that instead of being to leeward of the fleet we were now well to windward. No one was able to catch us. The finish gun was for *Fleetwing* at last.

And thus did the great Padanaram crew return home with an unearned prize and a memorable experience tucked away in the bilge along with the clutter of our cruising gear.

Herreshoff's S boats were also popular among Buzzards Bay sailors of the 1920s and 1930s and as a teenager I used to race them often. In this 1928 photo, Colonel Green's Round Hill "cottage" shows over the bow of Percy Chubb's "S-43."

2
Father's
Boats

i

After selling *Alert* Father acquired a boat that my disrespectful Mattapoisett friends immediately named "The Holy Roman Empire." Her actual name was, and still is, *Great Republic*, and as of 1975 *Great Republic* had been voted an "Historic Vessel," thus making her eligible for registration with the National Trust for Historic Preservation.

It was in 1927 that Father bought this little vessel from her third owner, the well-known naval architect William (Billy) Atkin. I am quite sure Father's friend Major William Smyth engineered this happy transaction, but why the boat was listed in Smyth's name for the first year I have never quite understood. Years later, when I asked him about it, the Major just smiled.

Great Republic was already famous and justly so. In overall length she was a modest 25 feet, but she had sailed across the North Atlantic. Her principal designer and original owner was still living, and had I only known about him at the time, I would surely have made a pilgrimage to the seagoing saloon he operated in his home town of Gloucester, Massachusetts. A privilege and a rewarding experience it surely would have been to meet and talk with this unique voyager.

Howard Blackburn must have been one of the greatest small boat sailors of the last one hundred years. Born in 1859 and a professional seaman by training, he made his first single-handed ocean crossing (to Gloucester, England) at the age of 40. This was in a small sloop to which he gave the large name *Great Western*. Then, in 1901, he made a second Atlantic crossing, again alone, this time in our *Great Republic*. The passage (from Gloucester, Massachusetts, to Lisbon, Portugal) was a good one, taking him but 39 days. He shipped *Great Republic* back to New York, and the following year proceeded to sail her up the Hudson, through the Great Lakes, down the Mississippi, and finally across the Gulf of Mexico to Florida. Yet again, in 1903, he planned a single-handed

The 25′ sloop *Great Republic*, which in 1901 had taken the great single-handed sailor Howard Blackburn from Gloucester to Portugal, became the Howland family yacht in 1927. Although she wouldn't always drive to windward through a steep chop, we found many other ways to enjoy sailing and cruising in her. Recently, in cooperation with the National Trust for Historic Preservation, *Great Republic* has been restored as a tribute to Blackburn and placed on exhibit in the state armory at Gloucester.

voyage across the Atlantic, this time in a 16-foot Swampscott dory. The undertaking failed in its purpose because of unbelievably bad weather, but both man and boat safely and miraculously made port in Nova Scotia. Such single-handed cruises are in themselves an accomplishment. When, however, you consider that Blackburn had previously lost his fingers and toes in a seagoing episode that would have been fatal to a lesser man, it becomes hard to imagine that he had the will even to start, let alone the ability to complete, such ventures.

I have read a number of grueling sea stories, some true, some fictional, but never one that affected me more deeply than Blackburn's own account of being separated from the Gloucester fishing schooner *Grace L. Fears*.* This occurred in the winter of 1883 on the Burgeo Bank off the south coast of Newfoundland. Blackburn and his dory mate, Tom Welch, were out one cold but calm morning hauling their trawls, when quite suddenly it breezed on from the northwest and began to snow heavily. Head winds and seas, bitter cold, and zero visibility made conditions all but impossible. That evening the air cleared briefly and the two dory men could see the *Fears*'s lights, but they could not reach her or attract her attention. They never saw her again.

It was five long nights and unmerciful days of freezing weather before Blackburn reached an isolated river settlement. It was more months of suffering before the ice finally left and gave him a chance to get to St. Johns and, at last, to Gloucester. How a human being could have the courage, strength, and stamina to watch his shipmate freeze to death, see his own mittens wash away and his hands turn white, arrange to let his fingers freeze around his oars so that he could row...how he could go without food or water for so long, and still keep his sanity, seamanship, and determination to live, it is indeed hard to understand. This is the type of man who designed and first sailed *Great Republic*.

Great Republic, a modified Friendship sloop, was built in 1901 by Archibald Fenton in Gloucester. She resembled a miniature of her clipper ship namesake, having a clipper bow, a graceful sheer, and a stylish overall appearance. By the time Major Smyth negotiated her purchase for Father, the original flush deck had been altered by the addition of a small cabin house. A two-cycle, one-cylinder engine had also been installed. These changes would not have been improvements for Blackburn. But for the Howlands and the cause of gentle summer cruising, at least the house was useful.

For our initial expedition aboard *Great Republic*, Father decided on a voyage to Nantucket. I had never been there, and he had the time for a fortnight's vacation. The first day saw us working south across Buzzards Bay on a close fetch to Quicks Hole, and then west in a number of short tacks under the beautiful boulder-strewn north shore of Nashawena Island. We sailed by

*See *Maine Coast Fisherman*, February 1961.

Merrill's Harbor with its partially hidden shallow creek, its rambling white farmhouse, and the last anchorage of the old Forbes cutter *Hesper.**

The sun was getting low as we drifted through the narrow channel into Cuttyhunk Pond. Here on the southern perimeter were several little pole docks to which a small powerboat or skiff could tie up, but the deep-water anchorage itself was very restricted in those days: *Great Republic* using 30 feet of anchor warp fairly well filled the whole area where a boat of five-foot draft would float at all tides in all wind directions. Alone though we were, Father still felt it wise to drop into the dinghy and do a bit of sounding with an oar before we turned in for the night.

Next morning we made a carefully timed start, drifting back to Quicks Hole and out into Vineyard Sound. Here a fair tide and following breeze met us and carried us along. A big old lumber schooner was also taking advantage of the favorable conditions. She slid silently by us during the morning, bound to the eastward around Cape Cod. When at last West Chop came abeam, we flattened sheets and headed into Vineyard Haven for the night.

Our third port of call was Edgartown, and to fetch in there from the outer channel buoy we had a long beat to the entrance of the harbor proper. These are sheltered waters in a summer sou'wester, and *Great Republic* stuck doggedly to her task. I'm sure a number of old-timers ashore must have stopped whatever they were at to take a second look at our little ship maneuvering her way in to Father's favorite Edgartown anchorage. (This lies a few hundred yards past the town proper under a sandy bluff close to the Chappaquiddick shore. It has sufficient water, even for a good-sized boat; the holding ground is excellent; and best of all, there is little current to contend with at any condition of tide. This can be said of few other locations in this often troublesome harbor.)

As the long leg of our voyage was to be on the following day, Father made up an ample batch of johnny cakes and bacon to put us in a proper frame of mind and stomach. Supper finished, I cleaned up the dishes, while Father made his usual elaborate ritual of preparing the kerosene riding light for hanging in the fore-rigging: cleaning the chimney, filling the fount, trimming and lighting the wick, and, finally, clicking the lens unit back into place. All in all, it was a lovely routine that naturally brought forth in spoken words those usually silent thoughts between father and son.

Come morning, with a light fair breeze behind us, we were not long in bringing Cape Pogue abeam. Soon we had sharpened up for Hedge Fence Buoy, the second objective on our course to Nantucket.

As the sun gained in altitude, so did the prevailing breeze gain in strength.

---

*In her declining years *Hesper* (a 53' LOA cutter designed by A. Cary Smith and built by Piepgras in 1879) was anchored at Nashawena and used as a summer guesthouse. The 1938 hurricane moved her up on the island; then the 1944 hurricane brought her once more to the water's edge.

Great Republic was quite willing to try to get to windward against the short head seas, but she couldn't seem to make much progress. When we hardened up a few degrees she just slid off to leeward. When we eased sheets she sailed better. On the other hand, her long tacks ended up about where they started. After perhaps six hours of patiently watching *Great Republic*'s bow climb up each oncoming wave and then whoosh down the back side of it, we still had Cape Pogue right there beside us. In a voice that endeavored to sound cheerful, Father finally admitted, "I guess we won't make it today, my boy." There was nothing for it but up with the helm. On Wednesday and again on Thursday we made an early start for Nantucket, but with unchanged weather conditions our progress was likewise unchanged. By Friday Father came to the conclusion that there were plenty of interesting things to do right here on Martha's Vineyard.

Thursday dinner and Friday breakfast, in particular, gave convincing evidence that a trip to the grocery store was overdue. In the calm of Friday morning we rowed to the west shore of Edgartown Harbor. Here, out of the worst of the current, we turned north and made our final leg into town. On the little crescent beach just to the west of the Edgartown Yacht Club landing I saw a small vessel lying on her side, above the high-water mark. She had a special look to her, and I questioned Father about her. Obviously she was a sailboat at heart. Only now the masts were gone, and just a short stub showed above her beamy flush deck. She was double-ended with a fair amount of freeboard. At first Father refrained from any comment. Then suddenly his oars stopped in mid-stroke. "My God, boy!" he half-whispered. "I believe that is my old *Fox*."

Then Father told me about Charlie Beetle, and how he himself had as a boy worked for Charlie when this craftsman and his brother John were on Clark's Point building whaleboats for the New Bedford whaling fleet. He described how Mr. Beetle had designed and built for him this little ketch: essentially a Block Island fishing boat, but fitted with a small cabin in place of a fish well.

Ashore we went. Father was like a parent finding a lost but never forgotten child.*

We never did get to Nantucket on this cruise, but it was an education and a joy for me to be off on a boat with Father. We worked our way back to Padanaram making one overnight stop at Menemsha, tucked in behind Gay Head on the north side of Martha's Vineyard. It was chancy no doubt to try to

---

*In his book *Sou'west and by West of Cape Cod* (Cambridge, Mass., 1947), Father included a charming chapter about *Fox*. On future cruises to Edgartown, I myself saw this wee ship often, and in more active occupations than sunning herself on the beach. She served her owner as ferryboat, bay scalloper, and general work boat. On one occasion I found her half hauled out on the Chappaquiddick shore. The owner was painting her decks. I admit there is nothing unusual about an owner painting a deck, but in this case the owner had to compete with a flock of hens that milled around the deck as he painted. In later years, when our boatyard painters grumbled about the terrible problems that beset their efforts, I could always offer them comfort by explaining that at least they did not have to contend with hens walking over their work.

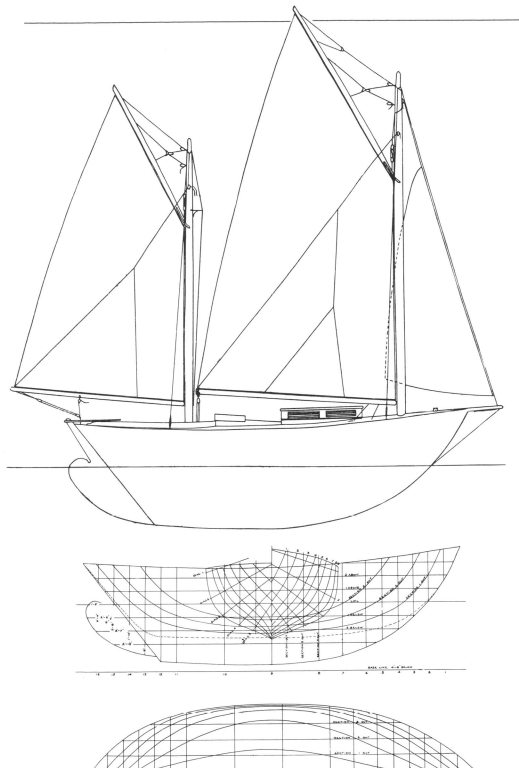

In his youth Father had
Charles Beetle design and
build for him this modified
Block Island boat, *Fox*, which
was fitted out for cruising. I
first saw her in Edgartown
while on our initial cruise in
Great Republic.

sail *Great Republic* into snug Menemsha that afternoon, for the breeze was failing, and a head current was running out through the jetties.

To be sure we had the "one-lunger." However, Father seemed loath to call on it, either by nature or because he could never get it to run (or for both reasons). I too had in the past tried and failed to get this noble piece of iron to start. Now, spurred on by what seemed like a sure catastrophe in the making, I ignored the great odds against me, gave the Barker a shot of ether and a spin of the flywheel that surprised even me with its determination. And then what a beautiful sound issued forth. Pop, pop, pop, and into the quiet waters of Menemsha we shot. But that was it. After that brief burst of purposeful popping, the Barker reverted to silence and never ran again for the Howlands.

Although we were often unkind to *Great Republic* by asking her to do things for which she was never intended, she always took good care of her crew, which often consisted of me and a college friend or two. If we would but listen, she would tell us where to go and when. It didn't matter that it was a long weekend and that we had made plans for Hadley Harbor. If there was a strong southeaster blowing, *Great Republic* just told us we couldn't go. She would, however, allow us to work our way out from our mooring to a safe anchorage under the Padanaram breakwater. Here the current was nil, the water was smooth, and the rain pattering overhead merely made the cabin below seem that much more cozy. The small coal stove warmed our hearts, dried our socks, and encouraged our culinary endeavors. The cushions on the low transom seats were neither soft nor wide, but they were finest kind for stretching out upon. With the wind whistling overhead, it was comforting indeed to remember that Blackburn himself had many a time rested in this very cabin and entrusted his life to this same little vessel.*

Great Republic taught me a simple, yet profound lesson: if you have a good stout ship, you can always enjoy her, provided you are willing to do things her way. The only other approach is to figure out clearly what you yourself most want a boat to be able to do, and then acquire one that fits your special way of doing things.

I last saw *Great Republic* off Mishaum Point in the summer of 1928. Father had already sold her to a Mr. McLean of New Haven. She was under power—I presume with the same Barker one-lunger that had defied Father's will and my own—pop-popping purposefully along to the westward as I in my dory sailed eastward toward Padanaram. Her blue topsides shone in the bright morning light, her sails were neatly furled, and all on deck was shipshape. Seated

---

*Howard Blackburn was in due course made an honorary member of the Cruising Club of America. He was more recently the subject of a full-length biography (Joseph E. Garland, *Lone Voyager*, Boston, 1963). In 1970, Mr. Garland found *Great Republic* hauled out and rotting away in her fifteenth owner's driveway on Long Island. Garland and others bought her and generously presented her to the Gloucester Historical Commission. By 1977, through the efforts of Garland and the boatbuilding skill of Laurence Dahlmer, *Great Republic* had been rebuilt.

upright on her wheelbox was my boatyard friend Harold Cleveland, derby hat securely planted on his head. As we sailed close aboard he reached for the old galvanized foghorn, raised it to his lips, and gave me three fine long blasts. And so *Great Republic* passed into my memory.

ii

With a change in Father's sailing objectives there came an about-face in his choice of boats. The next three were entirely unlike *Great Republic*. Following one another in rapid succession, they were essentially racing boats—what Professor Evers Burtner of Massachusetts Institute of Technology has taught me to call Open Class as opposed to One Design Boats.

The first of these we sailed for a single reason. She was *Mariana* (ex-*Timandra*), an R boat, which was a class that was extremely popular in the 1920s, especially in Marblehead. The fact that she had originally belonged to Mr. Charles H. W. Foster may well have influenced Father's decision to buy *Mariana*. Mr. Foster was not only a personal friend of his, but a most influential member of Marblehead's Eastern Yacht Club, a highly successful racing skipper, and a tireless and creative experimenter in hull and rig design. Anyone interested in boating history should read Foster's *The Eastern Yacht Club Ditty Box 1870-1900* (Norwood, Mass., privately printed, 1932), in which he faithfully and charmingly presents the events and attitudes of those years in American yachting.

Mariana's designer, John Alden, although a most successful creator of ocean racing schooners and other types, was never in my book a top designer of Open Class racers. On the other hand, Mr. W. B. Calderwood, who had done work on her, was a perfectionist in the construction of this type, and in this and other respects deserves far more general recognition than he has received.

During summer visits with John Noble at Prides Crossing, I availed myself of every opportunity to call on Mr. Calderwood. His yard was on the same neck of land at the head of Manchester Harbor that is now occupied by Manchester Marine Railway Company. I had no special business to discuss with Mr. Calderwood. I simply enjoyed nosing about in his building shed and listening to his yarns of boating pleasures and woes.

On one occasion I was questioning him about a number of little stock auxiliaries that had become popular in spite of various deficiencies. Compared to yachts built by Lawley, Herreshoff, or Calderwood, these boats appeared to me crude in construction, less than perfect in their building materials. "Well, boy," Mr. Calderwood allowed, "you just have to keep the likes of them in the air. That's all there is to it, just keep passing them around." It was his opinion that, saddled with a real dry-rotter, an owner might be wisest to halfway patch up the worst of the problems, enjoy the boat as much as possible for a spell, and

Mariana

LOA	38'2"
LWL	23'6"
Beam	8'0"
Draft	5'4"
Sail area	594 sq.ft.

Originally designed by Alden
with a gaff rig and well built
by Hodgdon Brothers in 1915,
the R Class sloop *Mariana*
(ex-*Timandra*, ex-*Banshee*)
had been converted to
marconi by 1928 when
Father bought her.

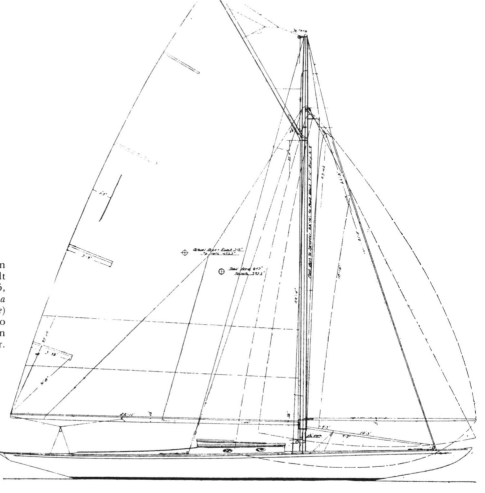

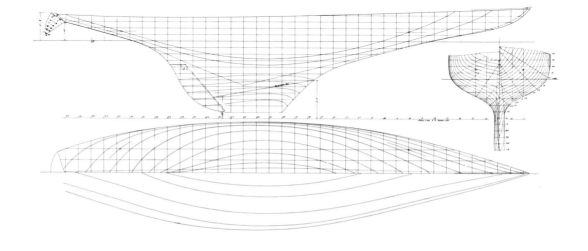

then pass her to someone else. In this way no one could get too badly hurt and everyone would have a little fun. Father sometimes expressed this same thinking in a slightly different way. "Whores of Babylon," he called these poor boats. "Everyone uses them," he said, "but nobody loves them."

Mariana was built to what was known as the Universal Rule. To me most rating rules form a big and confusing subject. However, they have over the years so materially affected the shape and type of yachts that it is important to consider them, at least in a general amateur way.

The commercial tonnage rules of medieval times had an influence on early attempts at rating yachts for racing purposes. In these rules a "tun" was a large cask of standard size for wine or other liquids. A vessel was taxed then according to how many tuns she could carry in her cargo space. To ascertain this number of tuns, merchants and customs people worked out a time-saving measurement method and formula in which cargo capacity was related to internal volume of the hull, i.e., length x width x depth. The distance between the stem of a vessel and her rudder post was the length dimension used in the formula. This length is what the old-timers called "Length Between Perpendiculars," as opposed to our "Length Waterline" and "Length Over All." The width factor was simply the beam of the vessel—a very easy thing to measure. The depth measurement was a more complicated dimension to get, because of 'tween deck, cargo, and other obstructions. Since most vessels in those days had a depth much the same as their beam, the measurers merely used the beam measurement twice to figure the cubic area of her hold—or "tunnage." It is not surprising that sharp traders tended to limit the beam of their vessels and add to their actual depth. In this way they cheated the tax man, even though they distorted the shape of their vessels at the same time.

Tonnage rules of modified form are still used as a measure of the size of commercial vessels. Early yachts were also measured by tonnage rules and raced against each other accordingly: ton against ton. This surely is a more informative way of describing the basic size of a boat than to speak solely of length. However, when yachts began to take widely different shapes, tonnage measurement rules no longer fairly rated them for racing. Waterline length then became the important factor, for boating people knew that the longer the waterline, the faster, all things being equal, a boat could go. (A specific rule of thumb is that the square root of the waterline length multiplied by 1.5 results in the outside limit of speed of a displacement boat. With a waterline length of 25 feet the square root would be 5, and this multiplied by 1.5 would indicate a top speed of 7.5 knots—1 nautical mile, or knot, being equivalent to 1.15 statute miles.)

The other most important factor in speed is the power needed to push a boat. For sailboats the power is the wind against the sails, and sail area becomes the

This photo shows *Mariana* with her marconi rig and also indicates a characteristic of some early boats designed to the Universal Rule. They appear to be afraid of the water, trying to lift their overhanging bows and sterns away from it, thus achieving a short waterline.

measurement of the power. And so a combination of waterline length and sail area became the primary factors in the early rating rules. Eventually, these rules resulted in boats with undesirable qualities, structural and otherwise. Designers of the late nineteenth century found that by making their waterlines short and their bow and stern overhangs long they got around the rules and produced boats that exceeded their rated speed. (When a long-ended boat heels, her actual sailing waterline length increases.) To correct the situation, the New York Yacht Club asked Nathanael Herreshoff to draw up a new rule. This Herreshoff did in 1902, and his formula soon became known as the Universal Rule, because it was more or less universally used in American yacht racing. This rule, which included the factor of displacement or weight of the boat in pounds along with the already accepted factors of length and sail area measurements ($R = \frac{L \times \sqrt{SA}}{\sqrt[3]{D}}$), resulted in a good, healthy boat.

The different sizes of Universal Rule boats were classified by letters. Of these, the largest and most famous was the J class. Popular smaller classes included M, Q, and R boats. Boats of any design could be measured under the Universal Rule and receive a rating (which in general would approximate the waterline length of the boat being measured). In this way boats of any rating could race against each other under a time allowance also worked out by Herreshoff and in common usage for many years. Rated boats of the same letter rating could also race as a class, boat for boat, without time allowance.

A second rule called the International Rule was developed at about the same time. It too attempted with considerable success to produce a healthier type of boat. It was widely adopted in Europe, and remains an influential factor in international competition.

iii

I feel disloyal not to remember more about the R boat *Mariana*. But I have no trouble remembering a great deal about Father's next Open Class boat. This was a Norwegian-built sloop that Father chose to call *Java* (after a lucky New Bedford whaleship of that name that had been owned by his grandfather Matthew Howland and his great-uncle George Howland).

For half a century I had been under the impression that this *Java* was a Seven Meter boat. The broker who sold her to Father had called her a Seven Meter. Indeed, there was such a class in Europe. Even if I knew of no American Seven Meter boats, who was I to question her identity? However, I never could quite reconcile her small displacement and hard bilges with those of a conventional International Rule meter boat. Now, thanks to the kind efforts of Mr. Frederick Denneche of Oslo's Norsk Sjofartsmuseum,* I have at last learned that *Java* was

*Mr. Arne Emil Christensen, of the University Museum in Oslo, helpfully introduced me to Mr. Denneche.

not a Seven Meter. Rather, she was a 75 square meter. The difference is instructive.

The International Rule aimed at making a fast-sailing boat, but also one that could be used for cruising. The resulting classes (which run the gamut from 5.5 Meters to the British giants *White Heather* and *Shamrock III* that for a time were designated Twenty-three Meters) developed fine boats. However, they were of fairly heavy displacement and expensive to build, and they depreciated rapidly in value when their time as racers ran out. This situation stimulated a demand for a cheaper, less extreme type of boat.

"In the winter of 1912," Mr. Denneche writes, "a committee was formed for working out a new rule. Among its members were Johan Anker, Christian Jensen, and Halvdan Hansen. The latter was a well-known regatta helmsman.

"The committee suggested two types of boats: a 75 square meter and a 50 square meter, corresponding nearly to the size of an International 7.5 and 6.5 Meter. This square meter rule was primarily a sail area rule, with certain restrictions, rather than a hull measurement rule. The 75 square meters turned out to be very popular. The last one was built in 1932. They took part in regatta years until after World War II. Following the trend of the period, the sail area was reduced, the first time about 1921 to 60 square meters and then about 1929 to 52 square meters. Today we therefore [call 75 square meters] 52 square meters.

"The smaller type of boat, the original 50 square meter, was not a success and soon vanished from regattas."

Mr. Denneche also emphasized that the square meter boats were not One Designs, but were "built to a restricted rule stating maximum and minimum dimensions and calling for a strict selection of materials...."

Piecing together information from Mr. Denneche and other sources, I can say with certainty that *Java* was a 75 square meter boat designed by Anker, and built by Anker and Jensen for their committee friend, Halvdan Hansen, who sailed and raced the boat as *Tamara III*. In 1923, she was brought to Long Island Sound by a Norwegian, Karl Krogstad, and made a fine reputation for herself, winning many prizes in handicap racing. Later she was bought by Herbert Stone, editor of *Yachting*. Somewhere along the line she acquired the name *Julita* and sailed out of New Haven under the ownership of Ralph Rowe. Still later, as *Miss Winsome*, her home port became Nantucket. Father bought her in 1929, after she had been refloated following a sinking accident. Major Smyth was again Father's helpful advisor and surveyor.

Johan Anker, *Java*'s designer and builder, was an outstanding Norwegian sailorman. Along with Colin Archer, about whom I will have more to say later, he might well be called the father of Norwegian yachting. To add to my own limited knowledge of Anker, let me quote once again from a letter from Frederick Denneche.

JAVA

Java's accommodation and sail plan fitted happily into the hull. Starting aft she had a steering well, a passenger cockpit, a main cabin with galley aft and lockers forward, and then an open fo'c's'le. (Originally she had two quarter berths aft. This arrangement was rather a trademark of Anker's and was greatly admired by Francis Herreshoff and others.) In the main cabin there was Howland headroom—low—that was enhanced by a good, sliding companionway hatch aft and a trim little skylight amidships. In place of wood panels in the locker doors there were mirrors with ornamental beveled edges. By day they reflected the sun as it streamed through the skylight; by night they cheered our lives with a double reflection of the central cabin lamp.

The cabin sole was set low in the hull, resulting perforce in a narrow floor. The transom seats were likewise narrow, but because of the low cabin sole, they were high enough to be comfortable and, at the same time, afford ample sitting room under the deck. (This was typical of the thought Anker put into planning and use of space.) The risers, or inboard faces, of the seats were angled outboard at the bottom and bore on the skin of the boat, allowing the seated sailor to draw his heels up for a change of position—or to prevent a passing shipmate from treading on his toes. The cabin table was of a simple folding type: for use, it rested on two removable pipe legs; for storage, the table and legs fit snugly beside the mast.

The seat backs folded down in an ingenious way to form wide, restful, safe berths. These backs were in effect rectangular wooden frames, hinged at the bottom. The frames were padded and upholstered on the inboard face for seating comfort and neat appearance. When they were hinged down about 60° from vertical, however, the backs revealed canvas berth bottoms attached on their inboard edge to the upper edge of the frames—and on the outboard edge to battens fastened to the skin of the boat. Good tautness of canvas could be achieved by lashing the berth back hard down. With thin pad mattresses and canvas berth boards, these berths were perfect for *Java*, because her greatest beam was at sleeping-berth level.

Forward of the deckhouse and cabin bulkhead was a pipe berth, and a throne. I must admit the throne was more usable when the forehatch was open. In the rain or in a seaway, one took one's chances.

By today's thinking the rig we had on *Java* would seem old-fashioned, but this does not mean it was inefficient or unsuitable. On the contrary, for a cruiser-racer, it proved an excellent arrangement. The hull had sufficient overhangs to enable the crew to handle sails comfortably, without falling overboard at either end from a bowsprit or overhanging boom. The mast itself was a built-up hollow spar that curved aft at the top. For its height, the curved spar provided for more sail area in the main than would have been attainable with a straight mast of the same length. Furthermore, it meant less need for long battens—nuisances for sailmaker and cruising sailor alike. Finally, as we tend to forget, a round curved mast is very strong—and will tend to bend like a bow rather than break. *Java* had no permanent backstay, and although we had several jolting unscheduled jibes in *Java*, we never had any problem with this spar.

Java's boom was about half the length of her mast. This 2:1 aspect ratio made for a good, efficient sail plan, especially for cotton sails (which tend to lose their shape if they are too narrow). The small working jib may appear to be a weakness to sailors raised on masthead genoas. Yet it was rewardingly effective when all points of sailing are considered. Just try tangling with a Herreshoff S boat—which has a similar sail plan—and you will find out what I mean.

In a boat the size of *Java*, a mainsail is an easy sail to handle. Being secured all along its luff and all along its foot, it cannot get out of hand, nor does it create undue stress to hull or fittings. On the other hand, a big genoa needs a taut luff and generates tremendous loads on its sheets and blocks that can be hard on boat and crew alike. Furthermore, when storage space is limited, a big stiff genoa can be a bulky and uncongenial bedfellow.

In addition to her jibstay, which was anchored well inboard, *Java* had a parallel running headstay that extended from masthead to stem head. On this long stay we could set a lightweight balloon jib for reaching in moderate weather. A ballooner is a good reaching sail; a genoa is not, for you can carry a ballooner when the wind is well aft. I admit that we did have a small flat spinnaker for going dead before the wind; its hoist was about two-thirds of the way up the mast. But even without it, *Java*, with her big mainsail sheeted well out, was a fast running boat and easy to handle.

All elements of *Java*'s design were skillfully worked out to blend into the final perfect whole. Her ends were stylish and beautifully balanced. Her transom was so small as to be merely a dainty carved arc. Her freeboard was low, graceful—exactly right for a boat with her overhangs and sheer.

Java's cockpit coamings, cabin house and forehatch, as well as her rails, were varnished mahogany. They were low and narrow, in keeping with her hull. Her topsides were painted a handsome green, and she had an artfully placed and carved cove stripe finished in gold leaf. Her narrow boot top was white and swept slightly upward fore and aft. Her side decks and house top were painted a sandstone buff. Rowing ashore from *Java* was never easy. You always wanted to circle her once or twice just for the visual pride and delight of it.

Not round and narrow in section like boats designed to the International Rule, *Java* had the moderate displacement of a handy cruising boat.

For three seasons starting in 1929 Father owned *Java*, a Norwegian-built 75-square-meter sloop and always one of my favorites.

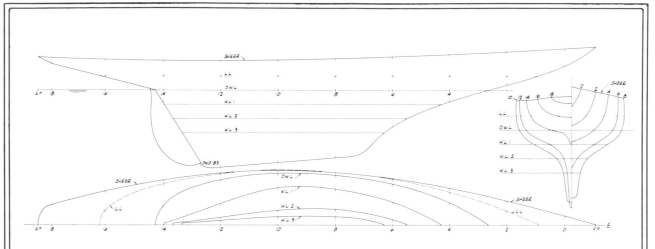

The steering well had a low coaming with two folding mahogany covers, which, when open, formed low seats on each side. Securely settled here, the helmsman could see over his guests seated in the larger cockpit ahead of and below him. *Java* heeled easily at first, quickly gaining in waterline length and potential speed. But as her rail approached the water, she stiffened appreciably and could carry sail well without dragging her decks under. Her helm was light and responsive, her motion easy and pleasing, in light airs or strong breezes. She was a joy to sail.

As with other Open Class boats, *Java*'s construction was light to allow for a reasonably heavy ballast keel. Her backbone was carefully designed so as to eliminate unnecessary joints.

Her steam-bent frames extended down alongside deep floor timbers. The planking was mahogany, fitted without caulking. (After a winter's haul-out, you could see through her open seams—a scary sight at first—and it took a little time for these seams to take up after she was launched. Once the swelling process was complete, however, her hull was very tight.)

Sailing hard on the wind, *Java*'s deck canvas would wrinkle slightly, the little valleys and peaks extending aft and to leeward. She was, indeed, like a porpoise, adjusting her shape to suit the conditions and thereby reduce her resistance. Limber she was, but like the bending reed, *Java* withstood the blows of wind and sea for many a year.

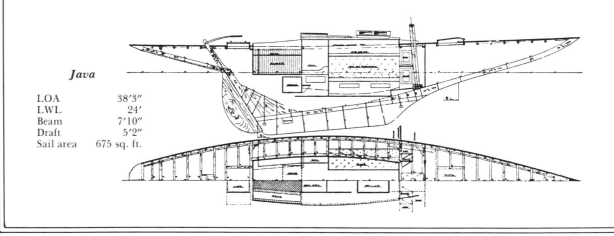

Java

LOA	38'3"
LWL	24'
Beam	7'10"
Draft	5'2"
Sail area	675 sq. ft.

"Johan Anker was born June 26th, 1871. He came from a well-to-do family. From his early childhood he was interested in boats and the sea, and both his father and his uncle owned yachts. His father even designed one himself....The family had a summer place on the east side of the Oslofjord (the Hveler islands), where Johan did his first sailing. His father, however, had plans for him to follow the family line and become a businessman. In spite of that his father agreed to his taking a technical education, first in Oslo, then at the University of Charlottenburg, Berlin, where he chose ship-construction for his major thesis. Until he was 34 years old, he worked in the pulp business.... He later stated that these years were the misuse of good abilities. They ripened him to take the great decision of his life: to go into partnership with Christian Jensen in 1905 to form the famous Anker & Jensen yard. In 1907 he moved to Vollen in Asker near Oslo where, with Jensen, he ran the yard until 1916. [Thereafter] he ran the yard alone until his death October 2nd, 1940.

"The Anker & Jensen yard was closed down in 1952. The buildings were later removed to give space for a new highway."

Anker's personal history bears out my general observation that few top yacht designers have gained their eminence through formal training in naval architecture or engineering alone. From the start Anker was a sailor. He learned much about hull form from his own early sailing experiences, from talking with older seamen who had spent their lives at sea, and from firsthand observation of the many vessels, large and small, that sailed in and out of Oslo, his home port. He knew well the skills and joys of sailing and cruising, and himself became a top helmsman and racing skipper. From such activities he acquired a solid understanding of what a sailor looks for in the way of deck and rig detail—detail that serves to further not only sailing efficiency, but the often forgotten ingredient of personal enjoyment as well. A boat designed with this true understanding, and for a well-considered purpose, is usually not just a good performer, but a delight to the eye and senses. Anker's boats were surely successful in both respects.

Boat design ability is incomplete unless it includes a full knowledge of boat construction. Johan Anker was an eminently fine boatbuilder. His Oslo yard was famous throughout the world for its well-planned and excellent construction. For his commercial craft he knew where strength, toughness, and weight were needed. For his racing types he knew where weight could be eliminated without the loss of essential strength and durability. Knowing that he would be building from his own designs, he took special pains with his construction plans, and I am sure that he did at times modify his lines in small ways to make construction simpler, better, less expensive.

Java was one of those rare complete units created by a master whose plans were not distorted by a rule. She has always been a special favorite of mine.

Johan Anker built his first boat in 1889 and formed a partnership with Christian Jensen in 1905. The Anker & Jensen yard built everything from dinghies to schooners, including several prize-winning International Rule racers—Six Meters, Eight Meters, and Twelve Meters. Anker's Twelve Meter design, *Smyrna,* of 1914 was the first of that class to carry a marconi rig. From 1915 to 1922 and again from 1931 to 1934, Johan Anker chaired the Scandinavian Yacht Racing Union. His best-known design is probably the Dragon class, which came out in 1928. His last boat was *Facit,* a cruiser, in 1939. (The above information was kindly furnished by Arne Emil Christensen, Oslo, Norway.)

Although she belonged to a racing class, I find that I think of *Java* more particularly as a cruiser-racer, as this combination can be one of the most satisfying and rewarding types for a sailing family. She was a practical size. She was for a happy period of time just right for the needs of Father and his two sons.

Although the 1930s turned out to be a decade of ocean racing for me, I did have my share of sailing in *Java.* One summer morning I organized a noon picnic to Red Beach across Buzzards Bay on the northwest shore of Naushon Island. The original aim was to get an early start, but this was just wishful thinking considering the pleasantly mixed company I'd invited. No matter. We swam at lunch time, ate at siesta time, and explored the island overlooking Robinson's Hole during the late afternoon when we should have been on our way home. So six o'clock arrived before we knew it.

In futile haste we weighed anchor and set sail. It was already too late to make the dinner gong. Further complicating matters, the wind did what it always does on such summer evenings. It died out completely. The sun turned a glorious red, then faded away below the horizon and left us alone in the luminous darkness of a starry night. Everything was lovely...everything except for one question. What would be the penalty our parents would mete out to us for causing them worry?

Father was not aboard, of course, but I seemed to hear him quietly talking to me. He was saying, "Get in the tender." Accordingly, we unbent the anchor warp from the anchor and fastened it to the lifting ring in the dinghy's transom. (This warp was a length of manila whale line made especially by New Bedford Cordage Company for the whaling industry. It was ³/₄ inch diameter, laid up loosely to prevent kink and provide stretch.) We paid out some 30 feet of the warp and made it fast to *Java*'s mooring bit. All hands were warned to sit still. After all, even on big ships that were attempting to get away from an enemy, it was the custom to order the men to their hammocks. Moving about slows any boat down.

Larry Grinnell took *Java*'s helm, and I commenced rowing with short, easy strokes. The dinghy had weight and momentum, the line gave at the right interval, and *Java* seemed in the quiet water to have little or no resistance. We slipped along easily, making good progress. I didn't have to ask my absent father what course to take. Years before he had shown me that at night or in a fog it was wise to head for White Rock. The gulls had given this peak of granite a luminous coat, and it was always a helpful marker on a safe course into Padanaram Harbor. If you weren't able to see it at first, you could often smell it or hear the waves washing around it.

It was getting on for eleven as we neared the anchorage. All was quiet except for some suspicious sounds to the west over in the direction of the Grinnells'

Birchfield Farm dock. We could see a light aboard their schooner and soon heard the sound of her engine starting; so we kept well to the east, close to the dark line of the breakwater, and I kept rowing.

As it turned out, the commotion we had heard had indeed been the result of an attempted search party mounted by various parents. However, it seems that those leading the rescue had had some difficulty of their own getting underway, and had fouled *Flying Cloud III*'s propeller in her mooring pick-up line, thereby swamping her tender. Or so Father explained the situation the following morning. (Father himself never worried when we youngsters were out in a boat. He only worried when we drove in cars to the movies.) Whatever befell *Flying Cloud III*, we arrived home before our parents.

My only conclusion from this well-remembered episode is that there is nothing like a nice, easily driven sloop and a suitable dinghy to make for a safe and happy amateur outing.

iv

Much as he enjoyed her, Father sold *Java* for a larger boat. The last of his Open Class boats was an Eight Meter.

As I've said, the International Rule to which the meter boats are built is primarily a European rule, albeit somewhat inspired by formulations of the Seawanhaka and New York yacht clubs. The Six Meters, in particular, have been very popular over a considerable period of time, especially in interclub and international competition. Many Eights, Tens, and of course Twelves have also been built and raced. Indeed, the International Rule, as wisely modified from time to time, has remained a significant racing factor longer than any other yacht rating rule.

Father's Eight Meter was christened *Balek* by her original owner, Tom Eliot, and I've been trying without success to find out what her name means. In one of her mystery novels, Agatha Christie describes a street scene in Baghdad where men in donkey carts shout "Balek, Balek." So perhaps it means "Make way." Way or no way, we all had some fine racing, sailing, and cruising aboard *Balek* during the three years that Father owned her, 1932 to 1935. But our most important *Balek* dividends came from the contacts we had with her designer, Frank Paine, and with others of his family.

I had for some years known Frank Paine's sister Georgina, then Mrs. Richard Thornton Fisher. She and her husband, who was for many years head of the Harvard forestry school, owned a summer house in Petersham, Massachusetts. My grandfather Charles S. Waldo also had a farm in Petersham, and just to the west of the Fisher and Waldo farms Harvard University owned a large acreage of virgin white pine, as well as areas of wetland. I assume my later intense interest in trees and wood must have started right there; for Mother and I

Father bought the 48′ Eight Meter sloop *Balek* for a mere $3,500 in 1932. His knowledge of Buzzards Bay and the boat's windward ability made them a hard pair to beat in the occasional racing that took place during the three years he owned her.

dearly loved Petersham and all that went with it. When Mother died just before World War II, our happy Petersham visits came to an end. Mr. Fisher also died before World War II. But about the time I came home from Navy service, the widow and the widower were married, and so it was that Nina Paine Fisher became my much-loved stepmother, and Father gained a whole new lease on life.

To go back a generation, Frank and Nina's father was General Charles J. Paine, one of the very greatest of American yachtsmen. In 1885 he was a member of the Boston syndicate, headed by J. Malcolm Forbes, which commissioned Edward Burgess, then a young and relatively unknown yacht designer, to draw plans for a contender in the upcoming *America*'s Cup trials. This became *Puritan*, which, as a Boston entry and flying the Eastern Yacht Club flag, won a decision over the New York entry *Priscilla* (designed by the highly respected and influential naval architect A. Cary Smith) for the right to defend the Cup.

With her deeper hull form and outside ballast keel, *Puritan* was a real departure from the prevailing American yacht type that had flat sections, long ends, a centerboard, and inside ballast. Managed by General Paine, *Puritan* outsailed the "plank on edge" English challenger *Genesta* and became the forerunner of a new and successful type of yacht. In addition General Paine started the trend toward Corinthian (unpaid, amateur) crews. In 1886 the General financed the Edward Burgess–designed *Mayflower*, which defeated the British *Galatea*. The next year, he successfully defended the Cup with Burgess's last great production, *Volunteer*.

During the nineties more large racing sloops were built than at any other time in history. Nine of them were over 80 feet on the waterline, and one of these was *Jubilee*, which was designed by Frank Paine's older—by some two decades—brother John, himself then only in his early twenties. Although *Jubilee* lost out to the Herreshoff-designed *Vigilant* in the Cup trials, she was—and remains—the only Cup contender to have been designed by an amateur.

By 1933, when I first became involved in the boat business, all these huge older sloops with their 7,000 square feet and more of sail had disappeared, and the equally majestic J boats, built to the Universal Rule, had taken their place. In 1930 Frank Paine was himself designing a Cup contender. This was the J boat *Yankee*, which, with C. F. Adams at the helm and Paine among others in the afterguard, sailed a most exciting series of trial races against the Starling Burgess–designed *Enterprise*, Clinton Crane's *Weetamoe*, and the Francis Herreshoff–designed *Whirlwind*. Sadly for the home team, Harold Vanderbilt's *Enterprise* was in the end selected and went on to defeat Sir Thomas Lipton's *Shamrock V*. Nonetheless, *Yankee*, in the summer of 1930 and later, established some remarkable racing records.

In 1931 Paine designed the 61-foot *Highland Light* for Dudley Wolfe and the Plymouth, England, ocean race of that year. In 1932 *Highland Light* made a record run to Bermuda that wasn't broken until the 1956 Bermuda Race, when the 72-foot *Bolero* made the run in one hour less. A less-well-known Frank Paine accomplishment is that he was involved in the design of the great Gloucester fishing schooner *Gertrude L. Thebaud*.

During the thirties, John and Frank Paine had an office on an upper floor of 11 Beacon Street in Boston. They made space there for Father to have a small room and desk, although Father's business was not boats, and he became much involved with boat talk. C. Raymond Hunt, who had already made a big reputation racing small boats out of Duxbury and, later, Q boats and Eight Meters in Marblehead, was constantly in and out of the Paine office. So was another young and excellent racing man from Marblehead, E. Arthur Shuman. And at times, someone in the office would move over to make a bit of room for me. To state it mildly, this was an exciting office to work in. Yachting history,

Balek

LOA	48′ 3″
LWL	30′ 0″
Beam	8′ 6″
Draft	6′ 5″
Sail area	833 sq. ft.

Balek was designed by Frank
Paine to the International
Rule and was built by Lawley
in 1930.

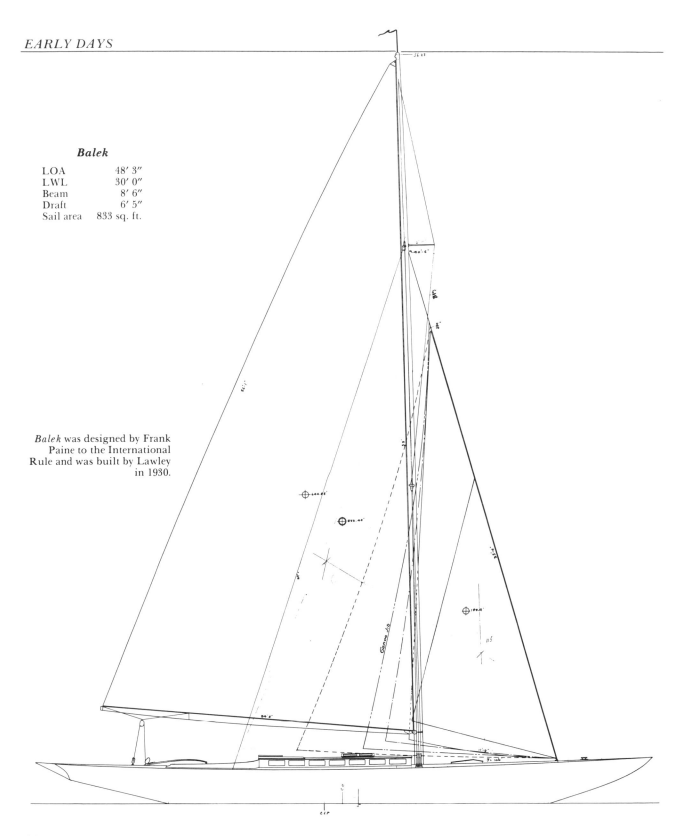

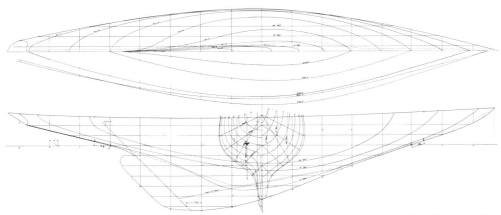

past, present, and future, was everywhere, although I fear that much of it passed by over my head.

I can see Mr. John Paine's desk now. It was one of those big rolltop monsters. The cover was kept down except for a brief moment every morning when the mail came in. Then Mr. Paine would roll the top back just far enough to permit him to stuff in the new letters underneath. Had he raised it any higher, a mountain of mail would surely have poured onto the floor. He explained that every so often and at random he plucked out a letter and attended to it.

Father had his own method for handling certain of his business matters, and Arthur Shuman has often regaled me with his version of this method. It seems that one day Arthur had joined Father in his little office and was discussing the latest racing results when an agent from the "Infernal Revenue" was ushered in. Father shut the door firmly and motioned this gentleman to sit down, but made no comment. Instead he went to the window and threw the bottom sash way up. Then he stuck his head out the window, looked down to the brick walkway below, and returned to his seat. The IRS man was beginning to look puzzled. However, he started his questioning. Father listened in silence for a few moments. Then once again he arose from his seat, deliberately and purpose-

Balek's round sections make an interesting contrast to *Mariana* and *Java*, both of which had harder bilges. This roundness was an attempt to achieve a boat that went fast yet rated low under the International Rule of measurement. That rule favored a larger displacement than other contemporary rules.

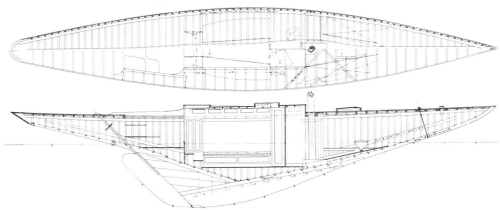

fully picked up the Persian carpet from the office floor, and with an ominous flourish hove it out the open window. By this time the man from the IRS was on his feet and backing warily toward the door. Art Shuman found this an unusual but effective way to handle unwanted visitors. When he asked Father how he took care of unwanted mail, Father explained that he had a rubber stamp made up with the single word "Deceased" on it. Stamped with this dolorous information the letter was "Returned to Sender." I am told Frank Paine was no less impatient with unwelcome correspondence. It was, as I say, an unusual office.

Frank Paine designed *Balek* in 1930 along with three other Eight Meter boats: a class that was growing in popularity at the expense of the Universal Rule Q class that had been so active, especially in Marblehead, during the twenties. He had all four boats built at George Lawley & Son's yard in Neponset (Dorchester), Massachusetts—a famous and fine firm in which he owned a majority interest and which he continued to operate, employing nearly 5,000 men during the height of World War II, until the postwar slump put it out of business.

When a good designer builds his own boats in his own good yard, the results can be great—and not necessarily exorbitantly expensive. The Herreshoff Manufacturing Company, Anker & Jensen, as well as Lawley's, all illustrate the point. *Balek* was a fine boat and as good as new when Father bought her in 1932 at the used-boat price of $3,500. She had beautiful Ratsey and Lapthorn sails made at the Ratsey loft in Cowes. With her Ratsey mainsail, *Balek* would stand up and go to windward like nobody's business. (This mainsail was cut down and used on Concordia Yawl No. 1 many years later.) With a lighter, fuller one that also came with the boat, she lay down and only slugged along.

Designed for racing, *Balek* would have been happier if she had remained in Marblehead, for we Howlands never gave her much of a chance to show her speed in competition round the buoys. I don't mean Father didn't sail *Balek*— and sail her hard and well. But the Buzzards Bay school of sailing was very different, at least when I was growing up, from the North Shore school.

In Marblehead, racing, especially class racing, is a very logical way in which to enjoy one's boating. With the exception of Manchester, Annisquam, and Gloucester a little farther east, there really are few harbors or beaches within range for weekend cruising or picnicking. So it seems to work out best to putter around your boat or yacht club during the prevailing morning calms, then go forth and test your skill and the speed of your boat when the light afternoon southwesterlies spring up. Certainly Marblehead has produced some of the finest racing skippers in the world, including Charles Francis Adams, Frank Paine, Charlie Welch, Ray Hunt, John and Charlie Lawrence, Dick Boardman, Brad Noyes, Ted Hood, and many others. Over the years, few harbors have seen so much fine competitive racing.

This sketch by Frank Vining Smith (one of his annual Christmas cards) shows clearly the snugness of Menemsha Harbor and its narrow entrance between the jetties.

In contrast, our beloved Padanaram is located on Buzzards Bay—one of the finest small boat cruising grounds in the country. Within a few hours run there exist some 17 or 18 attractive and safe harbors, as well as many a fine island beach. The water is warm and clean for swimming. The southwest breeze—rising before 11 in the morning, falling before sunset—is dependable, though often quite strong. The season is long—late May to late October. The conditions tempt sailors away from organized afternoon racing to less formal activities. Padanaram young fry learn to row, sail in rough water, reef sails, and poke around in fog and currents.

Balek did participate in a few days of racing when my brother and I and Father's professional skipper Martin Jackson took her on a cruise up to Marblehead. With Ray Hunt as helmsman, we sailed her to several Ladies' Plate victories. There was also a Whalers Race out of Padanaram when we had some rewarding fun with two Ten Meters. Father knew his Buzzards Bay, and *Balek* was a hard boat to beat in a breeze to windward. We finished the race on the last feeble puffs of a dawn breeze. Some two miles back of us off Dumpling Rocks the Tens lay utterly becalmed.

And Father and I had a most stirring weekend cruise in *Balek* to Menemsha Bight. It was a fine close fetch across the Bay, through Quicks Hole, and across Vineyard Sound. (The one event of note involved Father's Dandie Dinmont terrier, who chose during the passage to chew the cork off our drinking water bottle. The two were at the time sharing the open space under the stern deck.)

As we approached the stone jetties that form the narrow channel from the Bight up into the big Menemsha and Quitsa ponds, Father hove-to, and I took our Herreshoff dinghy *Nathanael* and rowed ashore to see how conditions were for entering.

Just to the east of the jetties there is a gently sloping beach on the neck of land that forms the northern side of Menemsha's deep-water harbor and also hides it from the Sound. Climbing up the rise I could look directly down on the tiny bowl of the harbor and on up its narrowing arm, which extends a short distance to the south. Here small working craft were tied up to the banks on either side. Immediately to the left was the little gas dock that ran parallel to the shore and was occupied by three or four local fishing boats. Conditions looked perfect. No boats showed any sign of getting underway. The lone mooring buoy in the center of the basin was clear. I rowed back to *Balek*, and Father mapped out our strategy for entering.

The tide was ebbing strongly from the main Menemsha Pond, and it would be boiling out the jetties against us. The wind was strong southwest. Our course was about south. Midway through these jetties we would have to make a 90-degree turn through a gap into the quiet water of the basin. Father worked to the westward a bit, then slacked sheets slightly and bore away for the jetties. By the time we reached them, *Balek* was well heeled over and going fast through the rough water. We were, however, barely creeping by the jetty rocks, and *Balek* slewed from side to side in the boils of the current.

Father continued slightly beyond our turn, then hauled the helm hard up. Simultaneously, I eased the main sheet to keep her moving. We shot across the current into the tranquil waters of the basin.

Before the wind and now moving very fast, we seemed certain to hit the gas dock bow on. I let go the jib halyard, and at the last possible second Father put the helm hard down and we shot upwind. By now I was standing at the main halyard. I let 'er go just in time to grab the boathook and scoop up the mooring. We still had far too much way on, but the mooring line was slack. This gave me a chance to take a turn on the mooring cleat. Thus snubbed and with the main under Father's control, we circled round the mooring till we lost headway and lay quiet and shipshape, head to wind. Not a word had been spoken between us.

All this while Gene Ashley had been standing in front of his shack on the dock. His short and imposing 300-pound figure was shrouded to some degree by a beautiful flowing nightshirt of tentlike proportions. In his mouth was a big "seegar"; in his hand a tall glass. As we set about furling *Balek*'s main, Gene hailed us. "That was a good show," he said. "Come ashore for a visit when you're ready."

Gene was a son of New Bedford's famous perennial mayor, Charles S. Ashley, and he was a good friend and business associate of Father's. Besides running an oil business he was the agent for the Boston-based Old Colony Insurance Company. In this latter capacity he controlled most of the New Bedford fishing fleet—and was valued and respected accordingly. One thing Gene would not do was go to Boston. If anyone wanted to see him, they could come to New Bedford. Period. Gene was a champion snorer whose ability in this line I learned to respect. On board his motor sailer he gave his guests 15 minutes to get to sleep before he shut his own eyes. This, however, was only a gesture: after the 15 minutes were up, no one on board, and few in the harbor, could get any rest. In working out the plans for his motor sailer, Gene gave Bill Hand very few instructions, but these few were very specific. He knew what he wanted (as all too few do). The length of the boat was to be 45 feet. She was to have a big icebox. She was to have a spacious head. These requirements he got, and he was entirely happy with them. When I asked him why he named the boat *Night Hawk*, he told me that he had named her after his wife.

There are many more stories I could tell about Gene Ashley. But to get a compliment from a man of his caliber was something to savor.

Although I have been back to Menemsha many times, we never did so in *Balek*. What happened was that after a visit at Gene's wharf, we rowed up to the little grocery store at the head of the creek to buy provisions. Dandie Dinmont came with us. All would have been well, I am sure, had not the one-room store been full of cats. Things ended up with all shelves empty and the floor completely covered with crushed tomato cans, broken cereal boxes, spilled milk, and worse.

The manager shouted at us to get out and stay out, as Dandie fought his way backward toward the door. Dandie had been designed and built in England for hauling small animals from their holes, but an open engagement against a dozen cats was well beyond even his courageous spirit.

Father's Dandie Dinmont in our Herreshoff tender. The boat, which once served H. S. Vanderbilt's M class boat *Prestige*, is now at the Herreshoff Marine Museum in Bristol, Rhode Island.

Part II:

OCEAN RACING

Brenton Reef Lightship where many an ocean race began.

3
The 1928 Bermuda Race:
Flying Cloud III
and William Hand

i

In the fall of 1927 my schoolmate and friend Larry Grinnell invited me to join him for a first go at a real offshore trip. He had earned his father's blessing to take over the family schooner *Flying Cloud III* for the upcoming Bermuda Race.

At the time Larry was a Harvard freshman and I was a Harvard sophomore (this from the Greek *sophos* meaning wise—and *moros* meaning foolish). Already I had been the former by signing up for Samuel Eliot Morison's course "New England Maritime History"; soon I was to be the latter by failing Morison's course. Had I but paid attention during lectures I would have learned some useful and interesting facts about Bermuda, especially its strategic significance in our national history. As it was, come spring, I knew only that Bermuda was an isolated British colony located some 600 miles east of the stormy capes of Hatteras and across a warm but fickle current of water known as the Gulf Stream. It took the school of ocean racing finally to teach me a thing or two about Bermuda's 25 miles of paradise.

The Bermuda Race was still a relative novelty in those years, as, indeed, ocean racing itself had been during the previous years and decades of the early twentieth and late nineteenth centuries. There had been ocean yacht races as early as 1866. However, the racing was generally between large schooners owned by wealthy sportsmen who left the management of their yachts to professional skippers and crews. Prizes were in the form of big wagers and big purses. The course was usually across the North Atlantic to Europe. At least two of these great schooner races took place in the winter months, severely trying ships and crews alike.

My first Bermuda Race was as a college sophomore in 1928 aboard the 67' Hand-designed schooner *Flying Cloud III*. She is shown here at the New London starting line (second from right) along with the other schooners, while the eventual winner, yawl-rigged *Rugosa II*, a Herreshoff New York Forty, is at the far left.

Not until the early 1900s did amateurs in their own small boats venture offshore on even informal coastwise races. Thomas Fleming Day, founder and great editor of *The Rudder*, was responsible for sparking enthusiasm for these early sea trials. The first of the Day-inspired races started from Brooklyn, New York, proceeded outside Long Island and around Cape Cod, and ended in Marblehead, thereby joining the two most active yachting centers of the day. This was in 1904. Six boats, all under 30 feet of waterline length, participated, with the winner being a 22-foot sloop designed by Boston's George Owen. Day's own *Sea Bird*, a 19-foot yawl, was last. Day had designed this V-bottomed boat himself. He later proved her worth by sailing her to Naples, Italy. An able little boat, inexpensive to build, she was the forerunner of a long line of successful V-bottomed Sea Birds of one size or another.

In 1905, 12 small boats started out, again from Brooklyn, on a race south to Hampton Roads, Virginia. On this occasion, Tom Day was the winner—in *Tamerlane*, a 29-foot yawl designed and built by L. D. Huntington of New Rochelle, New York. This was the same good friend who had built *Sea Bird* for Day.

The following year, Day organized a more ambitious race. The starting line was still off Brooklyn, but the finish was some 660 miles away across the Gulf Stream. Only three boats entered this first Bermuda Race. All three were small; all had participated in the Hampton Roads Race. Day and his *Tamerlane* were again victors. *Gauntlet*, a 23-foot sloop also designed and built by Huntington, took second place. The 30-foot yawl *Lila* had rigging and mast troubles and dropped out early. Hard as the 1906 race was for these three small boats, it had its own special rewards, and it was the event that really launched ocean racing as a popular sport worldwide.

For the 1907 Bermuda Race, specifications were changed and professionals were permitted to serve as crew. The whole complexion of the fleet changed with the rules. There were 12 entries in the 1907 race and these were divided into two classes. In the big class there were eight boats. Of these, five were schooners—and of these five, three were designed and built by Lawley. Four of the five schooners were 55 feet or more on the waterline. Then there were two cutters (both over 45 feet), one designed by the late Edward Burgess, the other by the Scotsman Will Fife. The smallest entry in the class was a yawl of slightly over 40 feet on the waterline.

Of the four boats in the small class, one was a 25-foot Lawley schooner, one a 38-foot Huntington yawl, one was the 30-foot yawl *Lila*. The final entry was a 29-foot cutter named *Zena*. *Zena* was the sole Bermuda-designed and Bermuda-owned entry; she was also the first ocean racer to have a jib-headed Bermudian rig.

I have used waterline lengths in describing these boats because this measurement is generally more indicative of actual size than is length overall. Most of the boats I mention were, however, of the modest-freeboard, long-overhang type so soon to be discouraged by the Universal Rule. For instance, the winner in the big class, *Dervish*, a schooner designed by Clinton Crane, was 56 feet on the waterline, but some 30 feet longer overall. Ironically, *Lila*, which overcame her bad luck in the 1906 Bermuda Race by winning the small class on corrected time in this 1907 race, was relatively moderate in overhangs, being less than 40 feet overall.

Tom Day did not sail to Bermuda in 1907. He powered there, in a race against one other motor boat. (Both entrants were 60-footers.) This match was a first attempt by Day to promote ocean racing for powerboats. He tried again in 1909, with four entries, then finally in 1910—two entries. But his effort was to no avail. No matter how you slice it, going to sea in a small powerboat is bad enough in itself, without the added inconvenience of racing. It can be done, but the problems are many and the pleasures too often are few.

Bermuda races under sail continued for another three years. In 1908 the start was from Marblehead with five entries (four of which were schooners, of which three were over 55 feet). The starting line for the 1909 race was back in Gravesend Bay, Brooklyn. Again there were five boats, four of which were schooners. Again, they were, with one exception, big boats of 60 feet and more waterline and up to 100 feet overall. Again, they were mostly older boats, well designed and well built, but sailed by owners who were trying out a sport that was new to them.

In 1910 the character of the Bermuda Race changed once more. There were only two entries. Both were big boats—some 75 feet overall. Each was schooner rigged. However, both were newer boats with more freeboard and shorter ends—ones better suited for offshore work than had been the previous type. And their owners were both what I like to call "sailors for keeps." *Vagrant*, owned by Harold S. Vanderbilt of New York, was a brand-new Herreshoff boat. *Shiyesa*, owned by Demarest Lloyd of Boston, was only four years old and was designed and built by Lawley. The race itself turned out to be a good one, and fast. *Vagrant* caught a lucky wind break near the finish and won by a few hours only. *Shiyesa* had aboard as crew a young man who six years later was to design an 83-foot schooner for Mr. Lloyd: John Alden.

By 1911 it was obvious that enthusiasm for ocean racing was, at least for the moment, petering out. The bigger boats with their paid crews were discouraging the smaller boats handled by amateurs—and were accomplishing this without giving their owners the special satisfaction that comes from winning by one's own efforts.

For the next three years there was no serious ocean racing, and in 1914 World War I put an end to any possibility of it. Right after the peace was signed, however, the sport sprang to life once more with added enthusiasm and new types of boats. It was the editor of a second boating magazine, Herbert Stone of *Yachting*, who was chiefly responsible for reviving the Bermuda Race. The first postwar sailing of the event was run in 1923.

What had prompted the renewal of interest? During the war and shortly thereafter, there was a great expansion in various forms of offshore work. Many men, including Herb Stone himself, had been in the U.S. Navy. In command of submarine chasers and other small vessels, they had crossed the Atlantic to foreign ports and had acquired not only a new knowledge of the sea, but, more important, a love for the seagoing life.

Additionally, in 1921 two small fisherman-type yachts—the schooner *Lloyd W. Berry* and the ketch *Typhoon*—each made successful crossings to Europe and return. The *Berry* was a 60-footer designed and built in 1920 by Charles A. Morse of Thomaston, Maine. In design she was similar to a Maine lobster smack. Her owner, Roger Griswold, and the very capable crew were all Bostonians, all Harvard graduates and U.S. Navy veterans. The *Lloyd W. Berry* sailed to the Azores, then to France, and finally to England, where Griswold and his friends had a fine old summer of it. Like many a vessel before and since, the *Berry* lingered too long before starting home, and paid the consequence. Fortunately, both the men and their boat were equal to the violent weather. Following a logical stop in the Canary Islands, they picked up the northeast trade winds and made a good passage to the West Indies and then north and home to New England.

Typhoon was a short-ended 45-foot ketch designed by William Atkin and built in Baddeck on the Bras d'Or Lakes of Nova Scotia. Her owner—yes, it is true—was yet a third influential yachting magazine editor: William Washburn Nutting, managing editor of *Motor Boat*. With the help of his friends Casey Baldwin and James Dorset he sailed his new boat to England. There he met the noted English cruising man Claud Worth, author of that great boat Bible *Yacht Cruising*, with whom he had some pleasant visits and much talk about cruising in general and about the already established Royal Cruising Club in particular. Because Baldwin had to return home early by steamer, Nutting took on as a replacement a young Sea Scout master from Cowes, Isle of Wight: Uffa Fox. The voyage back to the States turned out to be a rough one. Approaching San Miguel in the Azores, *Typhoon* ran into a gale—and at the same time ran out of food. Here again was the case of a boat that had tarried a bit too long in England. It was mid-November before *Typhoon* reached the Gulf Stream; in northern climes this is too late for a small ship to be making a crossing. *Typhoon* encountered strong gales and head winds, and suffered a near capsize. She was lucky to make landfall at all.

It was shortly after Nutting arrived back in New York that he and a few friends, in the cabin of his storm-pounded *Typhoon*, outlined an early plan for an American cruising club. Formal organization of the Cruising Club of America actually took place the following spring—or in 1922.

The newly formed CCA had 36 charter members. Rereading the list of these names I am struck with how familiar most of them are. In the 1920s the American offshore racing and yachting fraternity was a small one. And if many of my sailing memories of the period involve this small group, here is the reason why.

The CCA did not in itself sponsor the revived Bermuda Race of 1923. However, the race committee that did was headed by Herbert Stone and included such men as Bill Nutting, Bob Bavier, John Alden, my fellow townsman Allen Weeks, and other Cruising Club members. Indeed, the only member of the committee who was not at the time a member of the CCA was Kenneth Trimingham of Bermuda.

The 1923 fleet was divided into two main classes of schooners, ketches, and yawls: Class A for those between 53 and 70 feet overall; Class B for those from 35 feet to 52 feet overall. However, provision was made for single-masted boats and for any entries over 70 feet in overall length. Prizes from various sources were put in contention: among them, one from *Yachting*, one from the Royal Bermuda Yacht Club, and one from Paul Hammond, then Vice Commodore of the Seawanhaka Corinthian Yacht Club. (Captain Hammond's prize was for the first boat to finish with an all-amateur crew.) The simple racing formula gave a handicap of six minutes per overall foot of length, for the total course distance. In addition there was a propeller allowance.

An unexpectedly large number of boats signed up for this race—22 in all. And where most previous ocean races had set forth from New York's Lower Bay, this one was to begin from a starting line off Sarah's Ledge at the entrance to New London Harbor.

The 1923 Bermuda Race had a decidedly New Bedford flavor. In the first place, it was a "schooner race," and Padanaram Harbor was very much a schooner anchorage. In fact it may well be that there were more small cruising-type schooners moored in the harbors of Padanaram and Salters Point than on all the rest of the Atlantic coast put together. Of the 17 schooners entered, five were from the board of New Bedford designer William Hand, Jr., and four of these flew the New Bedford Yacht Club burgee. Of the four yawls and ketches, one, the 32-foot ketch *Sea Call*, was Hand-designed and locally owned. The sole sloop, *Flying Cloud*, was formerly a Padanaram boat.

The only entry that might be termed a racing yacht was the converted Herreshoff New York Forty *Memory*. Originally rigged as a gaff sloop, she now was a yawl with the only marconi sails in the fleet. *Memory* was well sailed by owner Bob Bavier and was not just the first boat to finish, but the winner in

Class A. It could surely be said that *Memory* started the trend toward the development of special designs and rigs for ocean racing. Before her outstanding performance, owners were content to enter the boat they happened to own, with the idea of trying out her speed over a long course.

The 1923 Bermuda Race was a notable success. The competition was good. The finishes were close. And Bermuda gave her guests a delightful welcome. No wonder another race was promoted for the following year.

There was a Bermuda Race in 1924. However, only 14 starters showed, of which a scant four were repeaters from 1923. It became apparent at this point that an annual race to Bermuda was too much of a good thing.

In 1926, the Cruising Club of America officially took over management of the race. The starting line was again set up off New London. Most of the fleet continued to be schooner-rigged (13 out of the 16 entrants). In spite of this, more important changes were taking place: a majority of the boats were new; an increasing number sported marconi rigs; and Paul Hammond's new One Design Seawanhaka schooner *Cygnet* and Everett Morss's *Malabar III*, following a current design trend, tried out double-staysail rigs. The race was an easy one and slow. *Malabar VII*, gaff-rigged and a schooner, was the winner in the big class and also took the overall trophy. Another slightly smaller Alden gaff schooner, *Black Goose*, had the best corrected time in Class B.

In 1928 the Bermuda Race start followed on the heels of the Harvard-Yale crew races, also held at New London. Those pre-Depression days brought out some strikingly beautiful spectator craft.

ii

The 1928 Bermuda Race was my first exposure to a real offshore sailing trip. From beginning to end it was an eye-opening experience.

For several days just before our June 23 starting date, all sorts of pleasure craft were collecting in New London Harbor. The railroad bridge tender was some busy, as most of the yachts were there to watch the Harvard-Yale crew races, and sailed up-river to anchorages above the town. Only the really big yachts such as *Corsair* and *Nourmahal* moored below the bridge.

By comparison, our Bermuda-bound fleet was unimpressive. Most of us dropped anchor off Burr's dock on the west side of the lower harbor. Still, above the bridge or below it, a busy confusion and a holiday "skimmer" spirit were the order of the day. In small rowboats or fancy power launches, or on foot along the railroad tracks to town, everyone was hustling somewhere or hurrying to get back.

My sea bag and I were already settled aboard *Flying Cloud III*, both of us having sailed over from Padanaram with a home crew that included Larry, as skipper, two professionals (Captain Roy Wall and the cook) and our Nonquitt neighbor Channing Frothingham. Other crew members were showing up one at a time, by boat, train, or auto. There was Mr. W. D. Stearns from Milton, our school science teacher and, for the trip to Bermuda, our senior navigator. Why we always knew him as "Bonzo" I cannot explain, for we respected him and

Flying Cloud's crew numbered 10 for this ocean race. Those shown (left to right) are L. Grinnell, Jr.; W. Story; W. D. Stearns; C. Frothingham, Jr.; S. Lane; the author; A. Hugeley; Captain Wall; and S. Batchelder. The cook is not shown.

loved him dearly. The others were Milton Academy and Harvard classmates of Larry's: Sam Batchelder and Arthur Hugeley, who were on their way to becoming famous athletes, and Sam Lane. As time went on, Sam was to take part in more than his share of ocean races and to cruise many offshore miles before he was tragically lost at sea—bound to Nassau—on a single-handed winter passage. Bill Story completed our 10-man roster.

The crew races were held the day before our start, and with a few exceptions all spectators did their level best to instill "speed, strength, and endurance" into their favorite oarsmen by drinking to their health. This they accomplished aboard moored yachts or moving along the river banks on special spectator trains. All this imbibing had a tendency to complicate our efforts the following day, as we tried to get organized for our own sailing race. Fog and drizzle added to the solemnity of this, the beginning of a serious offshore venture. Indeed, except for Captain Wall, a Maine schoonerman from way back, this was the first offshore trip for any of *Flying Cloud III*'s crew. (To his great credit, Captain Wall had kept his promise to remain aboard for the duration, thus avoiding the chance of running into his old friend John Barleycorn.)

What we found as we worked our way out to Sarah's Ledge was a schooner fleet for sure. Of the 24 entries, 16 were schooners, all but three of them gaff-rigged. Eight were of Alden design and of moderate size—between 47 and 57 feet. Another four were fisherman types designed by Hand, and on the average 10 feet longer than the Alden entries. At 67 feet, our *Flying Cloud III* was the largest boat in Class A.

Never having seen most of them before, I found it very difficult to tell all these schooners apart. *Malay*, a 45-footer designed by the Nova Scotia naval architect William Roué, was one exception, as were the Alden-designed *Teal* and the new Hand-designed *Yankee Girl II*. (All three had jib-headed mains.) Bob Bavier's two-year-old *Dragoon* was also easy to spot, as she was a marconi-rigged ketch. But the boat we knew best, and wanted most badly to beat, belonged to Larry Grinnell's uncle Russell Grinnell. Uncle Russy's *Rugosa II* was one of the grand, fast New York Forties designed by Herreshoff—a sister-ship to the Bavier-owned *Memory* that had won the 1923 Bermuda Race. She was virtually a new boat (one of two built in 1926, 10 years after the rest of the Forties), however, and at Mr. Grinnell's request had been rigged from the start as a marconi yawl. Our only hope against her was to have a fair wind—and lots of luck.

During and after our start we rushed about doing our best at a game that was strange to us—a game made the harder because we had to play it in thick, damp fog. Almost immediately a southeasterly wind drove us off our planned course. This discouraged us inwardly. Then a drizzle came on and soaked us outwardly. At every change of watch, a pile of wet clothes found its way below

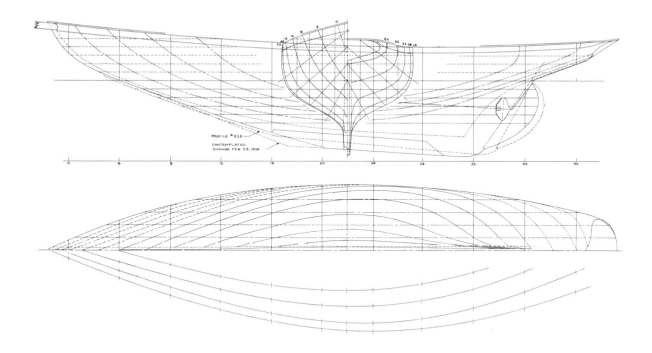

decks to end up on the leeward edge of the cabin sole and there to squeak underfoot odoriferously.

Next morning the wind came around enough to let us swing over on the starboard tack and resume our course. It also came in with more strength, building up a bit of a sea. With all working sail, club topsail, and fisherman staysail pulling, *Flying Cloud III* was in her element and going fast. At intervals her lee rail would dip under and fire a jet of water at the two nested Hand dories lashed on deck. In my mind's eye, I can still see old Captain Wall in his boots and oilies and black sou'wester hat, standing by the main rigging watching her go and, at the same time, keeping a weather eye on the man at the wheel and the prone bodies curled up on the after deck.

When night fell, the darker gloom of Gulf Stream rain squalls showed up ominously on the horizon all around us. This did little to improve lethargic spirits or racing efficiency. At the wheel, I, for one, didn't know whether to change course to dodge the squalls or to head for them and hope for a boost. (Prudence suggested the former.) All this while "Bonzo" Stearns in conference with Larry kept good track of where we were. (Bonzo never got in our way or interfered at all with the sailing of the ship. Except when taking sights he remained dry and comfortable below on his own bunk, and ate what was

Flying Cloud's lines are typically Hand's (although these have been kindly redrawn from the tattered original by my friend Fenwick Williams). Her bow is high, her freeboard generous, and her bilges firm—altogether a stout vessel quite at home offshore. These are substantially the same lines that were used for Hand's own schooner, *Black Hawk*.

61

available with obvious satisfaction. Idle talk about salt pork on the end of a string and such-like seasick remedies bothered Bonzo not in the least.)

At long last we emerged from the glooms and rigors of the Gulf Stream and found ourselves sailing in sparkling new colored waters. Variable light breezes were followed by calms. These new conditions really put the crimp in *Flying Cloud*'s speed. On the other hand, they raised the morale of her sodden crew. Eagerly watching our noon positions, we hoped at one stage to see Bermuda on the fourth day out. However, it was not until the fifth day that we sighted land. Even then, after the first magic thrill was over, it seemed as if the finish line just kept moving away from us. We finally crossed late that evening off St. David's Head, but the news called across to us from the Committee Boat was not encouraging. Uncle Russy Grinnell's *Rugosa II* had been the first boat to finish. She had come in the previous evening, closely followed by *Yankee Girl II*. *Malay*, a much smaller boat than *Flying Cloud III*, had crossed the line some eight hours before we did.

After the then-required native pilot had come aboard and guided us up through the long channel to Hamilton Harbor, we carefree amateurs quickly jumped ship and headed for shore. Up Queen Street at the New Windsor Hotel, hot baths and cold drinks flowed in various strengths and to our hearts' content. Henry Wise Wood was absolutely right when in a 1923 "Plan and Scope" report, he urged his fellow Cruising Club members to plan only ocean races that were sailed "between ports of two or more countries." For a chance to enjoy such pleasures as Bermuda affords, who wouldn't race there, even if he were at heart a cruising man?

When the time came for the great awards banquet, it was held during the cool of the evening in the lovely garden-banked halls of the New Windsor Hotel. Top honors went to the few marconi-rigged boats and especially to *Rugosa*, which had accomplished the extraordinary. Not only had Uncle Russy finished first, but on corrected time he had taken Class A and the overall first as well. *Malay* was some 20 hours ahead of the next boat in her class. *Flying Cloud III* might have won an award for having the youngest crew in the fleet; but there was no prize offered for this special distinction. (We did receive recognition for winning a special match race against the schooner *Alamyth*. At 82 feet, *Alamyth* was too big to contend in the regular classes.)

During all this dinner sparkle of silverware and silver-tongued eloquence, I sat next to a pleasant gentleman who—to me, at that time—seemed quite elderly and quiet. When I accidentally struck my spoon against a wineglass, he reached over with his hand to stop it ringing. He warned me that if it rang to the end, it could mean death for some poor sailor. To this day I worry when I hear a ringing glass, and I always silence it, if I can reach it.

Just who my new acquaintance was, I had no idea, until he rose to accept the prize for the first in the "Under 35-Foot Class." The name of his boat was *Islander*. Then it came to me. He was Harry Pidgeon, the American sailor and photographer-writer who several years earlier had completed a single-handed circumnavigation in this, his 34-foot gaff-rigged yawl, which he had built with his own hands. (*Islander* was, incidentally, an enlarged sistership of Thomas Fleming Day's *Sea Bird*.)

After talking with Mr. Pidgeon that evening, I came away with my first faint glimpse of how important it is to work out one's boating ventures one step at a time. As a young man, Harry Pidgeon had learned to build and sail boats. By middle age he carefully considered his own goals and studied special boat plans that had practical connection with his own abilities and pocketbook. Before making any long voyages, he made short ones. He learned to navigate and take care of himself as well as his boat. It was no accident that his voyages were uniquely successful.

iii

Larry Grinnell's father had inherited an appreciation of good boats. He first owned the Herreshoff 40-footer *Bambino*, and then in 1919 had Captain Nat design and build for him the bigger cutter *Flying Cloud*. Of first-class composite construction, she was a fine, able boat, and stylish as well. None of her dimensions was extreme or exaggerated to fit an artificial rule. Overall she was 58 feet 6 inches, with a waterline length of 44 feet. For this length she had a moderate beam of 14 feet and a draft of 8 feet. Surely she was one of Herreshoff's finest designs; so it puzzled me that in 1920 Mr. Grinnell sold her to Mr. Frank Draper, a charter member of the Cruising Club and spokesman for the CCA faction that believed "Cruising," *not* "Racing," to be the primary object of the Club. To compound my confusion, Mr. Draper campaigned his new purchase in the 1923 Bermuda Race.

Doubtless the designer of Mr. Grinnell's next two *Flying Clouds* had a great deal to do with his decision to change over from cutters to schooners. William Hand, Jr.—"Bill," as his friends all called him—was not originally from New Bedford. He was born in Portland, Maine, in 1875 and then moved to various seaports up and down the coast as his father's Navy and Coast Guard assignments dictated. From the very first he had ample opportunity to observe boats and to sail them to his heart's content. Although he spent several years as a student at Brown University, his involvement with sailing and cruising, and his natural inclination toward boat design and the seafaring life, led him to cut short his studies and settle down permanently in the harbor area of New Bedford.

Like so many other successful naval architects, Bill Hand spent little time at formal training in his chosen field. His own observations and his firsthand experience on the water automatically made him a good judge of useful work-boat shapes. Starting with sound commercial designs, he modified them in detail to suit his own objectives. Today he is best remembered for his motor-sailers, but this specialized reputation did not come to him until later in his life. Actually, the pattern of his design work closely followed his own wide-ranging boating career. When he was interested in a particular kind of craft for his own use, that was the type he developed and sold in his business. With him, theory and practice worked together. As Hand grew older, his needs and limitations changed, and so did the nature of his boats.

As a youth, when he was doing considerable sailing of his own, Hand designed and produced very successful small racing boats. Deservedly these brought him wide recognition not only throughout this country, but abroad as well. Likewise, his early cruising boats showed a thorough understanding of the essentials. When one of my sons questioned me recently about a possible boat for general family use, I thought immediately of the 30-foot Hand-designed *Sea Call*. As a boy I had saved pictures of this boat, clipped from boating magazines. In the 1920s *Sea Call* not only raced to Bermuda but took her New Bedford owner Dr. Lothar Neitch on some long offshore cruises. Forty years later, in the 1960s and under new ownership, this same boat sailed south, to visit again in the Caribbean. In the intervening decades, I sold her twice to friends of mine for family cruising in Buzzards Bay.

When gasoline engines became practical in the days before World War I, Hand dove wholeheartedly into the motor-boat business. Starting with the well-proven Chesapeake sailing boats of V-bottom design, he modified their lines for power, and developed a design (which, incidentally, he patented) that has to this day proved hard to improve upon. Initially, he concentrated on open 20-footers; then he progressed to larger cruisers. These "Hand V Bottoms" were fast—very fast—and made records that surprised the experts. At the same time they were of reasonable beam and displacement and otherwise fine healthy craft, performing ably in smooth water or rough. George Bonnell, a charter member and later Commodore of the Cruising Club, owned several of them. In one, *Old Glory*, he made at least two remarkable offshore trips. In spite of these notable successes (and Hand was world famous by the time of World War I), Hand never seemed anxious to race his fast boats for the sake of silverware. Rather, his interest lay in proving that it was possible to incorporate speed in a good, useful boat.

It was only after World War I that Hand really began to focus his attention on schooners. He had been interested in fishing for many years, but now he went seriously at the business of developing a good offshore boat in which to practice this, his favorite sport and avocation. It turned out to be a lifetime project, and he went about it as only a good seaman would.

SEA CALL

Sea Call is a development of an earlier and similar Hand cruiser, *Fundulus*, that was built in 1913. Some 36' overall, she is short-ended and essentially a double-ender. With her moderate displacement, modest beam, and long lines, she slips along easily without the need for a lot of sail. Underwater, she is, in many ways, much the same shape as a New Bedford whaleboat or seine boat, and these types by necessity had to be easily driven and yet very able at sea. In place of a centerboard, *Sea Call* has a long (but not deep) keel that has its greatest depth aft. This feature adds to the hull's already good shape for nice handling and steady steering. As a dividend, the keel shape protects the propeller—and helps slide the boat off a sand bar or shoal in the event she is grounded.

The rig is simplicity itself. Two short, solid masts, simply stayed, no backstays needed. Three small sails, easily handled, raised, or stowed by one person. Short bowsprit. (No need to go out on it, but it helps in handling the anchor.) Clear decks and a little capped rail for safety. Lifelines that can be rigged easily with a line between the main and mizzen rigging. Short house for standing room in galley area. Deep self-draining cockpit, with an athwartship seat at its aft end. Long bridge deck. (In the case of the original *Fundulus*, and her sistership, built by Joel White in Brooklin, Maine, in 1981, this is 10' long: very useful for carrying a dinghy or for a rest or work area above deck. This proved an excellent feature for a small crew on an extended voyage. However, the longer house and shorter bridge deck on *Sea Call* has obvious advantages for weekend family cruising.)

The construction plan is equally well considered and thought out. The keel is of uniform width (an uncomplicated shape). The mainmast goes through the deck with its strong mast partners (does not strain the house). The bridge deck holds the boat together amidships (and allows for simple engine installation). No winches. No tracks. No engine control or exhaust problems. With such straightforward planning, the original building costs and future maintenance of *Sea Call* were bound to be relatively inexpensive for a wooden boat of her size. Only an experienced sailor like Bill Hand who appreciated the simple pleasures and modest needs of the cruising life—and had enjoyed these pleasures himself over a period of years—could create such a complete little cruising vessel as *Sea Call*.

William Hand was a prolific designer whose work before World War I focused on fast V-bottomed powerboats, such as *Lornina*, while in the 1920s, wholesome cruising schooners such as *Black Hawk* (facing page) received his attention. He was an accomplished draftsman with a fine eye for a good-looking boat.

He started with a proven type: the Gloucester fishing schooner. Then he gradually modified size and model to fit his needs. His first schooner was a 47-footer named *Andiamo,* which he sailed and experimented with for several years and then sold. His second schooner was 61 feet overall. This was *Whistler,* and I remember her well. Rigged up for swordfishing, and beautifully maintained, she was a vessel to catch any seaman's eye. After working with *Whistler* for a season, Hand sold her to Mr. Edward Brayton of Fall River, who continued to sail her out of Padanaram for another 20 years. And so it went: Hand perfecting schooners according to his own judgment and needs, then selling them to others who found them as enjoyable and dependable as he had worked to make them.

Bill Hand and Mr. Lawrence Grinnell were friends, and both were members of the New Bedford Yacht Club. Although at heart Hand was never a racing man, he did skipper his third schooner, the 63-foot *Black Hawk,* in the 1923 Bermuda Race. Mr. Grinnell was Commodore of the NBYC in 1923, and he must have caught Bill's "schooner fever" pretty bad, because before he sold his Herreshoff cutter, he had ordered the Hand-designed 55-foot *Flying Cloud II* in time to sail her against *Black Hawk* and *Whistler* in the 1923 race. Then he went on to order the bigger *Flying Cloud III* for the 1924 Bermuda Race.

During the remainder of the 1920s Hand continued to produce his special type of schooners. These were for commercial customers as well as yachtsmen. (His *Bowdoin* became celebrated as the ship in which Admiral MacMillan carried out his Arctic explorations.) Dr. George W. Warren's *Yankee Girl II* showed yachtsmen that she could sail with the best of them. As I've mentioned, she finished less than two hours behind *Rugosa* in the 1928 Bermuda Race. In the 1930 race, she was the first boat to finish. But along with Hand's many

successful schooner designs, his design activities tended more and more toward the heavy, sea-kindly type that was to become the chief source of his fame in the years that followed.

In a way that few other designers made time for, Hand lived on, and with, his own boats. Almost every year he built a new one aboard which he would spend much of each summer, often swordfishing out of Menemsha on Martha's Vineyard. For him this latter occupation was more than a hobby. It was a serious—albeit very enjoyable—business proposition. Very few professional swordfishermen, if any, were more successful at it than Hand.

In the early 1920s, he carried on this fishing business from one of his own schooners. He cruised at slow speeds and under power. On calm days, all sails were furled. If there was a breeze and a bit of a sea, the foresail was set and trimmed flat as a steadying sail. The swordfish pulpit was mounted at the end of the bowsprit and forward of the jibstay. The fore-rigging was rattled down to allow the lookout to reach the crow's nest easily. This lofty station was fitted with a series of lines and canvas straps for the safety of the user as he stood his watch.

As time went on, Hand realized that a deep-bodied schooner hull made a fine steady platform for harpooner and lookout, but that deep draft and large sail areas were not needed. By 1927 power once again became the main driving force for Hand-designed boats, and Hand retained sails primarily as a safety factor, and for steadying and heaving-to. He also changed rigs—from schooner to ketch (gaff at first, then jib-headed for greater handling ease). His hulls continued to have easy sailboat sections and long runs, but lost their deep outside ballast keels. Ends, short initially, he lengthened slightly. These ketches soon became known as Hand Motorsailers. They had good but not excessive freeboard, a strong, graceful sheer, and well-balanced, moderate ends. Sterns went from transom to double-ended, then finally back to transom—a small heart-shaped counter.

Hand was always a believer in plenty of power. He realized that, once it was available, he himself and most yachtsmen and fishermen would use a reliable power plant more, sails less. He favored heavy-duty gasoline engines and often used Hall-Scotts hooked up with big reduction gears and big propellers. Although not fast like express cruisers, Hand Motorsailers were fine passage-makers. They drove easily without dragging a big wake and would carry on when others were being drowned out or were running for shelter.

During the winter months Hand spent his working hours planning new boats. He worked out of a neat, small, and old two-story house that backed up to the Fairhaven shore of New Bedford Harbor. The house was located a few hundred yards below the Fairhaven Bridge. South of it along the waterfront came Kelly's yard, then Casey's (with the biggest old-time marine railway left in the area), then Hathaway Machine Company and finally Peirce and Kilburn's yard.

For his office Hand used a small sunny room with a view of the harbor. His drafting room was long and narrow, taking up a good part of the north side of the house. Whenever I visited there, Hand's assistant, Richard O. Davis, was always hard at work, leaning over one of the long drafting tables. Davis was a pleasant and interesting man to talk with, and a most conscientious and reliable draftsman. I feel sure he was a big factor in Hand's success in business. During the years of World War II Davis moved to City Island, New York, and eventually became a respected designer of motorsailers in his own right.

Just to the north of the Hand office was his marine railway extending up into a complete boatshop of modest proportions. The whole facility was about the right size for the building and launching of a 45-footer. However, most of Hand's boats were larger than this, and a majority of them were built by Hodgdon Brothers in East Boothbay, Maine. The Hand-Hodgdon team cooperated in working out an excellent system for building that had advantages for all concerned. The standardizing of methods and materials saved time for the designer. It simplified construction for the builder. And the owner ended up

WILLIAM HAND

Hand always had a clear picture of what he was after. He planned one boat at a time. He carefully thought through each boat from keel to cabin-door hinge. Good features he retained, not only of lines or rig, but also those countless elements that make for a first-class finished boat. Hand developed his own design for houses, hatches, rail caps, and guardrails. He worked out a standard method for handling anchors and dories. His friend Eli Braley of Hathaway Machine worked with him in the manufacture of his own rudder fittings, engine controls, and deck and cabin hardware. Even his paints and paint schemes were carefully planned out. (If my memory doesn't fool me, there was a paint manufacturer that offered a "Hand Tan Deck Paint.") There was never much brightwork on Hand's boats. He favored white paint for houses, rails, and topsides (although a few of his hulls had black topsides). Everything was shipshape—easy to maintain and easy on the pocketbook.

In later years, from 1927 to the Second World War, Hand specialized in the design of comfortable seagoing motor-sailers. The 63' *Anzac* is shown here fitting out at the East Boothbay yard of Hand's favorite builder, Hodgdon Brothers, in 1936.

with a good complete boat at a reasonable price; he was not faced with years of ironing out bugs.

Hand had a rather set cabin arrangement, which he knew from experience best suited a particular boat. If a buyer wished to proceed in directions of his own that Hand felt would not work out well, he would urge the prospective buyer to start all over again with another architect. I have learned to my own sorrow that one planning error or misjudgment often necessitates another, or a succession of them. I favor Hand's seemingly over-independent attitude, because I sincerely believe in the value of an honest opinion that is backed by experience.

I sometimes hear the complaint that Hand Motorsailers won't sail. Well, Hand never intended them to, in the ordinary sense. If he had, he would have given them more sail. Other designers, after all, have taken a modified power-boat hull, rigged it with all the complications and sail area of an ocean racer and thus made her sail. This sort of motorsailer no doubt is what the owner thinks he wants. Perhaps occasionally it works out the way the owner hopes it will.

iv

Bill Hand was Commodore of the New Bedford Yacht Club from 1928 through 1930, and during those years a few of us younger fellows had a chance to get to know him a little. It was, as I remember, in the summer of 1934 that he asked me off for a week of swordfishing.

At the time he owned the *Seal*. She was a 63-foot double-ender with a jib-headed ketch rig. She was one mighty fine vessel, as many sailors have come to know. Although a bit bigger than his earlier motorsailers—and most of his later ones, for that matter—*Seal* survives as a splendid example of Hand's art.

The crew for our trip consisted of four men and a boy. Hand himself was captain; he always was captain on his own ship. A pleasant young redhead with a strong pair of arms was the professional crew and cook. As was usual on these expeditions, Herbert Flanders came aboard as first mate. Herb was not only a fine man and a topnotch commercial fisherman, he was also one of Chilmark's most respected town fathers. For relief helmsman Captain Bill had with him his old friend Dr. Frank Stetson. The doctor in fact was almost a regular member of Hand's crew. Year after year, come spring, he would drive down to East Boothbay to help sail a new Hand ship back to New Bedford. I completed *Seal*'s roster. My duty was to take orders.

Early each morning, *Seal* powered out of Menemsha and headed in a general westerly direction. The Hand dory was hanging in davits on the port quarter all equipped and set for launching. The kegs (clearly showing the Hand colors) were handy forward by the rail, with line bent on. The harpoon, with line and lily attached, hung in its brackets on the pulpit, in readiness for immediate action. The Captain was at the helm in his spacious deckhouse. The doctor was taking his ease below on the main cabin settee. (Dr. Stetson had a bad heart and was supposed to stay calm and quiet.) The cook was washing up after breakfast. Herb was soon to climb the ratlines to his lookout at the masthead. I was to follow Herb.

The first morning out was completely calm, perfect for spotting the single fin of a resting swordfish. There was a big old swell running diagonally across our course, and this rolled us around a little. At first I wondered about my breakfast, but actually the motion aloft was merely a slow arc back and forth through the soft air, and there was no evil snatching at either end of the roll. I doubt if the doctor noticed much of any motion at all, down low as he was in the main cabin.

As the morning wore on, what struck me most were the clearness of the water and the myriad forms of marine life to be seen from my lofty position. I found it difficult, even impossible at times, to concentrate on my around-the-horizon lookout duties, because often right below me would be scattering schools of fish of all sizes and colors, or big hammerhead sharks (and once a great blue shark that, as he went down, seemed bigger than our ship).

Working over toward Block Island we began to see various commercial swordfishermen. Compared to *Seal* they were a rough-looking lot, and I wondered if Hand would back off, in the event one of them spotted a fish at the same time we did. Contact with one of these work boats could not do our rails or topsides much good. (In theory, the boat that first saw and headed for a fish had certain moral, and for all I know legal, rights; but in the end, determination and savvy also entered heavily into the situation.) On several occasions I was like to fall overboard with excitement. But Hand had the skill and the reputation, and *Seal* had the power and the maneuverability, to keep us clear of collision.

When Herb did spot a fish, he signaled by phone down to Hand, and between them they worked *Seal* toward the fish. At the right moment the doctor popped up the companionway to take the helm, and Hand made "fast walk" out onto the pulpit. I don't understand why a swordfish will allow a boat to come up on top of it, but it does, or at least waits until the last moment to move off. Hand was a natural athlete, and was especially good with a harpoon. *Seal* cooperated by being steady. When the doctor, directed by Herb, maneuvered the pulpit near a fish, Hand usually got the lily into it. The attached line would go over the side followed by its keg, and poor swordfish was left to tow its floating tormentor around till exhaustion finally overcame it.

Occasionally, *Seal* would have two or more kegs out at once, but the system was the same whatever the number. In due course the keg would lie quiet in the water. The dory would be put over the side. Herb would climb in, row to the keg, and start hauling the fish to the surface. It was generally just a matter of time before *Seal* came alongside and the fish was hoisted aboard to join the other handsome, big-eyed victims lying at the aft end of the cockpit. To keep their skin damp and their meat fresh, Hand had a pump going and salt water flowing over them at all times, until he got them to market either in Menemsha or New Bedford.

The still air of the morning often changed to a fresh sou'west breeze in the afternoon, and this meant choppy going. Even under these conditions, however, being aloft on *Seal* was not bad at all. A good sailboat hull, when going into a head sea, tends to pivot from a point just aft of amidships. The narrow stern goes down into the water gradually as the bow comes up. The movement at the masthead is slow and sawing—up and aft a bit. A motor boat hull, on the other hand, usually has a wider stern and tends to pivot from well aft. This exaggerates the pitching and creates a quick whip action that is mighty uncomfortable, especially aloft.

On the way back to Menemsha in *Seal* on the evening of that first day, the cook told me that he was the one who usually hauled the fish. However, he wasn't allowed to go in the dory just yet, because he was fresh from the hospital. He explained that on the previous trip he had been a little hasty hauling in a fish. Although he did not realize it, the fish had some fight left in it; and, terrified, it sounded just before reaching the dory gunwale. A bight of the line caught around the cook's leg and jerked him overboard and down. He said he remembered reaching for his knife, but had grabbed the lanyard of his cigarette lighter by mistake. Not wishing to lose the lighter, he took the time to put it back into his pocket. All the while he was being dragged deeper and deeper. He vaguely remembered getting hold of his sheath knife but then lost consciousness. He said he had no recollection of cutting the hauling line, but that he must have done so. His clothes had enough air in them to bring him to the surface. And then a fisherman from another boat rescued him as he floated face down in the water. Aboard *Seal* they rolled him over a keg, got the water out of him, and finally brought him back to life. I have always wondered what drowning was like. I assume it must be quick and reasonably painless, because this cook had no comments about the discomfort of becoming unconscious. He did say that coming to had been excruciatingly awful, but that he wasn't feeling too bad now, several weeks after the mishap.

But enough. I hope it is obvious by now that I admired Hand and continue to admire his boats. To me he is one of the great American designers. He developed a type of vessel that for commercial or pleasure use was first-class and unique. A Hand Motorsailer was a good boat 40 years ago. It is still a good boat. I presume it will be a good boat 10 years hence. Hand gave his customers excellent advice and sound boats without regard to fads and fashions. Hand's example should be an inspiration for serious designers now and in the future. That William Hand did a large and profitable volume of business with a very small overhead is just one further reason why designers would do well to pay attention to his methods and his work.

4

The 1929 Gibson Island Race: Early Schooners, *Fearless,* and John Alden

i

After the festivities of the 1928 race had simmered down, my old crewmates weighed anchor and sailed away from Bermuda without me. *Flying Cloud III* was headed for a summer's cruise in the Bras d'Or Lakes. I had reasons to get home and so sought other means of transportation.

It was July 3 when I moved aboard *Black Goose,* a 52-foot schooner that was bound for Gloucester, the home of her ancestors. Her skipper and owner, Everett ("Emo") Morss, and her crew put me right to work to make me feel at home, then rewarded me with one of those offshore experiences that never grow stale in memory.

In later years, whenever I saw Captain Emo at a yachting gam, he made it a point to introduce me as his "underwater crew." On the occasion when I earned this title, the sea was proper Gulf Stream rough and the wind was rising. The jib was, as usual on these Alden schooners, the first sail to come in. I was out on the end of the bowsprit endeavoring to help with this maneuver when—precisely at the wrong moment—*Black Goose* shoveled into a steep one. At first Emo feared he had lost one of his crew. Then he was delighted to observe that at least no time was being lost in the sail-shortening operation: the jib continued to come down, albeit under water. Although I held on, I did lose my treasured English sea boots. You can be sure the incident lost nothing in the retelling.

Later during the trip, out on the back side of Cape Cod, with darkness coming on and the big can on Rose and Crown Shoal surging ominously up and down, I experienced one of those stormy-weather sinking spells that all sailors feel at one time or another, whether they admit it or not. The depression passed, and in a matter of a few hours we lay at anchor in the sunny peace and quiet of Gloucester Harbor. But even now I marvel at the speed with which

The 54′ Alden schooner *Fearless* at the start of the 1929 Gibson Island Race. She was built in 1927 by F.F. Pendleton, Wiscasset, Maine.

dark thoughts and dire forebodings come on one at such times—and at the speed with which they depart, once conditions have eased.

It was Sunday morning in Gloucester, and the customs officer was in a sour mood. He went through a thorough Prohibition search routine. "It's here, boys," he finally said. "I know it's here, but I can't find it." Emo took the calculated risk. "How about I show you," he said, "and we all try it out for quality." The idea turned out to be a happy inspiration indeed, and it put all hands in a proper Sabbath spirit of brotherly love. That evening we drove to Beverly to spend the night with the Morsses. After a refreshing welcome in the baronial hall, Emo's father ushered us up to the third floor. I'd heard many tall tales of the great North Shore mansions; now I was beginning to believe them. With some interest Mr. Morss surveyed his gallery of beautiful guest bedrooms. "Odd," he mused, "I don't think I've ever been up here before."

ii

The designer of *Black Goose* was John Alden, and at least in our yachting world, the years of the 1920s could rightly be called the "Alden Era."

Behind the Alden Era lay two and more centuries of evolution of the schooner rig. As America's colonial days were too long gone for even my father to remember, and having flunked Samuel Eliot Morison's course in maritime history, I must now venture my own interpretation of those vanished times.

Certainly, coastal life in the colonies could not have been too specialized. Farmers not only had to clear and protect their lands, plant and harvest their crops, build their homes and churches; they also had to set forth on the water to fish, to transport supplies, or simply to get from here to there. For these coastwise undertakings, families had to model and build their own boats. Great distances weren't usually involved, nor was sailing speed a dominant factor. Limitations were more directly imposed and defined by what a man and a boy could conveniently build and handle.

In shape and construction these early boats no doubt followed practices brought over from the old country. I visualize a 30-footer, short-ended, fairly deep in the body, on deck full at bow and stern, with nearly straight and parallel sides. Under water she would be of average fullness and short in the bow, and have a fairly long run aft. This was the cod-head and mackerel-tail model that had endured for generations with only slight modifications. Construction must have been simple indeed, but strong. A single smallish oak tree hewn to shape for a straight long keel. A vertical oak post well kneed onto either end of the keel, to form stem and sternpost. Sawn frames set up on the keel—these of a shape, deep or shallow, wide or narrow, to fit the owner's local needs. Planking would have been secured with nature's best fastenings, treenails.

The most common early rig was two masts of about the same height, one stepped in the eyes of the vessel, the other a little aft of amidships, with boom and gaff sails set on each. Somewhat later, it became a common practice to move the foremast several feet aft and to add a bowsprit and jib. This arrangement improved the deck layout for different uses and was a very logical evolution; for I venture to think that, given the same living conditions as faced the colonists, we would, out of common necessity, go at our boat planning just about the way they did. Easier it surely is to make and rig two small masts than one big one. The divided rig is also easier for a small crew to handle, as well as being the most efficient rig for passage-making up and down the coast. (The amount of sail area in relation to mast height is especially impressive.) Changing times and requirements resulted in changing shapes and sizes of vessels. However, the fore-and-aft schooner rig understandably remained the fisherman's favorite for as long as sail dominated the fishery.

During the Revolution many existing boats were destroyed or otherwise lost to their owners. To meet the urgent need for replacements, commercial building yards soon sprang up in likely locations. With its rivers, marshlands, and surrounding forests of good oak and pine, Essex, Massachusetts, became one center for this new industry, and the area continued as a shipbuilding capital throughout the remaining years of commercial sail. To be sure, fine wooden ships were built elsewhere in New England and all up and down the eastern seaboard. Yet the major development of our great American fishing schooners took place at Gloucester's back door, in the Essex shipyards operated by such families as the Storys, Tarrs, and Jameses.

The first Essex-built schooners were small—30 to 40 feet. There were two main models: the sharp-sterned vessels without bowsprits that were known as Chebacco boats (from the name of the parish in which Essex lay); and the square-sterned vessels with rig similar to the Chebacco boats, these being known as dogbodies. Pinkies were a third type. They had a full schooner rig with jib and bowsprit, and their rails extended aft on each side of the rudder head to join at a narrow V—or pink—stern. This pink member was shaped very much like the narrow transom of a Banks dory. Never, even in later years, much over 50 feet in length, the pinkies were fine, useful little vessels and did a bit of trading as well as fishing. Although their bows were round and their forward sections full as tradition decreed, pinkies were built with a raking sternpost, and later models also had a strong drag to the keel. Many of these pinkies worked quite a distance offshore, but very few had serious accidents or loss of lives.

When the canals and railroads began to open up the West, the market for fish expanded accordingly. Fishermen now had to sail beyond the local fishing grounds and out to the Banks. This meant longer trips, bigger vessels, and larger crews. The dogbody types were stretched out to 70 feet and more. Designed to stay out summer and winter until fully loaded, these schooners

The American schooner rig had its beginnings on the shores of New England and its development, at least for working vessels, had always been centered near Essex, Massachusetts. Crude colonial craft became more refined with the passage of time, yet remained simple to build and operate. The Essex-built pinky schooner *Maine* of 1845 (this page and facing) is an example. She was built mostly of local wood, such as oak and pine, and although 53′ long on deck, could, with but three moderate-sized sails, be single-handed.

carried salt to preserve the fish until it could go to market. Designers gradually gave these bigger boats a bit more overhang forward and aft. Underwater they cut away the bow profile to some degree, raked the sternpost, and gave additional drag to the keel. These modifications were all made to improve the handiness and sailing qualities of the schooners; although it must be said that it wasn't until the 1880s, when the ever-mounting loss of Gloucester men and schooners on the Banks led to a major design reform, that fishermen and builders woke up to the fact that refinements to the traditional fishing model that gave increased speed did not necessarily mean increased safety at sea.

Why was speed considered so necessary to fishing schooners as the nineteenth century wore on? I feel I can speak with some expertise on this question, because, in the living room of our house in Padanaram, there stands a pine chest of drawers, four full-width drawers below, 12 smaller drawers in a double bank above. To the small drawers are tacked metal name plates on which, in gilt letters on a black field, are painted the following: BANGKOK, BOMBAY, CAL-CUTTA, CANTON, LONDON, PANAMA, RIO DE JANEIRO, SHANGHAI, SINGAPORE, DOMESTIC, COSTS, INVOICES.

For many years this chest belonged to my mother, but it originally served as a file cabinet for the Tudor Ice Company. As early as 1805, Frederic Tudor of Boston pursued his dream of selling cold ice to warm cities—this for the pleasure of fashionable drinkers, as well as to retard the spoilage of meats and other foodstuffs. It was a problem-filled promotion, but in the end it did succeed. Abundantly. Tudor cut his sparkling natural ice from the clear waters

Small working schooners were occasionally used for pleasure outings early on, well before the schooner-yacht, designed by such men as John Alden and William Hand, came into being.

of Wenham Pond. Sailing ships transported the novel delight to faraway places. (The ice was successfully preserved in special holds insulated with sawdust, half hardwood, half soft. And while not all the ice came from Wenham Pond, I am told that within certain London circles it was generally believed that Wenham Pond was one of the biggest bodies of fresh water in America.) The prophetic dream of Frederic Tudor, "The Ice King," not only prolonged the lucrative East India Trade, but encouraged the home folks to cut their own winter ice and store it in their own insulated icehouses for year-round use in preserving their meats and dairy produce. As a small boy I well remember digging chips of ice out of my grandfather's Petersham icehouse. Some of the great blocks had been stored there for two years and more, surviving hot summers with very little loss of volume.

In any event, it was the advent of ice in the fishery that gave such urgency to the search for speed among the Banks schooners. Fresh fish was far more palatable than salt fish. The fresher the fish, the higher the price. With loose ice aboard, it obviously didn't pay fishermen to dally on the way to the Grand Banks; once loaded with fish, it was money in their pockets to beat all rivals back to market.

Here, then, is where the evolution of the Gloucester schooner made its most dramatic leap. For while vessels of relatively shoal draft—stretched-out versions of the very able small schooners of earlier days—possessed the speed, the carrying capacity, and the *initial* stability that the Gloucestermen wanted, they were sadly deficient in self-righting ability. The Gloucester fishing schooner of the 1860s and 1870s was, indeed, a deathtrap. As such, it represented an evolutionary blind alley.

Credit for the development of a healthier type belongs to several remarkable men, among them Dennison J. Lawlor, Samuel Pook, and John William Collins. The story of their contributions is finely told in Howard I. Chapelle's last book, *The American Fishing Schooners 1825-1935*. But the point I find especially important is easy to overlook. It is, simply, that form and function cannot be separated when it comes to the design and construction of worthwhile vessels. Just because a hull type is "traditional" does not make it good in all cases or for all purposes. Once Gloucester faced up to the limitations of one type of traditional vessel engaged in a new type of fishing, it was well on the way to creating a fine new generation of vessels that represented a great tradition all its own.

By the end of the nineteenth century, a number of top naval architects were being called on to design fast fishing schooners. Most of these designers lived in the Boston area. Some—George McClain and Thomas McManus, for example—were primarily designers of commercial craft. (However, I also think of McManus as the designer of Cruising Club Commodore Marty Kattenhorn's shippy little 44-foot schooner yacht *Surprise*,* which was built in Rockport in 1918 and was still going strong and without motor many years later.) William Roué, a Canadian from Halifax, was another most successful commercial designer. It was he who drew the plans for the celebrated Canadian racing fisherman *Bluenose*. More important to me personally, Roué designed an impressive number of successful American sailing yachts. Raymond Ferris's 45-foot schooner *Malay* is the Roué design I remember best, because she had the habit of beating us in so many Bermuda races.

A different group of naval architects who were at the time deeply involved in commercial sail were men whom most of us think of as yacht designers. These would include Edward Burgess and later his son Starling. Arthur Binney would be a third. However, it is Benjamin Bowdoin ("Bodie") Crowninshield whom I've been working up to in this fish boat story. I wish I knew more about him than I do, because along with Roué and Herreshoff (and Alden and Hand) he was in the forefront as a popular designer of Bermuda Race entries in the 1920s.

---

*Rebuilt in 1982 in Falmouth, Massachusetts, this little schooner was a true transition from commercial craft to yacht. Although she looked quite similar to the early Alden schooners, she was built like the big commercial fishermen with sawn frames, keel, and keelson.

B. B. Crowninshield was a member of a colorful, wealthy seafaring Salem family. As a young man he did his share of yacht racing and was very successful at it, too. His inherited interest in maritime matters led him to a draftsman's job, and shortly thereafter, in 1897, to a naval architect's office of his own. In his pleasure boat designs he continued on with many of the features seen in racing yachts of the Gay Nineties. *Black Duck* would be a fair example of his work. He designed this schooner for Dr. Alexander Forbes in 1909, and she was queen in Hadley Harbor for more than a generation. Many of us younger folks had some memorable sails aboard *Black Duck*, which was a 65-foot centerboarder with long overhangs, low freeboard, displacement on the light side, and no motor (but plenty of sail).

Among Crowninshield's many commercial ship customers, Thomas W. Lawson stands out particularly. For this Boston speculator, Crowninshield designed the only seven-masted cargo schooner ever built, as well as an entirely different type of boat, in the form of the *America*'s Cup contestant *Independence*. *Independence* was not a success. (As a matter of fact, she was, in part because of major structural defects, a solid failure.) But in drawing up her lines, Crowninshield could hardly have failed to study the shapes of earlier Cup boats, back to and including the yacht *America* herself.

Crowninshield's influence on the final flowering of the Banks schooner was considerable. He developed a profile for his fishermen that was generally considered an improvement over previous practice and was, thus, often copied by other designers. It came to be known as the "Fisherman Profile." In it, the bow was fairly well cut away to a point about under the foremast, then it abruptly joined a straight keel that had a strong drag to it. The rudder post was raked; part of the counter aft of the rudder was under water. A number of schooners were often built from a single Crowninshield plan, and at least two of his plans appeared in trade papers. This publicity enhanced his reputation, greatly influencing designers such as Hand and Alden who followed after him.

I feel very safe in saying that the good Gloucester fishing schooners were among the finest and fastest fore-and-afters that ever sailed the seas: an amazing culmination of several different lines of approach to design and building, from the most traditional to the most radical, from the "Centerboard School" to the "Cutter Cranks," from shipyards of Essex to classrooms at M.I.T. English designers contributed their share to the shape of these vessels. So—perhaps more than any other single designer—did George Steers, whose *America* had a shape and sections strikingly similar to successful Banks schooners being launched 50 or even 75 years after *America* swept the fleet at Cowes. In view of all this, it is not at all surprising that our sailing parents, when they returned from their World War I duties, looked first at the fisherman rig and hull shape for their offshore cruising yachts.

The Banks schooners were, of course, too big to serve as family cruisers. However, smaller versions (for use in light freighting and inshore fishing) had developed along similar lines. Thinking back to a few of these smaller commercial boats that sailed frequently into my view, I keep running into the name "Morse." Mr. Roy Wallace, partner in the once active Thomaston boatbuilding firm of Newbert and Wallace, tells me that the five Morse brothers were uncles of his. Their original home was on Bremen Long Island in Maine. This little island is in Muscongus Bay not far from the village of Friendship.

Wilbur A. Morse was the oldest of the boys, and he moved over to Friendship on the mainland to set up his boatbuilding business. Quite a few of his boats found their way to Padanaram. The 35-foot Friendship sloop type *Sea Fox* was

The most famous of all schooners developed in America were the Gloucester fishermen, which reached their zenith in the first quarter of this century. These schooners were fast, weatherly, and supremely beautiful. *Elsie,* shown here, was Essex-built in 1910 by A. D. Story. As young men, yacht designers such as Alden and Crowninshield were profoundly influenced by offshore trips in these big vessels.

83

built in 1910 and was used mostly as a family pleasure boat. Then there was *Edna*, a somewhat similar 39-footer that Wilbur built in 1916 for George Sistare, a New Bedford sailorman and the contractor who built the half-size whaleship *Lagoda* for the New Bedford Whaling Museum. It was also in 1916 that Wilbur built Mr. Ricketson's schooner *Dorothy B*. What a fine little ship she was, with her well-balanced ends, strong sheer, divided houses, and low simple rig!

Charles A., a younger Morse brother, set up his shipyard in Thomaston, Maine, just a few sea miles from Friendship. The 41-foot *Pennesseewassee* was one of his boats. Built in 1914 as a commercial boat, she came to Padanaram a few years later converted to a yacht and owned by Earl Smith. I also knew the 38-foot schooner *Rescue*, built in 1915. She could usually be seen in Manchester, Massachusetts. I have already mentioned the famous 60-foot Charles Morse schooner *Lloyd W. Berry*.

The *Pennesseewassee* was memorable to me not solely for her name. In the mid-thirties I had occasion to sell her on Earl Smith's behalf to Mr. Tudor Gardiner, then the Governor of Maine (and a descendant of "The Ice King," as well as a cousin of Starling Burgess). Governor Gardiner signed me on for a Jeffries Ledge ocean race out of Manchester. His crew consisted of older men, all interested in Canadian gold mines. One of them, a Mr. Brigham, was, I believe, president of the great Hollinger Mines. At that time in his eighties, he had never done any sailing, but his long experience of roughing it as a prospector had made him fit to be a useful crew member even on a small boat under stormy conditions.

As in all Jeffries Ledge races, we started according to our handicap, smallest boat first, largest last. All boats had to be at anchor, crew below, for five minutes prior to their starting gun. Tudor gave each of us a pint of champagne to be handled as best we could during our five minutes. I wish I could say that these happy bubbles blew us into a first place win. In fact, the *Tudor Rose* (ex-*Pennesseewassee*) ended up some hours after the start in Gloucester Harbor, a scant 10 miles distant. This was not her fault. She was a fine little schooner and an able sailer. The problem was simply that the winds were real strong and the sails she carried were as aged as her crew, and blew away one by one.

The Morse brothers contributed more to yacht design and construction than most people realize, and this fact brings me back, at long last, to the designer of *Black Goose*.

iii

John Alden originally came from Troy, New York. Just the same, most sailors thought of him as "John o' Boston." For some strange reason we, in our small circle, called him "Honest John."

John G. Alden, who was as good at sailing and promoting his boats as he was at designing them, is shown at left with Major William Smyth, one of the many skilled master builders who created the countless Alden-designed yachts. This photo was taken in 1930 while the Alden schooner *Teragram* was being built at Dauntless Shipyard in Essex, Connecticut.

As a boy, and throughout the later years of his life, John Alden enjoyed much the same breezy waters for his small boat sailing as I did. The only difference is that he started his boating some 20 years earlier than I, and that his summer home port, Little Compton, Rhode Island, is at the open western end of Buzzards Bay rather than in the more protected middle reaches where Padanaram lies. When John ventured forth from the Sakonnet River, nothing was there to greet him but the wide Atlantic Ocean.

By the time I had permission to sail my skiff all by myself, John was already in the boat business, working in Bodie Crowninshield's Boston office. Here as a draftsman he had the perfect chance to assimilate what the boss was doing, both in yacht and commercial design work. While overseeing the building of various Crowninshield boats, John automatically became well acquainted with the best New England shipyards. At least once, he even had the rare opportunity of experiencing a wild winter voyage on a big Crowninshield Banks fisherman. Thus he learned firsthand how able these schooners actually were. In 1909, after four years of apprenticeship with Crowninshield, Alden opened his own Boston design office. There he stayed "right with it" until his retirement in 1955.

Before World War I, Alden designed a variety of daysailers, a goodly number of sloops, and a few yawls as well, in the 30- to 40-foot range. A small proportion of these were of modified fisherman model, forerunners of his later cruising boats. Most designs, however, were of the shoal-bodied, light-displacement type that was the usual poor man's family boat of the time. I'm not sure whether Father's *Alert* was designed by Alden or not—for Hand, Crowninshield, and a number of other designers produced very similar boats. Alden also designed a few schooners before the war—mainly 60- to 80-footers.

During the actual war years very few big yachts of any type were built. This was a period when practicality and patriotism suggested that yachtsmen do their boating in a modest way. Along with other designers, Alden took the opportunity to win his share of yacht club contracts for small One Design racing classes. In 1916 he produced the Indian Harbor (Greenwich, Connecticut) One Design, which was 28 feet overall, 21 feet 10 inches on the waterline, 8 feet in beam, and 5 feet 3 inches draft. Designed for Long Island Sound, these boats had lots of sail area—some 550 square feet of it. Of the old light-displacement, fin-keel type with long overhangs and a small cuddy cabin, the Indian Harbor ODs were well built, and they well served their purpose for local racing and day sailing.

In 1917 Alden came out with a class of boats for Biddeford Pool, Maine. These had many of the characteristics of the great One Design class that Nat Herreshoff had designed for the Seawanhaka Corinthian Yacht Club the previous year—sixteen-footers we always knew as the Herreshoff Fish Class, which incorporated the qualities of seaworthiness, safety, and lively sailing ability so characteristic of the earlier Herreshoff 12½-Footers. Although the Alden class were short-ended like the Fish Class and had outboard rudders and watertight bulkheads for flotation, their keel construction was different by comparison, being of the old built-up fin type.

A couple of years later Alden had Rice Brothers in East Boothbay build a slightly smaller version of the Indian Harbor Class—this for the Stamford Yacht Club in Connecticut. Then in 1923 he designed a centerboard version of the Biddeford type. These were 18 feet 3 inches overall, 15 feet 6 inches on the waterline, with 6 feet 2 inches of beam. They became popular in a number of our New England harbors. (In Padanaram we knew them as Alden O boats, but although they were active for a time at Nonquitt and Salters Point, they never took hold in Buzzards Bay as well as they did in more protected waters. The Herreshoff Fish Class, on the other hand, like the Herreshoff 12½s, was always much sought after in our area.*)

---

*I can't leave this topic without putting in a word about the Seventeens, many of which were built in the early 1920s. (Seventeen was a waterline length. Only in recent times have we tried to impress buyers by using misleading overall length to identify the size of class boats.) B. B. Crowninshield designed at least two versions of the Seventeen sloops. All were on the narrow side, had moderate overhangs, a shallow watertight cockpit, and a tiny cuddy cabin. Their dimensions were 25'10" LOA, 17'6" LWL, 6'3" beam, 4'3" draft. There were long-lived classes of Seventeens in Cohasset, Manchester, Dark Harbor, and elsewhere. They made a fine boat for us young folks to grow up with. Many remain active in Maine waters today.

Although the period 1910-1920 saw a real boom in powerboat building, Alden himself never went into this field too deeply. What he loved was sailing and all that went with it, especially ocean racing. He was one of the original organizers and a Charter Member of the Cruising Club of America. In 1923 he and C. D. Mower (they were the only yacht designers involved) were on the committee that ran the revived Bermuda Race. Counting the 1910 Bermuda Race, John Alden eventually competed in this event 12 times. Thinking back, I can't remember ever going on a major American ocean race, or for that matter a big yacht club cruise, without seeing old John right there in the middle of it.

After the signing of the "peace to end all wars," activity in boating took a big jump. The homecoming boys were ready to go to sea, this time for their own pleasure, and Alden was ready and well equipped to help them get there. His recommendations were timely and good. In general he suggested a hull type that was about the same as that of the small commercial craft that had proved themselves over years of actual use. His rig was that of the time-tested schooner—two short masts, gaff and boom main and foresail, and single jib on a club. His cabin layout was specifically arranged for family cruising: a forecastle with stowage space and one pipe berth; then a full-width galley and a jogged-in enclosed toilet room; a main cabin with transoms and uppers that slept four; and two good quarter berths aft.

Alden had most of his first small schooners built at the Thomaston yard of Charles A. Morse. Here again his choice was excellent, because Morse, having already built very similar boats of his own design, knew well his costs and construction details.

For the schooners he himself owned, Alden chose the pleasing name *Malabar*; and in a few short years, this trademark became famous throughout the boating world. Alden's approach to selling his schooners was strikingly similar to that of Bill Hand. He would build a *Malabar* for himself, shake her down, tune her up, then sell her and start on a new improved one. Sisterships of the various *Malabar*s were built for interested customers; and of course Alden quite often drew up a custom design to fill an owner's particular requirements.

Because Alden's *Malabar*s and their sisterships played such an important role in the ocean racing and cruising picture of the 1920s I have included a sort of chart of them. As the chart shows, there was a new *Malabar* practically every year, and almost every one of them did well in one or more of the Bermuda races. Alden himself was usually skipper aboard the top performer, in spite of the fact that others of his schooners were well sailed by able racing men. With all the wins Alden and Alden-designed schooners (and latterly the ketch *Malabar XIII*) amassed in ocean racing, it isn't easy to pick a year or a boat of particular note. But the 1932 Bermuda Race was probably Alden's finest hour: *Malabar X* won first overall, followed by two Alden schooners in Class A; an

	Year Built	Dimensions	Designed Displacement (pounds)	Rig	Sail Area (square feet)	Builder	Sisters	Bermuda Race
Malabar I	1921	41'3"x31'10" x11'7"x6'2"	29,100	bald-headed schooner	963	C.A. Morse & Son Thomaston, ME	none	
Malabar II	1922	41'6"x32' x11'3"x6'2"	28,600	bald-headed schooner	938	C.A. Morse & Son Thomaston, ME	three, including *Mary Ann*	
Malabar III	1922	41'6"x32' x11'3"x6'2"	28,600	bald-headed schooner	938	C.A. Morse & Son Thomaston, ME	three, including *Mary Ann*	1926
Malabar IV	1923	47'x35'6" x12'x6'11"	37,200	topsail schooner	1,220	C.A. Morse & Son Thomaston, ME	*Felisi* (*Toddywax*)	1923* 1928
Malabar V	1924	49'x36'9" x12'x7'3"	38,540	topsail schooner	1,307	C.A. Morse & Son Thomaston, ME	one	1932
Malabar VI	1925	52'3"x38' x12'x7'4"	46,250	topsail schooner	1,337	Hodgdon Bros. East Boothbay, ME	eight, including *Merry Widow*, *Black Goose*, *Adventurer*	
Malabar VII	1926	53'9"x37'11" x12'5"x7'3"	43,300	topsail schooner	1,406	Reed-Cook Marine Construction Co., Boothbay Harbor, ME	six, including *Teal, Fearless*	1926*
Malabar VIII	1927	54'x39' x12'9"x7'4"	48,000	topsail schooner	1,464	Hodgdon Bros. East Boothbay, ME	*La Goleta*	1928 1930
Malabar IX	1928	57'11"x44'3" x14'2"x7'9"	53,000	topsail schooner	1,620	Hodgdon Bros. East Boothbay, ME	none	1928*
Malabar X	1930	58'3"x44'2" x14'2"x8'1"	61,700	topsail schooner	1,637	Hodgdon Bros. East Boothbay, ME	one	1930* 1932*
Malabar XI	1937	44'x30'6" x10'3"x6'	23,750	yawl	1,084	Casey Boatbuilding Fairhaven, MA	six, including *Dorothy Q., Sirocco*	
Malabar XII	1939	46'8"x34'3" x12'x6'9"	34,700	ketch	1,043	Morse Boatbuilding Thomaston, ME	two	
Malabar XIII	1945	53'9"x40'8" x14'3"x7'4"	55,200	ketch	1,221	Goudy & Stevens East Boothbay, ME	three	

A SUMMARY OF THE MALABARS

* *Alden schooners carrying the* Malabar *name won or placed second or third in these races.*
Malabar *sisters won their share of prizes in the years between 1923 and 1932 as well.*

Information excerpted from John G. Alden and His Yacht Designs, Robert W. Carrick/Richard Henderson, International Marine Publishing Company, Camden, Maine, 1983.

Alden schooner got a second in Class B; and, of the 27 boats entered in this race, 10 were of Alden design.

The burgeoning interest in cruising during the twenties was not confined to schoonermen. There were plenty of other enthusiastic sailors who either wanted a smaller boat, or couldn't afford a big one. Alden had a good solution for these folks in the form of "Malabar Juniors." I thought they were very distinctive little ships. To me, the earlier versions with their saucy sheers were more attractive than the later models. But public demand is always calling for more cabin space, and something has to give, usually at the expense of performance, looks, or cost. Between 1925 and 1930 Alden must have sold hundreds of these and similar little cruisers in one form or another. The only Malabar Junior I sailed aboard seemed a mite heavy on the helm. But all in all the boats filled a real need and many are still in use.

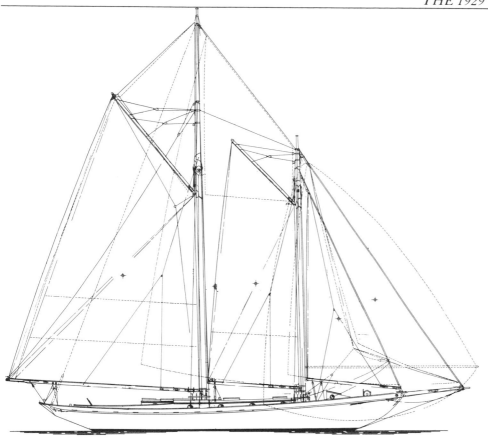

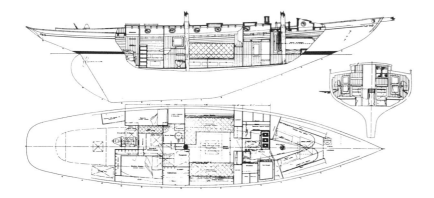

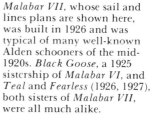

Malabar VII, whose sail and lines plans are shown here, was built in 1926 and was typical of many well-known Alden schooners of the mid-1920s. *Black Goose*, a 1925 sistership of *Malabar VI*, and *Teal* and *Fearless* (1926, 1927), both sisters of *Malabar VII*, were all much alike.

For New England shipyards Alden and his boats certainly had to be real lifesavers. The demand for commercial wooden sailing craft was at this time fading fast; Alden boats took up much of the slack. Some might think that Alden was a miracle man to have turned out so many boats in such a short time—perhaps 150 or more between 1922 and 1926 alone—and also to have been able to take in so much sailing and racing. However, a visit to his office at 148 State Street in Boston revealed some of the ways he achieved what he did.

Entering the office, I usually found myself talking with John Robinson, who had been at Milton Academy a few years before I had. He seemed to be the silent business partner, and he also handled all the firm's brokerage and insurance business. For many years, John owned one of the best of the small Alden yawls, a 34-foot Malabar Junior type named *Shag* that had been built by Lawley in 1928. Good construction obviously has a great deal to do with happy sailing and a long boat life. *Shag* was still going strong in the 1960s, and Concordia Company had a hand in putting her back together after a brush she had with the 1954 hurricane. Robinson was a vitally important cog in the Alden wheel, being both a shrewd businessman and an adept student of public relations. He knew what he was about and did it well. When John finally retired he followed the old sea captains' path and went back to the farm and let the boating world take care of itself.

In addition to Robinson and a formidable office general in the person of Ethel Bacon, Alden had during the 1920s a powerhouse of some nine or ten yacht designers working for him. Some of these men eventually left to set up their own offices; others remained to play their important part in future Alden design work. Even a very long book could not include all the salient information about, or credit due to, Alden's early design staff. But no book on the subject should ignore a few of the high points.

Number One man was probably Dwight Simpson. He was the overall supervisor of construction and drafting room operations. He was also Alden's chief designer of powerboats. S. S. ("Sam") Crocker left Alden in the mid-twenties, but not before he set his mark on such types as the Malabar Juniors. On his own, Sam designed many small to moderate-sized cruising boats. He is, for example, the one who created *Roarin' Bessie* for my friend Burnham Porter, who has owned and sailed this little cutter forever, plus a few years. *Roarin' Bessie* has the nearly plumb stem, wide stern, and ample beam that have been characteristic of many Crocker boats. (Palmer Scott used this design for his series of charter boats called *Amanthas*.) Another Crocker type I admire (and which continues to be a popular production boat known as the Stone Horse Junior) has short ends, a raised deck, and a full-width cockpit. These boats have an amazing amount of useful room, yet they sail well and look well and keep their owners happy year after year. It was always fun and profitable to visit with Sam in his Boston office, or later at the Crocker boatyard in Manchester. He knew the basic cruising boat problems, handled them well, and was most generous in sharing his insights with me.

Clifford Swaine, Bill McNary, Carl Alberg, and Charles MacGregor are all

MALABAR JUNIORS

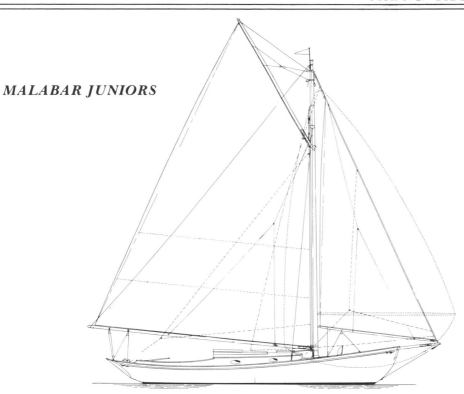

The Malabar Juniors had a profile very much like that of the early *Malabar* schooners: short ends, good sheer, and a bit more freeboard (particularly forward) than was common at the time. The first ones were 29'9'' LOA, 23' LWL, 9'8'' beam, and 4'11'' draft. They had a good cockpit and a short, lowish house rounded at the forward end. The mainsail was gaff-rigged, and there was a single jib set on a partial club at the end of a short bowsprit. Below they had 5'2''

headroom, and the cabin as a whole was well worked out for so small a cruising boat. Forward a pipe berth was hung to port, and the toilet was under a box to starboard. Two good transom berths in the main cabin were followed by a short galley area aft. The engine was under a hatch in the cockpit. As time went on, the freeboard was raised somewhat amidships and the house lengthened. The rig became marconi and provided for a mizzen if wanted.

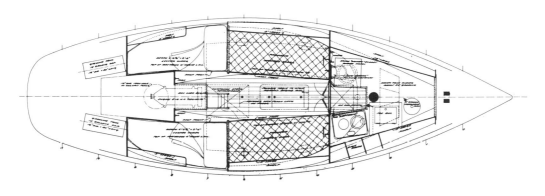

ALDEN SLOOPS

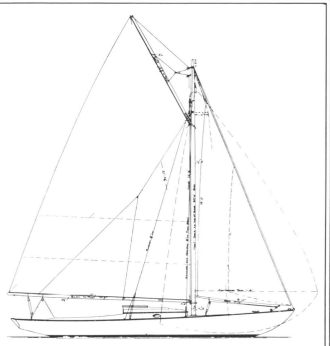

These all had low freeboard, relatively long overhangs, and built-up ballasted, finlike keels, to which the rudder was attached. The cockpits were long and usually watertight. The cuddy cabins were short with scant sitting head-room. They contained no facilities whatsoever except two low transom seats and perhaps a shelf or two. The mainsail was gaff-rigged; the jib usually had a light club lashed to the aft three-quarters of its foot. Some of these boats had bowsprits and were called "raceabouts." Others didn't and were known as "knockabouts." Little old flat triangular spinnakers and storm jibs were usually aboard, but nothing like a genoa. A whole generation of us grew up on these sloops. We raced them on a simple handicap basis, and cruised on them with the help of a blanket, a bucket, and a box of crackers. Equipment always included a portable brass bilge pump, a boat-hook, and a fisherman anchor and warp. I don't know if there is such a thing as a nostalgic smell, but if there is, the cabins of these sloops surely had it. It must have been the combination of the unpainted cedar of the interior hull, the damp oak of the bilge, plus the pleasant oil paint of gray seats and white overhead, all spiced up with a whiff of manila rope and a salty canvas bag or two. A fair proportion of Alden's sloops were built by Calderwood in Manchester, Massachu-setts, or by Lawley in Neponset. Others were turned out by Maine and Narragansett Bay yards.

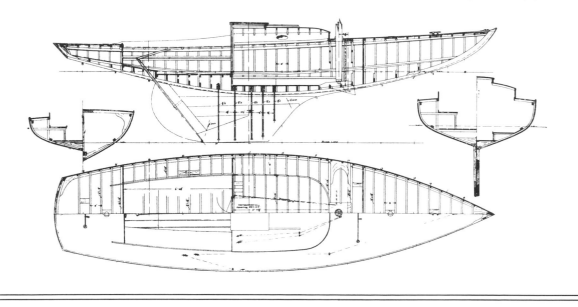

designers whose work I have known and respected, but I never knew them personally. They all joined Alden in the early twenties. In fact, 1923 and 1924 were years of great expansion in Alden's overall business. Fenwick Williams came in 1923, and to my great pleasure and advantage I saw a lot of him in later years when he was working under his own name in Marblehead. K. Aage Nielsen came from Denmark in 1924; Murray Peterson, from Portland, Maine, also joined Alden that year. Later, on their own, those two excellent designers worked out many first-class and distinctive boats. Murray is best known for his beautiful little coasting schooners. Aage, in addition to his handsome cruising boats, designed a number of highly successful ocean racing yawls, cutters, and sloops. Wilder B. Harris is yet another talented architect who worked in Alden's office for a time. He later joined Concordia Company for four years just before World War II.

iv

In 1929 sailing fortune struck my way again, in the form of an ocean race to Gibson Island, Maryland. It was aboard another Alden schooner, this time the *Fearless*, a member of the *Malabar VII* family.*

The owner of *Fearless* was Ralph B. Williams, Jr., a friend of a lifetime. It was in the winter of 1929 that Ralph bought *Fearless* secondhand for some $16,000. John Robinson handled the transaction. The boat had been built the previous winter by F. F. Pendleton in Wiscasset, Maine. Alden had ordered her on speculation and had sold her to a Mr. Baker, who kept her but one season.

Fearless was stored in the Peirce and Kilburn shipyard the winter of 1929 and was thereby subject to the Fairhaven property tax, which was levied as of May 1. The fact that we sailed *Fearless* out of Fairhaven in April may have had something to do with a sudden change in the assessing date from May 1 back to January 1. But tax or no tax, this early sailing proved once again that spring boating weather in Massachusetts is chancy at best. No sooner had we left the dock and hoisted sail when we found ourselves charging along through a blinding snowstorm in a ship channel we could only hope was free of traffic. The melting snow eliminated all traction underfoot, and the wet cold discouraged any use of one's hands. Nothing serious actually happened. However, it was one of those occasions that make you wonder where your brains were at the time of your departure.

---

*We never hear about *Malabar VI* on the ocean racing lists, but this is because she was sold out to Chicago right after she was built. Her sistership *Black Goose* did the honors for her by winning Class B in the 1928 Bermuda Race. That same year *Malabar VII* took first in Class A and top overall prize. There was very little real difference in the design of these two *Malabar*s, but the fact that *Malabar VII* was about a foot longer overall than *Black Goose*—that is, 53'9"—qualified her to race in Class A, whereas *Black Goose* fell just shy of the 52' dividing line that for many years separated the two classes. In racing, especially in ocean racing, it can make a real difference if you are rated in the top or bottom of your class. With these two boats, Alden successfully covered his bets both ways.

Gibson Island is a beautiful spot some 10 miles as the crow flies north of Annapolis, Maryland. In 1929 the yacht club there was but a few years old, and its members felt that a visit from outside sailors might be a good idea. They organized a race for June 1929, and asked Herb Stone and John Alden, among others, to serve on their race committee.

The fleet gathered in New London, as it might for a Bermuda Race. A record number, some 48 boats, had signed up. Forty-one actually started. There were 18 boats in Class A, all but one of them schooners.

Our Saturday start was another of those foggy ones. The wind was mostly "up and down the mast," but with a fair tide we drifted over to Montauk Point. It was an eerie evening. We could hear action of one sort or another all around us, but saw only the occasional gray shadow of a drifting competitor. When the tide began to turn, our lead line proved conclusively that in spite of slight headway through the water, we were actually going backward over the bottom. In silent secrecy we slipped a light anchor over the side at the leeward forward chainplates, and thus held our position. With all sails set and pulling, our helmsman played his misleading part. We made astonishing progress through the fleet until the clank and splash of many anchors spoiled our little game.

As darkness came on, so did a light southerly, and we all began to sail up on our anchors, some sooner than others. The fleet became confused, to put it mildly. Some were still ringing fog bells to indicate they were anchored. Others blew horns to signal that they were sailing on one tack or the other. An especially puzzling set of sounds turned out to be the schooner *Malay* drifting ashore (fortunately without damage).

Once around Montauk we set our fisherman staysail and reaching jib, and fetched along on our course for several hours. By Sunday noon the weather had cleared, although the wind was still light and pretty much ahead. These were conditions that the lofty marconi-rigged boats liked. They could nearly keep to the rhumb line while the gaff-riggers tended to sag off. Finally, late Monday, the wind came around to the southwest and freshened. Conditions were stacking up against the trailing boats, of which we were one. Those ahead and to windward soon fetched the lightship and barreled up Chesapeake Bay before a strong breeze. We, on the other hand, had a long rough beat to the turning mark. By the time we had the lightship abeam the wind slacked way off and then left us becalmed.

The 65-foot Alden yacht-type schooner *Sachem* finished Tuesday morning, followed by Paul Hammond's famous *Niña* and a Ten Meter boat later in the day. Many of the bigger boats finished Wednesday. At the time of the dinner and dance on Saturday evening we on *Fearless* were anchored in a flat calm, in easy sight of the finish line, but not over it. Some charming young ladies came out in a powerboat to urge us to hurry ashore. Would that we could have.

Conditions did play a big part in the outcome of this particular race. *Niña* won in Class A and overall. As a new boat in 1928 she had won the Transatlantic Race to Spain. One of the bigger boats, she had the then-ultramodern staysail rig, and was very well sailed. *Teal* took second in Class A and finished three days before we did—this despite the fact that she was a sistership of *Fearless*. (In her favor, she had a marconi mainsail and also the advantage in any schooner race of having John Alden aboard.) The Alden-designed *Merry Widow*, a near sistership to *Malabar VI*, took first in Class B.

Rather than leave *Fearless* sitting ignominiously off the Gibson Island finish line, I wish to add that during 1929 she sailed some 2,500 miles, cruising as far east as Halifax and picking up silverware in Padanaram's Memorial Day Race, a Boston Yacht Club race, and the Jeffries Ledge Race. She also did well in the 1930 Bermuda Race. More important, she made a fine seagoing teacher for her owner, Ralph; his brother Tom; John Hallowell and his two brothers, Bill and Roger; as well as Roger Warner, my brother, me, and others. Various *Fearless* graduates were to meet again on many another future ocean race.

Ralph sold *Fearless* in 1932 for $4,000—a sign of what the Depression was doing to the yacht market. But she was to enter the life of my family some 40 years later, when, in the early 1970s, my son Kinny helped bring her north. She was then rigged as a ketch and was in the charter business.

v

John Alden retired in 1955 and joined his ancestors some six years later. His influence is still being felt, however, for he most certainly had a good eye for a line and a real desire to turn out the best boats possible. I personally never thought of him as a genius of the drafting board. Rather than being an innovator, he was, to me, an excellent judge of what people wanted and needed. In addition, he had the wisdom and ability to follow through with the goods. The organization that he built *produced*; it is one of the very few boating concerns that has continued to carry on in a substantial way after its founder's death.

The name *Malabar* will forever be a part of America's boating history. The name *Fearless* is a part of mine.

5

The 1930 Bermuda Race: *Flying Cloud III*, the Grinnells, and Donald McKay

i

One more milestone! June of 1930 brought a welcome end to my formal and barely passing college career. (I still have nightmares about math exams and English composition.) That month simultaneously bore with it another Bermuda Race invitation, again from Larry Grinnell. Some basic decisions now certainly had to be faced, and I dutifully consulted my parents.

In their own very different but thoughtful ways, each of them sympathetically considered my serious personal wishes. Regarding the situation at hand, Mother wisely pointed out that the stock market disaster of the previous year should surely give all young men a positive cause to stop and think. Fellows who had graduated a decade earlier had, far too easily, drifted into a white collar job in the family business or the like. On credit they had bought expensive homes and habits. Thanks to a sharply rising market they had appeared to be reaping the rewards of sound financial judgment. After the crash, it was all so unkindly different. Budding magnates found themselves without funds—and often without jobs or homes. What was even more tragic, many of them had not acquired the willpower or any other mechanism with which to get started again, this time from a lowly and solid base. I was soon to see the sad truth that many of these men never really did recover, and this fact has caused me to bless the good fates that saw to it that my own business days began at rock bottom. There was only one way that my economy could move. It was hard, but it was up.

Mother had a strong and valid point, but happily for my own selfish

For the 1930 Bermuda Race, it was again my good fortune to crew aboard the Grinnells' schooner *Flying Cloud III*. Her name comes from a 229′ record-breaking, family-owned clipper ship of the 1850s.

seafaring enthusiasms, all such matters as concerned boating promotions were in the end passed along to Father for the final verdict. Father, God bless him, had an uncanny way of seeing beyond current conditions and ahead into things that were to be.

In granting his approval for this second trip to Bermuda, Father explained that Larry and I were not by any means the first young Grinnell and Howland shipmates to sail together across the Gulf Stream. It seems that in 1777, when the Revolutionary War was in full swing, my three times great-grandfather Cornelius Howland was 19 years old. In that fateful year, young Cornelius departed the home of his father, Gideon, on Round Hill, Dartmouth, to venture off on a privateering voyage to the West Indies. He was second mate on the vessel. A young Grinnell, also named Cornelius, was signed on as one of the crew. The whole story is too long for the telling here, but it turns on Cornelius Howland's imprisonment in Edinburgh Castle—a beautiful fortress to be sure, but not one arranged for easy escape.

Fortunately for my eventual creation on this earth, Cornelius survived a severe case of prison scurvy. His recovery was not thanks to British Navy lime juice, but rather to a basket of fresh cherries, which the prison doctor shared with him. There followed several months of frustrating incarceration, but eventually, with the help of a sympathetic washerwoman and her daughter, Cornelius did make an ingenious escape by donning the clothes of the younger woman. After many harrowing adventures, he returned safe and sound to his Round Hill homestead. His family had had no news of him for three long years.

I never did find out how Cornelius Grinnell made his way home, but there is no doubt that he did; for he subsequently married Cornelius Howland's sister Sylvia. This would indicate to me that Larry Grinnell and I have a common grandparent, if we but take the connection back six generations.

Within a few short years Cornelius Grinnell became Captain Grinnell. An excellent seaman from the first, he soon acquired prominence in New Bedford's whaling business and, later, in the merchant service. Several of his sons, including Henry and Moses, moved to New York and there established the great mercantile firm of Fish and Grinnell, shortly to be known as Grinnell Minturn and Company. This is the famous house that owned many a great clipper ship, including the *Flying Cloud*. A third son of Cornelius, Joseph, was founder of the cotton industry in New Bedford. It was Joseph Grinnell who established the prestigious Wamsutta Mills and who for so many years was its president. I more personally think of him as the man who built the stately mansion with the Classic Revival facade located on New Bedford's County Street overlooking the town. My grandparents lived there for several years. Later I too spent many a night within its granite walls as a guest of the Lawrence Grinnells.

A grandson of old Cornelius Grinnell moved from New Bedford to a large estate on the banks of the Hudson River. He became a prominent and influential yachtsman. Elected as the New York Yacht Club's first fleet captain, this Grinnell—Irving—was a member of the regatta committee that ran the early *America*'s Cup races.

To come down one more generation, we find Frederick Grinnell, my friend Larry's grandfather. He was the inventor of the automatic fire extinguisher and founder of the Providence-based Grinnell Sprinkler Company. Larry himself went to work for his uncle Russell Grinnell in this company and was sent by the firm to their San Francisco office. Not surprisingly, Larry has become one of the leading yachtsmen of San Francisco Bay. His first cousin Bill Severence has played an equally important role in the Los Angeles area and was for some years commodore of the Newport Beach Yacht Club. As in whaling days, New Bedford families continue to have seafaring interests in California.

The Grinnell Minturn ships were top performers during the high point of the clipper ship era, a unique period of less than 30 years that saw our sailing ship development ascend to its zenith. For speed, for beauty, and for perfection of wooden hull construction, these American clippers have never been surpassed. It is not, however, a simple matter to pinpoint the individuals who were most responsible for developing the clipper model. The fact is that a great many designers and builders, captains and shipowners, were involved and contributed their valuable share.

One such was John Griffiths. During the 1830s, Griffiths was working for the big New York shipyard of Smith and Dimon. His position gave him an excellent opportunity to see and consider the shape of a ship, and thereby to arrive at a number of specific conclusions of his own. These ideas Griffiths demonstrated in 1841 with a ship model and a series of lectures on marine architecture. He recommended several quite radical departures from the current practice. Briefly, he proposed the lengthening and fining out of the forebody of a ship. In doing this he carried the stem forward in a concave curve and hollowed out his waterlines, especially above the water. He also moved his center of displacement slightly aft of amidships by carrying aft the ship's greatest beam. Finally, he sharpened up his stern to get away from heavy above-water quarters. These suggested improvements are very similar to those made famous 10 years later by George Steers. (Was it a mere coincidence that George Steers's older brother James was superintendent of the Smith and Dimon yard from 1834 to 1839? It seems to me natural that James Steers and Griffiths should discuss design work together—and that later, and at second hand, the novel thinking of John Griffiths should filter through to the brilliant younger brother George Steers.)

A first noteworthy use of Griffiths's design theories was made by the New York shipping firm of Howland and Aspinwall, which, in 1837, purchased what might be called an experimental ship from the estate of a Baltimore merchant. This was the five-year-old, 500-ton *Ann Mc Kim*—the finest big ship built along the lines of the small, fast Baltimore clippers. *Ann Mc Kim* turned out to be not only a beautiful creation, but also an extremely fast and able sailer. However, being this fine in shape, she lacked the needed carrying capacity for economical operation in the shipping trade.

Smaller clipper-type vessels continued to be designed and built for operations requiring speed and weatherliness rather than large carrying capacity. Forbeses, Russells, and other Boston merchants sent out many a fine little 200-ton clipper, to be operated against monsoon winds and strong currents in the Indian Ocean and China Sea. The vessels transported quickly quantities of light opium from India to China. The vast profits and Eastern treasures came home more slowly in larger company ships.

After the *Ann Mc Kim* there were no further efforts to build a big fine-lined ship until 1843, when the persistent Howland and Aspinwall Company commissioned Smith and Dimon to build for them a vessel that would incorporate the recommendations of John Griffiths. Thus did the handsome 750-ton *Rainbow* become the first true "extreme clipper." In spite of outspoken reservations on the part of most shipping people, the *Rainbow* proved on her first trips to China and back that she was a great ship—and more important, that she was a model to be well considered in the planning of all future clippers.

As a shipbuilding center Boston did not come into its own until the mid-1830s. Earlier New England merchant ships and fishing schooners had been built in the outlying communities along the shores of Massachusetts Bay. To the south of Boston there were the boatbuilding towns of Scituate and Duxbury, and to the north Essex, Salem, and Newburyport. Nearer at hand Chelsea had a flourishing community. Farther east in New Hampshire and Maine were still more excellent builders. The event that actually sparked Boston on its climb to shipbuilding prominence was the timely creation of the East Boston Timber Company. It was in 1834 that its promoter, one Stephen White, and his associates bought a big piece of land in East Boston and established a lumber yard between Borden and Liverpool streets there. With great foresight White created his own source of supply for good shipbuilding timber by the bold action of purchasing the whole of Grand Island, located in the Niagara River near Buffalo. On its shores the Company set up its own mills and sawed out the lumber as specifically required by the shipbuilding trade. From Grand Island it went direct by barge from Buffalo through the Erie Canal to New York, and thence by coasting schooner to the Company docks in Boston. The importance of a specialized set-up like this may not seem obvious; but lumber does have to be sawed and handled differently for boat construction than for commercial shoreside or inland use. A house carpenter wants his lumber cut straight, while a shipbuilder often needs as much shape in his material as possible. The East Boston Timber Company knew what it was doing, and shipbuilders soon began moving in to Boston to take advantage of the favorable opportunities now available.

The building of wooden ships is full of fascination, and I wish I could write in detail of the booming era of clipper ship building in Boston. This, however, would be straying well out of my ken. Suffice it to say that of all the famous American extreme clippers built in the mid-nineteenth century, New England yards built a majority, of which Boston builders could claim the lion's share.

The foremost builder of clipper ships was surely Donald McKay, who originally came from Shelburne, Nova Scotia, and who served his apprenticeship in several of the big New York yards. In 1840 McKay came to New England, working for a time in Newburyport with John Currier and others. Here he created a strong reputation for himself and produced a number of fine ships. Here, too, he began his designing career. In 1845, with the urging and financial support of Enoch Train, who established a Boston-Liverpool line of sailing packets, McKay moved to East Boston. His initial building contracts were for Train's Liverpool Line. Later, however, he built a number of packets for the New York–based Swallow Tail Line owned by Grinnell Minturn. One of these vessels was named *Cornelius Grinnell.*

The McKay and Grinnell Minturn fortunes reached their flood during the years of the California Gold Rush. The situation was, of course, unique—with speed at any cost the objective. American shipping interests poured orders and money into the big yards of New York and New England. Bigger, finer, and faster clippers slid into the water and sailed south for Cape Horn on their way to San Francisco. First they were overloaded with just passengers and their gear. Soon they were carrying additional supplies and provisions to fill the desperate needs of the growing thousands of gold diggers who were getting rich, but starving at the same time.

The long passages out and back became true ocean races between rival shipping firms or individual ships. The marks of the race courses, especially on the California run, were often very specific: from New York or Boston to the equator; from the equator to 50 degrees south in the Pacific; thence to the equator; finally north to the finish line off San Francisco. Sometimes the races were boat for boat; more often the contest was against time—an attempt to set yet another new record. Considering all the variables of weather, great distances, different seasons, quality of crews and masters, it is amazing how close the actual competition was. An average voyage from New York to San Francisco took perhaps 120 days. A fast trip was 110 days or less. Some 20 or more clippers succeeded in reaching San Francisco in 90 to 100 days. Only three times did a ship make the passage in less than 90 days. The *Andrew Jackson*, built by Irons and Grinnell of Mystic, Connecticut, made it once in 89 days—in 1860. But it is the Grinnell Minturn clipper *Flying Cloud* that is credited with top honors for this California ocean race. She *twice* made the run in 89 days—first in 1851, again in 1854.

The *Flying Cloud*, that most famous of the California clippers, was one of a fleet of 10 that Donald McKay built at his East Boston yard between the years 1850 and 1853. They were all of the same general design and beautiful construction, but no two were exactly alike. Into each went McKay's best effort and talent. In each, the owners and captains took the greatest pride. Money was not spared. Every ship was strongly built and finely finished. Spars and rigging were carefully designed to withstand the extreme strains imposed by a stout ship with tall sails being driven hard around the Horn by a determined and able captain.

In size, Grinnell Minturn's *Flying Cloud* was, at 1783 tons, about the same as four of the other McKay California clippers. (Many New England–built clippers were smaller; a number of the New York–built ones were larger.) In length she was 229 feet, in beam 40 feet, in depth 21 feet. Like all the other extreme clippers she had a very tall rig and an enormous spread of sail to allow her to maintain speed in light airs, and, in the doldrums, to chase fickle airs. Her mainmast alone, not including topmast and topgallant mast, was 80 feet long and nearly four feet in diameter. (Compared to other ships of an earlier or later date, the clipper rigs appear narrow; but it is mostly the great height of the spars that gives this impression.)

Flying Cloud was assuredly a very fast vessel. However, credit for her unbeaten records must go not only to her designer-builder; it must also go to her owners, who had the fine judgment to employ Josiah Perkins Cressey to command her. Like so many of the clipper captains, Cressey was a New Englander with extensive and valuable seagoing experience dating back to his childhood days. After sailing dories in Marblehead, and venturing over to Salem Harbor where he could observe the merchantmen returning from faraway places and listen to the tales of sailors and watermen, he gained a basic education of great depth while serving as a ship's boy aboard a Salem East Indiaman. At an age when most of us are still in high school, he was rapidly, but surely, aboard different ships, climbing the ladder to the captain's position. By the time he was 37, Captain Cressey was recognized as one of the ablest officers in the ocean trade. I shudder at the responsibilities and skills that were required to run a big clipper. Successfully to cope with all the problems and difficulties—and then consistently to drive such a ship up to her limits in all weathers and conditions—represents ocean racing at an untouchable peak.

The ability, quality, and accomplishments of our extreme clippers, their

The Grinnells had an earlier
Flying Cloud (No. II), also
schooner-rigged and also
Hand-designed, which was
entered in the 1923 race. She
is shown here in contrast
(more freeboard, more stability, fewer modifications for
racing) to Alden's then-latest
schooner *Malabar IV*.

The year 1930 ended the schooner era for offshore racing. New names like Burgess, Rhodes, and Stephens were designing leaner craft with more efficient racing rigs— craft that could generally save their time on the heavier-built fisherman-type schooners and on the long-ended centerboard types such as the schooner *Black Duck* (shown here).

builders, owners, and captains, made possible a glorious sailing era in America, when our United States was, indeed, Sovereign of the Seas. History suggests that we had a chance to keep this supremacy. But somehow, in the years following the Civil War, the golden opportunity slid off to leeward, and we watched England, our chief rival, climb to weather of us.

ii

It is a steep descent, but not—I believe—a total fall from the lofty extreme clippers of the 1850s to the Bermuda Racers of 1930, including Larry Grinnell's *Flying Cloud.* In any event we were conscious of our boat's illustrious namesake and wished to do well by her.

Our start was essentially a repetition of the 1928 Bermuda Race start. We set sail from New London on the day following all the distracting excitement of the Harvard-Yale crew race. I remember a biased couplet that may suggest the general idea: "In the morning we went to New London, the sky it was blue overhead/At the time of our dinner that evening, it had turned a most glorious red." Certainly *Flying Cloud III*'s crew remained Harvardian in nature, although it differed slightly from that of the previous race in that Mr. Stearns, Story, Hugeley, and the green-faced cook were replaced by our S-boat friend

Johnny Stedman, by Larry's younger brother Peter, and by Ephron Catlin and Arthur Devens.

In the makeup of the fleet itself there were more basic changes. The stock market had crashed, but fortunately (as we saw it) too late for racing owners to cancel their plans. A record 42 yachts showed at the starting line. Most of them were relatively new boats, built, that is, after 1925. Of the 30 schooners, nine were either brand-new or only a year old. Alden's own *Malabar X* and *Dauntless* also of his design were 1930 boats; the Alden-designed *Teragram* had been built the year previous. *Mistress* was a new 50-foot length-at-waterline schooner designed by Sherman Hoyt for George Roosevelt and built at the Eastern Shipbuilding Corporation of Shelburne, Nova Scotia. *Cayuse*, belonging to my friend C. McKim Norton and his brother, and *Rose of Sharon* were both 50-footers built the same year at the same Nova Scotia yard but designed by Starling Burgess. Of the three cutters two were new: the Rhodes-designed *Skål* and the Wells-designed *Viking*. Of the five yawls, two were 1930 boats: the Olin Stephens–designed *Dorade* and Alden's *Sea Witch*. Important new names were showing up. This was the first Bermuda Race in which there were entries by Starling Burgess, Philip Rhodes, or Olin Stephens. A few older boats were still on hand, but not many. Three of these were Crowninshield schooners: *Black Duck*, built in 1909; *Shimmo*, built in 1907 (my brother was aboard her); and *Fame*, a 60-footer built in 1920. Among old-timers there were also a 1902 ketch and a 1903 yawl built by Lawley.

With so many new boats (there were only eight repeaters from 1928), it was difficult or impossible to identify most of the field. True, we had good friends aboard eight of our competitors, and we even placed a few side bets with *Black Duck*, *Black Goose*, and *Fearless*. Major Smyth had just built *Teragram* for George Mixter and was aboard for this race (and the following two, as well). I made a point of finding him to wish him well.

Our arch-nemesis, *Rugosa II*, was among the repeaters, and more than ever, her owner, Uncle Russy Grinnell, was the man we sought to beat. In 1928 he had finished a full 21 hours ahead of us (and this did not include his time allowance). Now he was even calling our beloved *Flying Cloud* the *Emily M. Pushwater*. (Emily was Larry's mother, and the *M* stood for Morgan. Charles W. Morgan of New Bedford whaling fame was Emily Grinnell's maternal grandfather.) It was now time for us to get on with it and straighten matters out.

The weather tended to be sympathetic to our aims. Although at times too light, the winds remained westerly, which helped us gaff-riggers on a south-southeast course. For our start on June 22, the morning was fair and the wind was free. Neither troublesome tide nor blinding fog showed up to confuse us as we approached Montauk Point. A calm area that we soon encountered merely gave us an incentive for a session of much needed sail drill. For once, this didn't

The main and foresail throat halyards were double-ended. One end came direct to the pinrail at the foot of the mast, the other end led to a jig which ran down parallel with the lower shrouds and belayed to a pinrail there. This made it easy to "change the nip," and thus avoid halyard chafe continuously working on any one spot. Every day the running end of the halyard was supposed to be slacked off a bit, and the jig set up an equal amount. The jig with its three or four parts took the place of a winch. In spite of this simple aid and precaution, a human error crept aboard and chafed through one strand of the main throat halyard. With our easy ship motion and a gaff rig, it was no trick to get aloft, seize two parts of the throat halyard temporarily together to hold the sail in position, slack off the damaged end, and, while thus free, cut out the chafed area, and lay in a long splice. Very quickly we were back in business without lowering the sail or losing time. It definitely is not that easy for an amateur to repair a damaged wire halyard on a light marconi-rigged racer.

precipitate the organized confusion that so often fouls up the early stages of a race. We just settled comfortably into a normal routine, groused about the other watch, and occasionally whistled for more wind. Each evening before the dew fell, we slacked away a few inches on all halyards. (A simple routine, perhaps, but not entirely without interest, because it involved jib and jumbo halyards, two halyards each on foresail and main, two more on the fisherman, one on the topsail, and several other lines for good measure. Plymouth-made yacht manila was a lovely rope to handle. But like other natural fiber lines it shrank in dampness, and this in turn created undue strains, especially with cotton sails, which likewise shrank when damp.) The reverse process—"setting up"—came with each dry morning.

Our rig and sail complement remained much the same as it had been for the 1928 race, except that the club topsail had been altered and cut down in size and now set only the yard that extended the sail above the masthead. *Flying Cloud* had an anchor windlass, but no other winches aboard; yet the old girl had better than 2,000 square feet of working sail and far more with all light sail set.

We ran into a second calm area on the third day out, which helped the slower boats catch up on the leaders. When the breeze came in again, it was from the southwest, and this gave us all a chance to fetch along in good shape. The result was a close and lively finish for almost everyone—and especially for us.

To add to the normal confusion of many boats in a small piece of ocean, there happened to be a cloud cover that last day. This unkind condition made it hard for navigators to know exactly where they were. Boats were approaching St. David's Head from every conceivable direction. It was about mid-morning when *Flying Cloud* received her big shot in the arm. Larry had estimated that the finish line was to windward and only some 10 miles distant. There were boats all around us—10 or 15, maybe more. Some we recognized, others not. They did appear to be Class A entries, and that was encouraging. All at once we identified the masts and sails of a white marconi yawl about a mile and a half to leeward of us. It was *Rugosa II*! We were ahead of Uncle Russy. Now all we had to do was stay there.

Hard on the wind we constantly trimmed sheets, coming about for real or imaginary puffs. On every tack our fisherman—with two halyards, a tack, and a sheet—had to be lowered and reset on the opposite side. In those days snap shackles were unknown to us. The fisherman halyard bends had to be untied from one end and retied on the other. During one tack, Sam Lane had a jammed knot; he whipped out his knife to cut it loose, but missed and like to cut his thumb off. Blood ran all over the deck, distracting us. When we looked around again old *Rugosa* was obviously gaining on us at an alarming pace. Had we worked half as hard during the whole race as we did during those last two hours we would at least have beaten Uncle Russy boat for boat. As it was, in the final

''Uncle Russy'' Grinnell's
Herreshoff yawl *Rugosa II*
was our arch rival in the 1930
race. We failed to beat her,
and a look at her sleek
underwater shape, as she rests
on the turntable at Peirce and
Kilburn's yard, helps explain
why.

20 minutes and with the finish line clearly in sight, *Rugosa* gracefully sliced by to windward and finished some four minutes ahead of us. Throughout a major part of the race we had undoubtedly sailed faster and more comfortably than those aboard *Rugosa*, but when it came down to a tacking duel, our able gaff schooner was no match for a New York Forty.

Race committees seldom have an easy time of it, but the Bermuda Race Committee at the finish this June 26 could never say that time hung heavy on their hands. Boats literally poured across the line. Three-quarters of the fleet finished within about 10 hours, and some 17 of these (including *Flying Cloud III*) within the first four hours. That evening a steady procession streamed into Hamilton, and by the next morning the shore celebration was in full flower.

For many of us the first shore stop was the narrow second-floor quarters of the old Royal Bermuda Yacht Club on Front Street. Here, after a rewarding pause within the small cedar-paneled barroom, we would drift out to the open front porch from which we could observe the passing scene below or gaze out across the blue-green waters of the harbor to the Paget shore beyond. Activity aboard the yachts in the foreground was mainly of a domestic or idle nature— sails half hoisted to dry, apparel and bedding of many colors airing on makeshift clotheslines. Here and there a man in a bosun's chair signaled instructions down to his helper. All was so rewardingly peaceful after the few somewhat strenuous days at sea that it was a great temptation to remain here at the yacht club indefinitely.

I had only one serious piece of business to attend to in Hamilton on this and other Bermuda races: a trip to Trimingham Brothers just west of the yacht club on Front Street, where a pair of London-made shoes from Fortnum and Mason awaited me. (By having the shoes delivered in Bermuda I saved the American duty on them. The duty would have amounted to as much as a dollar. Who knows? Even a dollar and a quarter.) It was a ritual of great satisfaction to me. And, of course, I never left Trimingham's without adding other items to my wardrobe as well.

When the evening came for the awards dinner, all hands donned their best and sauntered in small groups up Queen Street to the old Hamilton—a hilltop hotel that dated back to the days of our Civil War. Generally speaking, the prizes went to deserving winners. There were no great surprises, except, of course, for the amazing closeness of some of the finishes. Alden in his *Malabar X* had kept pace with many a fine boat of greater waterline length, and thereby won Class A by over two hours. The Alden schooners *Teragram*, *Teal*, and *Dauntless* took second, third, and fifth places respectively—and with only three hours between them. The Alden showing is convincing evidence that Alden carefully designed and made available excellent boats that were capable of winning races against current competitors. It shows too that he and a number of his owners really knew how to equip these schooners, to select good crews for them, and then race with skill and energy.

I'm sure that Bill Hand was much pleased that the schooner *Yankee Girl II* of his design was the first boat to finish. Performance even before prizes was his approach. And *Flying Cloud III* was tenth on corrected time, only two hours behind *Rugosa*. For the home team this represented great improvement. It allowed us to hold our heads high and quaff our side bets with relish.

In his six-year-old Roué-designed schooner *Malay*, Raymond Ferris showed us all a thing or two. He not only took his class, but was on corrected time nearly an hour ahead of *Malabar X*. This was the first time that a boat in the small class had won the overall prize in a Bermuda Race, and Mr. Ferris got the big cheers. Although the weather had been on the small boats' side during the 1930 Bermuda Race, it was an obvious omen of things to come that the new Stephens yawl *Dorade* and the new Burgess schooner *Rose of Sharon* placed second and third behind *Malay*, saving their time on all the Class A boats except *Malabar X*.

iii

The inevitable day of departure from Bermuda is always a trying one. It's much like the prospect of going for a swim in the Gulf of Maine. You are completely happy where you are, and Gawd! how you dread the first plunge into that dark and frigid water. To add to this mental anguish you find that the conditions aboard the boat are seldom what they should be. Those careful preparations made before the race are all too often neglected for the return trip.

On the morning of our 1930 departure the weather itself was none too good, and there were further aggravations to cope with. In the main cabin there were, to my thinking, too many cluttering cases of costly and worthless soda pop. In the galley there were too few signs of sumptuous provisions. And on deck it looked as if there might be too many cases of hangover. To top it all off, I soon felt ready for lunch. But as we made our offing from the North East Breakers, it emerged that the cook had failed in his half-hearted attempt to light the old Shipmate, and was himself having a snooze of uncertain duration.

There was nothing for it. I worked my way through the cases of soft drinks in the big main cabin and into the galley. Once there I firmly locked the door behind me. The cook had complained of a lack of dry newspaper and kindling wood as the reason why he had been unable to fire up the iron monster. Indeed, there may have been some truth to his complaint. But in any event, time itself did not appear to be of the essence. So I settled in for a session of experiment, science, and skill.

With my Ka-Bar knife I transformed a long piece of kindling into a pile of finger-length pieces. These I graded into two stacks: those less than four inches and those more than four inches. Next I removed the two stove covers and opened the draft door—the only way to get access to the baulky mess of char within and below the firebox. On the cleaned-out grate I laid a number of long pieces of kindling in three crossing layers. On top of this relatively flat grid I wedged two special pieces parallel to each other and about a quarter of an inch apart. Finally, over the slot formed by these parallel sticks I built a miniature criblike bonfire, using the four-inch or larger slivers of kindling for the bottom squares, the shorter slivers for the top.

The ship was jumping around now, and the construction job was somewhat like playing jackstraws on a roller coaster. For fear of unwanted and hazardous puffs of air, I closed both the ashpit door and the chimney draft, and replaced the rear stove lid. (I left the front lid off for access to my masterpiece, and to admit what gentle circulation of air was needed.) The match I held to the top cone of the elfin volcano flickered and wavered for a moment, but slowly caught on. The little flames crept down the pile of slivers and spread out rapidly as they reached the bigger ones below. Soon conditions became quite bright and active in the firebox, and it was time to replace the front stove lid and, by degrees, to open the drafts, both top and bottom. Lo! accumulated hot air from the firebox blasted up through the cold air block in the damp chimney, as new air flowed in through the ashpit door to fill the vacuum. The Shipmate was now in business and ready for the first few shovels' worth of coal.

Yes, I was proud of my handiwork, and I feel no modesty is necessary in writing about it. But I also tell the story to make a fundamental point. Proper ventilation and drafts are vital to the health and functions of stoves and boats alike. Many a promising craft has later proved to be a dismal failure because its designer or builder ignored this very basic truth. Why would factories have such lofty chimneys were it not for the fact that hot air rising has an elemental force all its own—a physical property that must be understood and utilized and not replaced by mechanical forced draft?

Fortified by an amplitude of fresh roast beef (I left my dishes for others to attend to), I found the voyage home went smoothly and happily. On the fifth morning out we sighted America with good old Block Island showing up right where it was supposed to be. We were sailing full and by, not quite fetching Mishaum Point. With the big black buoy abeam, we lowered the working jib and set the big full ballooner.

To any sailor watching from shore, and there was at least one for sure, this change of sail would have been a real puzzler. In fact, it made no sense at all. *Flying Cloud* wasn't even fetching the Sand Spit, and once we rounded that we would have the wind dead ahead for the final stretch into Padanaram. Mr. Grinnell, Sr., was quick to learn of our approach. From the end of his dock he watched his own schooner tacking pathetically back and forth, inching her way in against a failing morning northwesterly. His fears and curiosity were mixed in large quantities. Had his son lost his mind or had a gale of wind split *Flying Cloud*'s jib? The former guess came closer to the truth. We somehow figured that our supply of smuggled liquor would be unsuspected out on the bowsprit and furled carefully in the working jib. The bulge did not seem to concern the customs man. But thinking back, perhaps he was just a little on our side of the law anyway.

Flying Cloud never went to Bermuda again. For that matter, neither did *Black Goose, Black Duck, Fearless,* or several other old friends. Good boats often have to move on to poorer days. Fortunately, happy memories remain unchanged.

6
1931:
The Transatlantic and
Fastnet Races:
Landfall and *Highland Light*

i

My introduction to the lovely ketch *Landfall* struck out of the blue. Her owner simply phoned from his New York office and inquired whether I would sign aboard for the 1931 Transatlantic Race. At the time Paul Hammond was just a name to me, although I was, of course, well aware of his ocean racing victories with the schooner *Niña*. I accepted the invitation quickly enough, but all the same I did wonder what had prompted this famous sailor to offer me such a rare opportunity. Only as the years slipped by did I sense at least a partial answer to the question.

Paul Hammond had no sons of his own, and his fatherly instincts were therefore naturally and generously directed toward helping young men to climb their ladders of business and life. Furthermore, for his racing crews he seemed to favor fellows who had sailed on open waters and rowed their own tenders in preference to riding the club launch. I remember so well his great admiration for the impressive array of fine pulling boats that once graced the New Bedford Yacht Club floats.

Paul's intuitive seaman's line of thinking had very positive merit, and now in the 1980s, I observe ever more clearly that exposure to fundamental old-time training does stand a sailor in good stead, whether his final joy be buoy racing or ocean cruising. Somehow this simple reasoning about the basics keeps eluding parents and yacht club committees alike, to the real detriment of young sailors and all of yachting.

Searching for the finish line at Plymouth, England, are *Landfall*'s owner and captain, Paul Hammond (left), and four of her 11-man crew. From the left are Johnny Hallowell, J. Quincy Adams, Uffa Fox, and the author. As might be expected, it took a bit more than a sharp lookout to get us to our destination.

113

Paul Hammond (at right), owner of *Landfall*, had commissioned the building of the great schooner *Niña* in 1928 and was manager of an *America*'s Cup syndicate in 1930. In earlier years he had been a key promoter of international Six Meter competition. To me, he was a great friend and benefactor. He is shown here talking with N. G. Herreshoff, whose son, Francis, designed *Landfall*.

For a notable half century Paul Hammond cast such an obviously strong and beneficial influence over the general course of yachting and the lives of so many a young sailor that I now find myself eager to offer a few comments on his life.

Paul always enjoyed referring to himself as a New England farmer, and indeed he was born, in 1882, to Puritan parents on a working farm in Egypt, Massachusetts. His youth was spent in that small agricultural village, which lies in the back country between the South Shore harbors of Cohasset and Scituate. Neither his father, William, nor his mother, Adelaide (Nowell), was in any way sailing folk. Nonetheless, and early on, they gave to Paul and his twin brother, Noel, a genuine fisherman's dory; and all those local ponds, tidal marshes, and shallow reaches shoreward of Scituate Harbor certainly offered the finest kind of world for a venturesome boy in a real boat. Stephen Hammond, some 17 years older than Paul and Noel, introduced his brothers to the diverse wonders of rowing and sailing, teaching them the many skills and joys of trapping and shooting. (Paul later gained international fame as a top man with a shotgun, left shoulder or right.)

Paul graduated from Thayer Academy and attended Harvard, class of 1906; but always the outstanding athlete and man of action and never the top student, he soon left college to seek his fortune. His great ambition was, quite literally, to make a lot of money fast, and thereby at an early age achieve for himself a sound financial position from which he could substantially improve the lot of his whole family and, that done, follow out certain plans for his own satisfaction.

Choosing the great competitive battleground of New York City for his base, and industrial banking as his line of business, he remained from 1906 to 1965 concertedly and aggressively successful in his mission. All the while, I should add, his office door remained wide open, so that his protégés could enter at will and receive within the answer to any legitimate quest—and, as the system went, a mandatory bonus of a professional polish for dusty New England shoes.

Out on Long Island in lovely Locust Valley, Paul created his lifelong home by acquiring, in 1931, a generous portion of rural Muttontown property from his patron, friend, and Lord of the Manor, Bronson Winthrop. Two years earlier, in 1929, Paul had married Susan Sedgwick, the widow of Dr. Arthur Swan. Susan Hammond was a lady of uncommon grace and intelligence who was always affectionately known to us as The Admiral.

As a reserve officer in both world wars, Paul served in the U. S. Navy for a total of some seven very active years. In 1917-1918, starting as an ensign, he was assigned to destroyer duty and operated out of Queenstown, Ireland, where he was in close contact with British officers. During World War II he worked again with a destroyer fleet, but this time in the Pacific. Retiring as Captain, U.S.N.R., he was the recipient of many an honor, including a Bronze Star and a citation for development of anti-U-boat weapons and rockets. For notable assistance to the Royal Navy, he was given the coveted Order of the British Empire. In many ways both sentimental and practical, these wartime connections meant a great deal to Paul—and, as it turned out, to international yachting.

Admiral Susie Hammond explained his thinking, "Paul, after achieving his financial goal," she wrote, "was next determined to aid, abet, and take part in the racing of sailing craft: the peak to be in international racing." This action, he felt, "would be a builder of character and an inspiration to youth," while at the same time serving as a "deterrent to prejudice, greed, drink, wastefulness, and sloth." From his Puritan parents Paul had surely inherited a positive mission, one that he pursued religiously for the active years of his life.

As a new member of the Seawanhaka Corinthian Yacht Club, Paul at first crewed for other skippers whenever and wherever the chance presented. Following World War I, he promoted and joined in the racing of several small-boat classes including Gloucester-built "Kitten" cats, Herreshoff 16½-foot Fish Class boats, and Gardner-designed, raised-deck Victory sloops. In 1920 he pioneered the new Herreshoff S boats, owning one he chose to name *Spinster*. Designed to the Universal Rule, Paul felt that these fine 28-foot sloops would be ideal for foreign competition as well as for local racing. He was most disappointed when the European countries insisted that, for international racing, the International

Rule should be followed. In spite of his personal objections, Paul went along with the majority decision and bought and raced two Six Meter boats in succession: *Sheila* and *Cygnet*.*

Not content with small boats alone, Paul owned and raced two different New York Fifties. These were lively sailers designed by Herreshoff and were some 72 feet in overall length.(Joseph V. Santry's *Pleione*, rigged as a staysail schooner, was a fixture in East Coast waters—and won many a trophy—in later years, giving many of us an unforgettable reason for remembering the great New York Fifty class.) Although he was elected to serve a term as Seawanhaka Rear Commodore and, then, in 1923, as Vice Commodore, Paul found it awkward and in some cases difficult to crack the old-time Seawanhaka yachting establishment. Possibly this situation encouraged his natural desire to turn toward the wider field of ocean racing and even *America*'s Cup competition.

How did it come about that Paul chose L. Francis Herreshoff** and not Starling Burgess to design *Landfall*? Certainly Starling had done a beautiful job for Paul in working out a prizewinner in *Niña*; however, a glance at the 1930 Cup boat competition seems to answer the question. During 1929 and 1930, competing New York interests were monopolizing the services of Starling Burgess. During these years he was busy designing the mechanical sailing machine *Enterprise* and overseeing her construction at the Herreshoff yard in Bristol.

Paul, who was manager of the *Whirlwind*/*America*'s Cup syndicate, naturally turned to L. Francis, *Whirlwind*'s designer. One thing led to another. And while they worked together on J-boat details, Paul was further exposed to Francis's sound ideas about long-lined, easily driven cruising boats, and must have shared with Francis his plans for commissioning a boat for extensive Mediterranean and European cruising.

Landfall, as she developed, was definitely a member of the Nat Herreshoff 12½-Footer family, which included the Fish Boats with which Paul was so familiar, as well as the Newport Twenty-nines and other able and versatile Herreshoff creations. *Landfall* was modified, to be sure: her lines were stretched out, her wetted surface was cut away, and she had much new and ingenious rigging detail. In no way, however, was she a spartan ocean racer like *Niña*. With her 60-foot waterline and 18-foot beam, she was large enough to have accommodations for owner, guests, and crew that were not only ample, but luxurious, fitting, and beautiful.

Landfall was a 72′ ketch designed by L. Francis Herreshoff, built in Germany by Abeking and Rasmussen, and shipped to the United States in time for the race to Plymouth, England. In shape, she was not unlike the 21′ Seawanhaka Fish Class daysailer modeled by N. G. Herreshoff in 1916, and a boat with which Paul Hammond was intimately familiar. In accommodations, *Landfall* was luxurious, especially when compared to *Niña*, Hammond's previous ocean racer.

*To quote from a 1976 talk given by my long-time sailing friend Joseph W. ("Pat") Outerbridge before a Seawanhaka Corinthian Yacht Club meeting, "The decades of the twenties and thirties represented an era of international small boat racing that has never been equalled....With minor exceptions this racing was in 6-meters, and all of it in the United States was sponsored by the Seawanhaka....Paul Hammond with some wartime English yachting friends conceived this whole wonderful series of home and home team matches."

**Few people realize that the *L* stands for Lewis. Francis's grandmother was the daughter of Captain Joseph Lewis of Boston shipping fame, and one of Captain Nat's brothers was also named Lewis.

Landfall was one of L. Francis Herreshoff's finest ships, and it is more than a shame that racing rules necessitated the elimination of a graceful canoe stern that, although definitely a part of the original design, had to be cut short to keep overall length below 72 feet. In future great cruising boats like his *Ticonderoga*, Francis wisely stuck to his guns and carried out his lines to suit the flow of water—and the eyes of the beholder. His later boats (with the exception, perhaps, of the fine yawl *Persephone*) never did "fit" current ocean racing rules. Nevertheless they invariably matched in beauty and performance the excellence of those glorious clipper ships that he so greatly admired.

ii

In the fall of 1930, Captain Hammond arranged a Boston meeting for members of his *Landfall* racing crew. Except for the three English crew members, who were to arrive in this country at a later date, and for our navigator, Ben Ames, we were all known to one another. Larry Grinnell, Johnny Stedman, and I had, of course, a particularly close association. But Johnny Hallowell was also a Buzzards Bay sailor, had been a classmate at school, and had raced to Bermuda in 1928 on *Black Goose* and in 1930 with Ralph Williams on *Fearless*. Quincy Adams, a Harvard classmate, had raced to Bermuda in 1930 on Fred Ames's *Primrose IV*. Larry Pool and Kim Norton we knew and respected as Harvard upperclassmen. They had both raced to Spain in 1928, Larry aboard the schooner *Mohawk*, Kim aboard *Niña*. As for Ben Ames, we may not have sailed with him before, but we were mindful that he had only that summer participated in the Honolulu Race on *Mollilou*, a 46-foot yawl.

At the Boston gathering we were given instructions and information about the race. However, what remains more vividly in my mind is a picture of the Hammonds' niece Babs Clough and all the special equipment that she, as Paul's deputy, doled out to us. First, there was for each of us a heavy, white raw wool suit—button-up jacket and pants. Next were a somewhat less heavy wool jacket and red wool trousers; a light, white wool sweater with *Landfall* embroidered on it in red over the left breast; a heavy, Scandinavian, red and black sweater with white band at the bottom for tucking inside the pants and a tape tie at the top to keep things snug around the neck.

This was for starters. In addition, we each received a gaily striped wool watch cap, the newest fashion in oilskins, a sou'wester, and short Scottish deck boots. To hold all this gear, Babs Clough next presented us with what, at the time, was a new type of duffel bag. The old standard sailor's bag was little more than a sack with a drawstring opening at the top and the article you wanted always at the bottom. Our new bags (lettered with our initials and the name *Landfall*) were forerunners of the type that is popular today, having a zippered

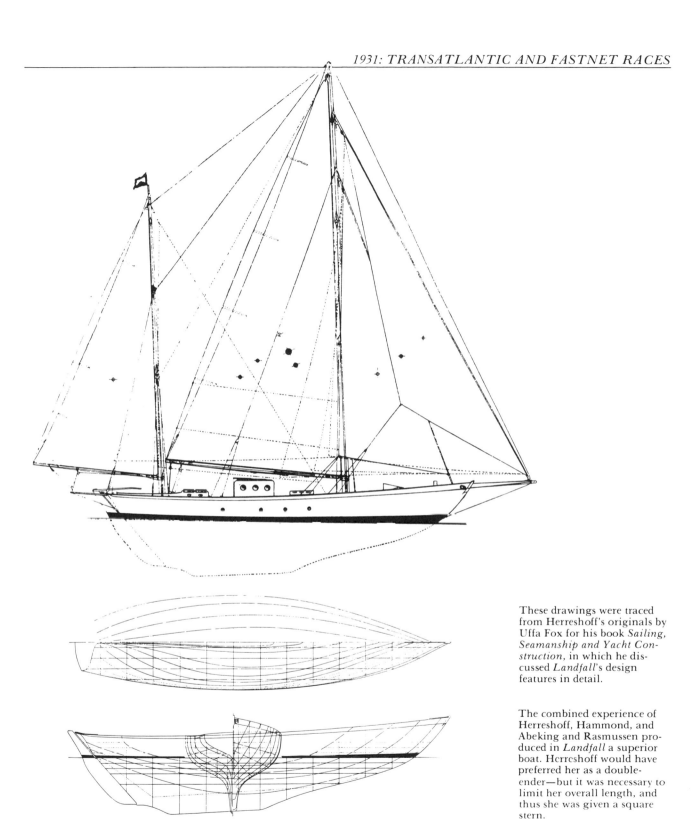

These drawings were traced from Herreshoff's originals by Uffa Fox for his book *Sailing, Seamanship and Yacht Construction*, in which he discussed *Landfall*'s design features in detail.

The combined experience of Herreshoff, Hammond, and Abeking and Rasmussen produced in *Landfall* a superior boat. Herreshoff would have preferred her as a double-ender—but it was necessary to limit her overall length, and thus she was given a square stern.

119

opening almost the full length and handles placed to allow for carrying the bag in a horizontal position. Hidebound and reactionary as I may be, I never refer to "good old-fashioned duffel bags." The new ones are far better.

As a final touch, Babs gave each of us two soft flat leather cases, one small for toilet articles, one larger for the safe keeping of a go-ashore shirt or two. How typical all this was of Paul's approach to life! From the first, we had suitable gear for use at the appropriate times that could be stowed neatly where it belonged. We never needed any words of instruction on this subject, then or later.

The next crew meetings were at Oyster Bay, where we had many a practice drill and sail. But again my memory clings not to boating activity, but rather to visits at Muttontown Lodge. This delightful Hammond summer home had the atmosphere of a New England farm, complete with rolling pastures, fences, outbuildings, and the fragrance of hay. The house, too, although somewhat larger than its prototypes, was very similar to the traditional Cape Cod type. As a Long Island contribution, the chimneys were painted white, as were the sidewall shingles.

The path to the Lodge led through a privet hedge and up to a white picket gate, in the structure of which was incorporated a varnished steering wheel complete with shined brass hub. (It sounds ostentatious, but it wasn't. Yet it certainly did give promise of something special within.) Indeed, everything about Muttontown Lodge was redolent of the fine old saltwater farms of southern New England, reminding one that water connections, in the early days of European settlement in America, were far quicker and easier to make than road connections, and that Long Island of past years had been more closely connected with the English settlements of Massachusetts, Cape Cod, and Narragansett bays than with the Dutch one of New York.

The food, like the setting, was something special at Muttontown Lodge, and I wish I could have a rerun of the fine fare that the Admiral's table provided. But there was one Hammond delicacy that I failed to relish—the "last course." This was Paul's special delight and consisted of an ominous, twisted green cigar that he always insisted that I light for him. I was not even a cigarette smoker at the time, and Paul's cigars offered nothing to further the temptation.

Sailors from near and far made it their habit to drop in at will at Muttontown Lodge. Boat plans and pictures, notes, and models were everywhere about. The big open fireplace consumed endless explanatory sketches and other finished business. Above the mantel hung a striking painting of Paul's World War I destroyer. A short walk from the Lodge stood a long, low, white-painted chicken house. No hen had laid an egg there for many a year, but the white-washed shelves were crowded to the roosts with boat equipment of every conceivable sort, from dinghy to J-boat size. There were stoves, lamps, cordage,

and canvas—you name it, it was all there, the useful relics of years of boat owning and dealing. Up on the hill behind the Lodge was a red barn topped by a fine weathervane to keep the skipper informed as to the true direction of the wind. In the barn were small work boats, a Herreshoff dinghy, tools, and the general appearance of a working boatshop—which, indeed, it was becoming, with the building of the 38-foot-overall sloop *Barnswallow*.

Our prerace routine called for daily auto trips to Fife's yard across the bay in Glen Cove. Here *Landfall* was receiving her final tune-up and outfitting. Given Paul's organizational ability and the general competence of all *Landfall*'s crew, our preparations were for the most part uneventful. However, one sail drill, occurring shortly before *Landfall* sailed for Newport, fell outside the routine. We were maneuvering in the open ocean off Montauk Point. It was early morning and the wind was still moderate. After trying out several light sails, Paul worked us through a man-overboard drill. Tossing a life preserver off the stern, he sang out the warning, and we jibed smartly around, so that we

Left—Final preparations for the 1931 Transatlantic Race were made at the Herreshoff yard in Bristol, Rhode Island. On deck is the usual prerace clutter.

Right—While *Landfall* is outfitting, it's a time for visiting (my mother and "Porthole Pete" Chamberlain are aft by the mizzen rigging) and fine tuning the gear, which is what my fellow crew member Uffa Fox seems to be engaged in near the base of the mainmast.

might come right up on our target on the first pass.* The life preserver, however, was not the only object that went overboard. Unbeknown to us, Paul had also directed Larry Pool to slip over the side into the water. The alarm was urgently sung out by the first observer, and around we came in earnest. It all went smoothly enough in spite of the real urgency we felt. Larry was helped aboard without problem. Paul had made his point.

Later on in the afternoon the faithful old southwest breeze came on with its usual authority, and our big genoa was a bit too much for us to carry. Ben Ames and I were ordered out on the bowsprit to smother the sail as it was lowered. By this time the ocean seas had grown to quite impressive size, and *Landfall* poked her nose well down into one of them. As the bowsprit rose again, I was still out there, hanging on for dear life. But Ben was gone.

Looking down, I could see Ben's form far below me in the water. The bobstay was now descending directly toward the middle of his back. Turning my head aft, I gave the cry "Man overboard!" Then glancing down again I saw to my horror that Ben had disappeared under the bow. My call was heard. All hands knew the routine. *Landfall* swung off sharply. The genoa came down behind the main. And by the time I got the genoa lashed, the ship, sails slatting, was gently surging up to Ben. Unaccountably, he was not seriously injured, in spite of an angry red stripe slanting diagonally across his back. I don't remember just how he was hauled aboard. I do know that when conditions warranted, none of us ever complained about making full use of our life belts.

The start of the race was not to take place until July 4, but by June 27 *Landfall* was on her way to the Newport starting area. By the time I joined her for the duration she was conveniently tied up at the Herreshoff yard in Bristol. Brian Waite, Uffa Fox, and Joe Fredericks had arrived from England. Brian, a well-known seaman and author of nautical articles, was a veteran of three Fastnet races, one of them on *Niña*. He was to be our first mate, in charge of the port watch. Uffa was not an ocean racer as such, but he was recognized as one of the best helmsmen on the Solent, and he had already made two transatlantic trips in small yachts. Joe, an English professional, who was about my size or smaller, was a first-rate cook and had also been aboard *Niña* in the 1928 Fastnet. Paul had obviously given much thought to the selection of his crew.

Thinking back, I'm amazed that I was not more excited about that day we visited the Herreshoff shop. I can only presume that I didn't know enough to be impressed. It seemed quite routine that there should be two great J boats, *Yankee* and *Enterprise*, looking down from their cradles above us. It was, to be sure, most interesting to talk with Captain Nat Herreshoff and have him show

---

*One must make this retrieving operation from the leeward and avoid bringing the ship into the wind (which would merely set you farther to windward and away from your target). The very moment of jibe is an ideal one for taking in a spinnaker or troublesome big jib, assuming everyone automatically does his job right at the right moment. We all know this. Nevertheless, the automatic part is not so easy, unless it is practiced.

Since *Landfall*'s propeller had been removed for this race, we took a tow from Bristol to Newport from Sidney Herreshoff in his lovely launch, *Bubble*. Paul Hammond (seated to port) and his wife, Susie, are also aboard in this photo.

us the many models he had made or was working on. But what struck me most about Captain Nat at the time was that in pointing out details his hands were so shaky. I wondered how in the world an 83-year-old man with such an apparent handicap could do such fine and beautiful work.

It seems odd now that we had to ask Captain Nat's son Sidney to start up his beautiful launch and tow us down to Newport. But on that evening of July 1, there was no wind at all, and *Landfall*, although she had a fine engine, was to keep her propeller officially stowed below until the ocean race was ended. That's the way it was in 1931.

Before a race there are generally many more things to do than there is time for the doing. But for the crew of *Landfall*, the waiting days of July 2 and July 3 seemed most relaxed. Paul's earlier preparations had been thorough. It was both pleasant and timely to have the Grinnells' *Flying Cloud III* and Father's *Java* anchored nearby. Ocean voyages in small boats have a way of drawing together those family ties that are too often forgotten.

As a sharply dressed crew, several of us at a time accompanied our Captain on formal afternoon visits to one or more of the many distinguished yachts that had gathered in Newport for the prerace festivities. Commodore Arthur Curtiss James, a special friend and admirer of Paul's, honored us with a memorable reception aboard the great 165-foot (218 feet overall) bark *Aloha*. With the help of his well-trained staff, he saw to it that we met his family and friends, had an

Landfall at sea. Although she was fitted with a huge overlapping mainsail that would sheet to the end of the mizzen boom, such oversized sails were disallowed by the race committee only a few days before the start. The decision was a blow to our chances of winning, since we were limited, and perhaps rightly so, to the regulation, boomed mainsail shown here. (We were, however, able to utilize the big mainsail as a balloon jib—and did.)

opportunity to tour his ship from bow to stern, and were treated all the while to refreshments varied and plentiful enough to satisfy the fussiest of fancies. Uffa and I requested and received permission to climb the fore-rigging and work our way out on the yardarms as we saw fit. Even with the ship at anchor my immediate reaction was one of great respect for the possibilities. I dared not look down for long, and as I hung on with both hands my thoughts went out in sympathy to the young sailor of years gone by, fighting his first storm at sea and endeavoring to stow a fore royal.

When the party came to an end and *Landfall*'s crew stepped down aboard the waiting mahogany launch, I was happy in mind and spirit. I never gave one thought to the fact that I was enjoying a glimpse of yachting on a scale of splendor that was fading literally before my eyes.

At the midday start of the race, the weather was fair and the breeze was light. Yet all that morning the crew of *Landfall* was aware that a storm was brewing in our skipper's mind. News reporters in their launches were continuously churning alongside taking pictures and requesting some comment from Paul. Paul held his peace as long as patience would permit. Ultimately, however, he rewarded his over-insistent questioners with a broadside that would not be quotable even in today's permissive press. Not until many years later did I piece together the factors that brewed up the tempest.

With a special staysail configuration, Paul had in *Niña* created a new and successful type of ocean racing schooner. Now with *Landfall* he had worked out a novel idea he felt would make a ketch rig competitive. For moderate weather, a big, light, long-footed mainsail was designed to hoist in the normal way to the masthead, but was rigged to sheet way aft to the end of a strong mizzen boom. This device would produce unmeasured sail area, just as did a genoa jib or overlapping staysails. The plan had been studied and accepted by the committee in charge of the Newport-to-Plymouth Race.

Unfortunately, just a few weeks before July 4, *Highland Light* blossomed out with a strange new cutter rig that included a boomkin of gigantic proportions. From this weird creation the owner threatened to sheet a large light-weather mainsail. I really do not know the details, but I somehow doubt that this *Highland Light* super sail would ever have been practical in performance. However, it was eminently successful in presenting to the committee, of which John Alden was an important member, a royal problem. In the end, the committee voted to bar all oversized mainsail rigs, including *Landfall*'s.

This decision was a lethal blow to Paul's strategy. But the episode, as it developed, convinced me then and there never to build a cruising boat to a specific man-made racing rule. The details of the rule may well—indeed, generally do—change, sooner or later leaving the owner with a boat that is out of the running. Even worse, the rule (or attempts to beat it) may adversely affect the design and result in a boat that is undesirable from the very beginning.

iii

After the high drama of those hours just before the start, the race to Plymouth proved largely uneventful. But I think this very fact is the best evidence of Paul Hammond's foresight, ingenuity, and skill.

To begin with, Paul set up his port and starboard watches in accordance with a timing arrangement that is known as the Swedish system. It is, I feel, the best watch system for a longish voyage. Starting at midnight the first watch of the day goes to 4:00 A.M.; the next watch from 4:00 A.M. to 8:00 A.M.; then another watch from 8:00 A.M. to 1 P.M.; and two final watches, 1:00 P.M. to 7:00 P.M., and 7:00 P.M. to midnight. This rotation gives all hands a chance to have meals together at normal times, which is good for the crew, good for the cook. (Breakfast: 7:45 to 8:15 A.M.; lunch: 12:45 to 1:15 P.M.; supper: 6:45 to 7:15 P.M.) With five watches in each 24 hours, we had our turn every other day to have a fine six-hour snooze. Having the 7:00 P.M. to midnight watch never seemed overlong, since the off watch usually sat around with those on duty for a spell, to enjoy the sunset or shoot the breeze. The midnight to 4 A.M. watch was seldom anyone's favorite (is it ever?), but still, watching a new day dawn is always something to look forward to. Besides, the hot water taps in the

---

Newport–Plymouth Race

This list of contestants in the Newport-Plymouth Race reveals that no two of the 10 starters were designed by the same architect, despite the fact that a majority of the boats were specifically designed for this one race.

Rig	Built	Name	Designer	Overall Length	Position in Race
Ketch	1920	*Lismore*	Henry Rasmussen	72'	10
Ketch	1931	*Landfall*	L.F. Herreshoff	71'	6
Cutter	1931	*Highland Light*	Frank Paine	61'	3
Schooner	1930	*Mistress*	C. Sherman Hoyt	60'	4
Schooner	1931	*Water Gypsy*	John Alden	59'	8
Yawl	1930	*Dorade*	Olin Stephens	52'	1
Cutter	1926	*Ilex* (English)	Charles Nicholson	50'	7
Cutter	1929	*Maitenes II* (English)	Harley Mead	50'	9
Cutter	1930	*Skål*	Phil Rhodes	48'	2
Schooner	1931	*Amberjack*	Boston Yacht Sales	42'	5

There are a number of published accounts of this race, including Alfred Loomis, Ocean Racing (New York, 1936), p. 201 ff.; Uffa Fox, Sailing, Seamanship and Yacht Construction (London and New York, 1934), p. 27 ff.; and C. Sherman Hoyt, Memoirs (New York, 1950), p. 118 ff.

---

wardroom gave every chance to enjoy a welcome mug of coffee, tea, or soup. The five-hour morning watch came at the right time of day for us comfortably to complete the routine inspections and carry out the daily chores.

In spite of sail changes, soft weather, squalls, or the unexpected, I fail to remember even once having been called from an off watch. (Excluding the navigator and the cook, each watch had five men, and with things arranged the way they were on *Landfall*—rig, winches, deck layout—five could easily handle any normal work.) There was a bunk for each crew member. All bunks were adjustable for a good sleeping angle, and all were clear of the dining area. In the aft stateroom on each side there was a fixed berth with Root berth* above, as well as a long settee inboard.

Being the smallest of the crew, I was assigned to a Root berth, and this was fine by me. Canvas is soft and gives to knee and elbow alike, but does not bounce with the motion of the sea as do springs or foam cushions. In one of these berths, with the side-to-side tension slacked off, one is cradled gently in the center with no risk of rolling out to leeward or being pitched to windward. As an added luxury, I was on the port side for a starboard tack trip. Finally, cool, fresh air—but never water—wafted down upon me by way of the aft companionway and spiral staircase. It is no wonder that the skipper on occasion wished to leave the wide open spaces of his built-in bunk for the snugness of a Root berth.

---

*A Root berth—so named for Elihu Root, Jr., who deserves most credit for its development—consists of a piece of canvas secured outboard to the skin of the boat. Inboard, the canvas is attached to a stiff pipe, the ends of which fit into one of three socket positions that control the angle of the berth and the tautness required of its canvas bottom.

My log of the race mentions quite a bit about food. Well it should. Paul had stocked his ship with experienced thoroughness, and Joe planned and prepared every morsel in such a way as to keep all stomachs happy and healthy. I may have been the most appreciative of the entire crew: If the race had been any longer I would have doubled my weight; as it was I gained 14 pounds during the 19 days at sea. But, then, I must admit that a little special duty in the galley has never bothered me. On a cold, wet night it can be a mighty pleasant place to be, especially when all is neat and orderly, and a Swedish Aga coal stove is quietly mulling along, keeping everything dry and comfortable.

I'm quite aware that memory has a most fortunate ability to retain the happy side of events and forget the less pleasant ones. However, aboard *Landfall*, I haven't even the slightest recollection of any real problem.

The detail of *Landfall*'s rig was a real change from what I had grown up with on *Flying Cloud*. It suggested considerable Starling Burgess engineering influence. *Landfall* had reel halyard winches, an abundance of winches for sheets, an internal sail track for the luff and foot of main and mizzen, and an internal bowsprit track for the forestay that allowed for easy handling of the jib. The gear worked extremely well, giving us mechanical advantage and very little by way of operating disadvantage. For racing, I am prepared to concede that the mechanical philosophy has its points, especially when the philosophy is as well carried out as it was on *Landfall*.

Being barred by the rules from sheeting our big light mainsail to the end of the mizzen boom, we tried an experiment that worked quite well in the right conditions. We hoisted the sail forward of the mast on a jib halyard, tacking it down through the forehatch to the reel anchor winch secured below. We sheeted it outside everything to the end of the main boom. In effect, we now had a big balloon jib set flying. (This rig reduced chafing dramatically. On the other hand, it put a tremendous strain on the head of the mast.) Another sail that I have never been shipmates with before or since was a raffee squaresail. In essence this worked like a flat spinnaker; but it was bigger in that it used not only a pole at the foot, but also one two-thirds of the way up the mast. With this and the light mainsail set, we spread a veritable cloud of canvas.

In spite of three weeks at sea and a bit of bad and rainy weather, *Landfall* (and her crew) remained remarkably dry and clean. The top of the doghouse was equipped with solid handrails designed to catch rainwater for washing purposes. In a good rain squall, a bucket hung under the gooseneck also filled quite rapidly. There was a proper place for hanging waterproofs, and proper stoves to heat the drying areas—and, most important, as I have said, there were proper bunks and a proper galley to restore the inner man and leave him fresh for each new watch.

On July 5 we had seen *Highland Light* just ahead. Thereafter we saw none

The 61′ Frank Paine–designed cutter *Highland Light* carried me on the Fastnet Race later in the summer of 1931. Like *Landfall*, she had been fitted for a giant light-weather, overlapping mainsail, which was to sheet to her outsize boomkin. But, like *Landfall*, she was not allowed to set it.

128

of our competitors until July 23, when, again, we saw *Highland Light*—this time just astern of us. At the finish of the 3,000-mile race, the two boats were separated by only 14 minutes of actual time.

The victory of little *Dorade* in this Transatlantic Race of 1930, not merely on corrected but on actual time, was a prodigious one. (She crossed the line 45 hours and 47 minutes ahead of *Landfall*, which, as scratch boat, had to allow her an additional 48 or so hours on corrected time.) That we did not fare well in the race was a disappointment, especially to our skipper. But in a sporting event, one wonders, at times, what winning is. For in many ways we were all sad to see England come over the horizon. It meant an end to a very special and isolated incident in our lives, one that could never be repeated. *Landfall*, unlike so many racing boats, was sound of build, beautiful and comfortable, fast and handy. She had won our affections, perhaps a more important victory than the race to Plymouth.

iv

After the race we cruised on to Dartmouth and while there explored its enemy-defying landlocked harbor and the beautiful historic buildings dating back to Elizabethan days. The Hammonds took a few of us up to Totnes to see an old friend of Susie's, Mrs. Elmhurst, who, within an old castle and its grounds, had established a self-sustaining community of great charm. More important for my story, we visited Brixham and there had a close look at a number of Brixham trawlers. These vessels are the English counterpart of American Gloucester fishing schooners. They had evolved over the years into their final perfection for the local fishing grounds of the North Sea and Irish Sea and the English Channel in between, just as our fishermen were built to sail fast. The trawlers aimed at being able to perform this task in rough waters.

Quoting from my log written at the time, "These Brixham (or Plymouth) trawlers are deep heavy boats, with the straight cutter bow. The fish is stowed amidships and the gear forward. Ballast takes up all the hold. Their nets go down thirty or forty feet and the boats stay out during the week 'til Saturday (Sunday is rest day) if they don't get a big haul first. The war has pretty well busted this business. Stern trawlers now do most of the work. Those left have the same old ketch rig, red sails, etc. The particular trawler we inspected was *Sheila*. The Captain told us he named his daughter after the trawler. I guess he was pretty proud of his old vessel. She was sure some handsome and able looking."

Next we went along to Cowes, a roadstead that did not seem like a good small-boat harbor at all. It is wide open to the north—Southampton on the mainland being some miles away. Both tides and breezes are inclined to be so strong that small American-type dinghies are all but useless. But the town itself

The cover of my diary for the season of 1931.

From my *Landfall* diary, August 6, 1931: "Had an early lunch on *Landfall* and then went up to Uffa's to *Huff*, a Fourteen Footer that Uffa let me have. We had an interesting race, as Sherman Hoyt was racing Mr. Ratsey's boat, Uffa was crewing for Mr. Richardson, and Tom Thornycroft, one of England's best helmsmen, was sailing his own. It was rather funny to have myself and Sherman going around the course twice in the lead. In the end Tom T. got first, *Huff* was second, Mr. Edwards was third, and S.H. fourth...." I have good cause to remember this dinghy race, because Sherman recalled it so often at later boating gams, and embellished it too, all for my benefit. In his own way Sherman was a very kind man. As well as being youthful in spirit himself, he knew well how to give a lift to other young fellows and enjoyed doing it.

I found to be most charming, situated as it is on the northerly shore of the Isle of Wight and separated into two parts by the Medina River. All the townsfolk there were more than friendly; and my own New England accent wasn't out of place at all, as it would have been in London or Oxford.

Uffa Fox, God bless him, saw to it that during this stay in Cowes I would have the opportunity to meet everyone, see everything, and participate in all boating activities. For lodgings, he put me up for several nights (what was left of them) at his own upriver home. This was as unique as its owner: an old Medina River chain ferryboat he had converted to include a fine dinghy-building workshop in the former center vehicle section; bedroom, drafting room, and kitchen on one passenger side; and living room, bathroom, etc., on the other. With only a portable gangplank connecting him to the open marsh, he paid no taxes, hunted with his two dogs on King's property, and was otherwise as free as the open air around him.

For the Cowes regatta he loaned me one of his famous International Fourteen Footers, complete with instructions, equipment, and, most important, a good crew. This racing was a revelation. I realize that many of our contemporary racing boats are light displacement and that they, too, have to be handled just like the Fourteens. But this type of racing was new to most sailors in the thirties. It was certainly new to me.

In addition to racing an International Fourteen, I had another first-time-ever experience in Cowes: the King of England nearly ran me down in his royal launch, as I, after a race, was making a clumsy effort to row out to *Landfall*. It would, I suppose, have been a royal way to die.

After I left *Landfall*, I made a London visit to Fortnum and Mason and ordered a pair of the handsome soft-toed brown leather shoes with large lacing eyelets of the sort I had earlier arranged to be shipped to Trimingham's in Bermuda. My special order—for a pair one size wider and shorter—was produced for me in two days. Fortnum and Mason shipped additional pairs to me in Bermuda in 1936 and 1938, and was able to keep my specifications on file through the war years and for a decade thereafter. It is sad that such great institutions are now a part of the past. However, I still have two pairs of the special shoes. These will surely see me on my way.

To the best of my knowledge *Landfall* never came back to the United States. Between 1934 and 1937 she took the Hammonds and some of their friends on four most interesting Mediterranean cruises about which Susan Hammond has written in her delightful book *Landfalls Remembered*. At one point and under very favorable terms, I agreed to charter *Landfall* for an Aegean cruise, but by that time Mussolini was making ominous noises and it was a family decision to cancel the plan. In 1938 she was bought by Richard C. Paine, who with his family enjoyed two years of very rewarding cruising aboard her. At the time

"Mike" Cumberlege, son of an English admiral, served as her sailing master. Then in 1940 *Landfall* was sold to a consular official at Nice and sold again to some wine merchants for trading up and down the coast. Next she was captured by the Germans and spent six months sunk underwater. By 1945 she was afloat again, but in sad condition. The last I have heard was that she was purchased by a Chilean and had been fitted out once more as a yacht in Villefranche.

As I write now after the passage of half a century, I am beginning to realize the unique and wonderful opportunities *Landfall* opened up for me. She introduced me not only to America's Nat Herreshoff, but then a few weeks later to one of England's greatest designers, Mr. Charles Nicholson, and to Germany's great designer-builder, Mr. Henry Rasmussen. I took little advantage of the situation in 1931. But in years to come, Fate was kind and gave me a second chance.

The 600-odd-mile Fastnet Race, from the Isle of Wight around Fastnet Rock off the Irish coast and back to Plymouth, usually has more than its share of heavy weather. We nearly lost the rig out of *Highland Light* by carrying sail too long in a gale of wind.

v

Being all too well aware of the possibilities in any Fastnet Race (sailed from the Isle of Wight down the Channel to Fastnet Rock off the southeast coast of Ireland and then back to Plymouth), Uffa Fox, with due brotherly concern,

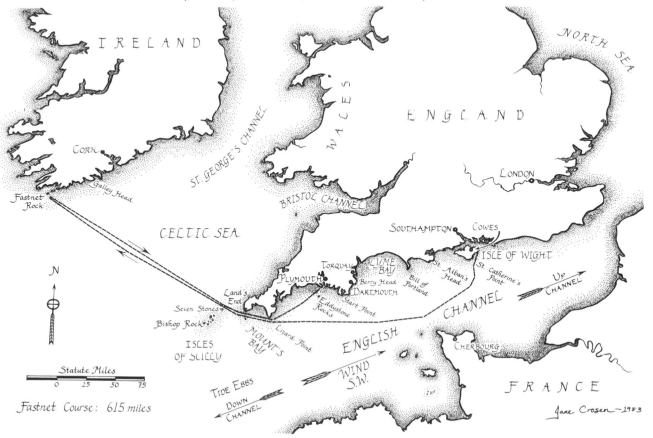

advised Larry Grinnell and me against signing up for the approaching sailing of it. Perversely, and at the moment asked, we both did exactly that, and aboard our old rival *Highland Light*, for good measure. Several of *Highland Light*'s regular crew, including her designer, Frank Paine, and Jack Parkinson, Sr., had jumped ship for other adventures, but owner Dudley Wolfe, his right-hand man, Harold Peters, and a major proportion of his Transatlantic team remained aboard. Larry and I plus two other sailors we knew from home— Robert Goodwin and Elliot Perkins—filled in for the missing.

The noon start of the race off Cowes that August 11 was not at all unlike the Sarah's Ledge start of a Bermuda race. As far as the eye could reach, not a ripple of air darkened the waters. Observing a strong tide, most skippers wisely held fast to their moorings well after their gun had gone, which in turn presented all hands with a perfect opportunity to take a good second look at the worthy competitors around them. Eight of the 10 Newport-to-Plymouth racers were on hand. (Only *Landfall* and *Lismore* were missing.) Five other able-looking boats proved to be veterans of earlier Fastnet races. Among these *Jolie Brise* had already been a winner on three occasions and a runner-up once. The famous *Amaryllis*, then owned by the Royal Naval College at Dartmouth, was also starting for the fourth time.

Beautifully conspicuous in the scene were two brand-new English cutters. One was *Patience*, a 68-footer designed by Nicholson as a fast cruising boat for Mr. H. E. West and being sailed by the famous English yachtsman George Martin. The second was *Lexia*, a 64 footer designed by Shepherd and owned and skippered by Major T. P. Rose-Richards. Both of these handsome great yachts were approximately 50 feet on the waterline, making them the same in that vital dimension as *Highland Light*.*

With the first faint stirring of an approaching breeze we slipped our moorings one by one and, as judgment dictated, trimmed our sails to work out around the east end of the Isle of Wight. We passed the Lizard two days later, according to my log. The log further notes: "*Patience, Water Gypsy, Dorade, Lexia* in sight. Double spinnaker, small spinnaker, broken pole, reefed mainsail by dark and then storm trysail the rest of the night. Barometer way down...."

It all sounds routine enough as written, but my memory brings up a far livelier picture of that particular stormy night in the Irish Sea. Early on we were carrying the number-two spinnaker in spite of confused heavy seas and an ever-increasing gale of wind. *Highland Light* was definitely being overpressed,

Built in 1913 as a French pilot boat, *Jolie Brise* became England's most successful and best-loved ocean racer. In 1931 she was one of our major competitors in the Fastnet Race. Today she is still in use and sails under the auspices of Britain's Exeter Maritime Museum.

---

* With a 14′ beam, they were narrower than us by a foot or so. Whereas old *Jolie Brise* was slightly shorter than 50′ on the waterline, she had a few inches more beam than we did. She and *Lexia* displayed carefully worked out gaff rigs, while *Patience* and *Highland Light* carried big marconi mains. A cutter race it certainly promised to be. In fact there were only three schooners entered; typically they were all American: *Water Gypsy, Mistress,* and *Amberjack*; and just two yawls, *Dorade* and *Amaryllis*. (From an international aspect nine of the contestants were English, six American, and two French.)

but daylight was fading and, running off as we were at the time, we didn't fully appreciate how fast things were getting beyond our control. At one critical moment the helmsman failed to heed that cardinal rule of all sailors to "luff 'er when she rolls," with the terrifying result that the outer end of the main boom and a considerable area of the mainsail itself rolled right under water to port. Our heavy wire foreguy was securely hooked into a rugged bale on the boom; but with the sudden and awful extra strain on it, it let out one unholy shriek, straightened its iron hook out, and let go.

By this time we were rolling wildly over to starboard, with the end of the boom free of the water and flying ominously skyward. "By God," I thought, "she's going to jibe and take the stick right out of her!" I gave one look toward Larry Grinnell as he rushed aft to the wheel, obviously intending to give the ship a luff up across the steep seas. Then I worked myself forward to the mast. I had halyards in mind....

It was too late. The end of the spinnaker pole drove down under water. With the horrendous added compression on it, that long, hollow wooden spar just exploded in the middle. Its jagged outer half catapulted in by the mast, missing me by inches, and then began flogging wildly from the clew of its yanking spinnaker.

The exact sequence of events I no longer recall, but with all hands on deck we were able to clear both pole ends and horse the spinnaker partway down before it wrapped itself around the headstay. Here was a proper lash-up and no mistake.

By early morning, and thanks mainly to the energy and seamanship of Harold Peters, we were finally pretty well squared away. It was about this time when, in the gray light of dawn, we saw a disheartening but stirring vision to leeward. Trim little *Dorade* was slowly but all too surely easing through us. She was carrying full working sail and appeared to be completely under control. It was obviously past time for us on *Highland Light* to shift from trysail to reefed main.

It is seldom easy to make the right decisions in an ocean race. Too much caution may lose you the race. Too little may lose you the race and a lot else besides. Nevertheless, that night I found myself wishing that Paul Hammond had been in charge of our watch. He would have seen to it that we shortened down before the wind and sea came on too heavy, thus saving us hours of time and much needed equipment. *Highland Light* was a vessel of unquestioned ability. She kept a-going and carried us through in good shape. But it takes trained judgment and a powerful, experienced team to drive such a racing machine in a real gale of wind. We didn't have enough of either on *Highland Light*.

According to my log, we rounded the Fastnet at about noon on August 14,

Patience, that great English cutter designed by Charles Nicholson, was brand-new in 1931. Our neck-and-neck race with her to the Fastnet Race finish line at Plymouth was a sight I'll never forget.

shook out the reef, and had a fine afternoon sail. August 15 was a different matter altogether. On the fast, close fetch back to the Cornwall shore and during the hours of darkness, we apparently passed *Water Gypsy* and *Dorade*. Dawn of the 15th we were off the Lizard, and a preliminary scan of the horizon revealed just one competitor—*Patience*, our closest rival, the scratch boat of the fleet. She was scarcely half a mile ahead and somewhat to windward. Perhaps we were still in the running! After bearing off for Plymouth, both of us soon had spinnakers drawing, and with the exhilarating surge of helpful white-capped seas we were boiling along in fine shape at close to hull speed. Inch by inch we gained on our rival. It seemed that we must surely overtake and pass her.

As we came closer still, Captain Martin of *Patience* made his gamble. He would shake out the single reef *Patience* was carrying. Handled in the normal way, this maneuver was bound to slow his boat down—at least for a few minutes. Martin did not, however, take the normal way. Instead of flattening the boom so his crew could reach the outer reefing gear, he gave the nod to a volunteer, who thereupon crawled out on the broad-off spar and, methodically, commenced to accomplish the impossible.

And so we watched as the sailor worked his way along the swaying boom, all the while loosing the reef points until he reached the clew. How he accomplished his mission without being tossed overboard, I will never understand.

With her whole mainsail drawing, *Patience* picked up just enough speed to hold her own with us. And as we approached Plymouth breakwater, conditions became even more painfully exciting. Both of us were rolling along with a tremendous overpress of canvas. We were sailing dangerously by the lee, constantly confronted by the very real prospect of an unwanted jibe. A scant 100 yards remained between us as we bore off into the harbor channel. In the end *Patience* crossed the line 1 minute 50 seconds ahead of us. I've enjoyed other match races. None could compare to this.

vi

Before winding down my *Landfall* and *Highland Light* summer, I proudly presented £25 of good English money to the Ocean Racing Club, and in return received a most rewarding life membership. Almost simultaneously King George V honored the club by his patronage, thereby designating it forever after the Royal Ocean Racing Club. There was no connection between the two transactions.

I departed England in September, on the Cunarder *Mauretania*. To be a first-class passenger on such a top transatlantic liner was, in 1931, to be a well-attended and respected guest. *Mauretania* was an exceptionally fast ship. However, the speed of her passage was not what mattered to me. Just being aboard her was a happy and satisfying business.

Not knowing any of my fellow passengers, I followed an old custom and sought out the ship's butcher, who, among his other important duties, was charged with the care and welfare of all canine travelers, especially those in transit without their owners. At my request I was granted limited custody of a young Scottie that was blessed with a friendly face and a curious nature. The Scottie was only too happy to walk with me in the designated areas, and as we walked we both achieved lightning success in meeting other dogs and their owners. It was through Pamela, a black Labrador, that I came to meet a tall and amiable Yale undergraduate bound home with several convivial classmates. This was Percy Chubb II, whose family summered at Mishaum Point, only a few miles west of Ricketsons Point on Buzzards Bay.

My next project was to consult with the head dining room steward regarding a birthday party. In a most attentive and efficient manner the steward made the necessary preparations, which included a special printed menu and a selection of appropriate music to be played by the ship's orchestra. The predinner refreshments were underwritten by another new shipboard acquaintance, Charles Francis Adams, Jr. Percy Chubb paid for the banquet champagne.

All in its proper time the great frosted cake appeared, a creation of regal beauty, decorated in pink letters—"Many Happy Returns to Kitten." The arrival of the cake did, I admit, present a minor, and temporary, problem. Where should it be set, who should cut it, and, for that matter, who was Kitten? Being in London, Cousin Kitten (Ellen Howland) could not come forward. But numerous toasts could—and did. And so the four-day sea voyage passed much too quickly, a fitting finale to a fine seagoing summer and the beginning of several new and valued friendships.

While *Landfall* was not a winner in her one and only race (sixth out of 10 boats in the 1931 Transatlantic Race to Plymouth), she was, as intended, a most wonderful boat for extended cruising. Paul and Susie Hammond spent four summers aboard, visiting historic Mediterranean ports, before they sold the boat in 1938. Miraculously, *Landfall* survived World War II, but in spite of this, she never returned to the United States.

7
The 1932 Bermuda Race:
Lexia

i

In 1932 it was my good fortune to enjoy Bermudian hospitality during a third racing visit. Paul Hammond, my generous promoter, laid the groundwork for me to race there with Major T. P. Rose-Richards aboard his new *Lexia*.

It pleases me to look back at random over some of Bermuda's intriguing history—a history that rightfully makes her a top location for the finish of a top ocean race.

On any small-scale map of the Western Ocean, Bermuda appears as a mere isolated dot. Her nearest neighbor, North Carolina, is some 600 miles to the west-northwest, and the Bahamas are several hundred miles farther away to the southwest. On all sides, Bermuda is surrounded by exceptionally deep water. In fact, she perches in solitary splendor atop the oblong rim of a high and ancient volcano, the northwest perimeter of which fails to show above water, but does present an imposing barrier for the approaching waterborne visitor. Her scant 20 square miles of usable dry land are nowhere more than 300 feet above sea level and are composed of many separate islands.

Considering weather conditions, Bermuda is situated too far from the equator to be tropical. (Her latitude is 32 degrees north, which is about the same as Savannah, Georgia, or, across the Atlantic, a point somewhat south of Gibraltar.) In spite of this northerly position, however, her climate is noticeably more evenly comfortable throughout the year than that of other land masses that lie in her zone. She enjoys the leveling effects that come from being entirely surrounded by water, and is even further protected from cold northerly and westerly winds by the warm waters of the Gulf Stream, which flows north from

Bermuda, with its temperate climate, clear water, and natural beauty, makes an ideal finish for an ocean race. The city of Hamilton, shown in this mid-1930s photo with the vessel, *Queen of Bermuda*, in the foreground, especially caters to visitors. Bermuda racers and their families have always enjoyed being there for a few pleasant days before setting out on the return trip.

the Caribbean, brushes the east coast of Florida, then continues inside and west of Bermuda before veering off toward northern Europe. Really, it would be hard to conceive of a finer location than Bermuda for the year-round enjoyment of boating.

From the day nearly four centuries ago when Admiral George Somers first rowed ashore from his wrecked *Sea Venture* and made his landing on what is now St. George's Island, all Bermudians have realized the essential need for water transport: small boats to carry them between the many Bermuda islands, and larger ships to keep them in touch with the outside world. In 1609 there were no native craft on Bermuda either to commandeer or to copy. Building new boats to their own design was the Bermudians' only solution. Under these circumstances builders started from proven English shapes and construction methods, then added practical modifications as needed. The first significant Bermuda-built boats, *Deliverance* and *Patience*, were created as replicas of English craft of the time.

Bermudians then and later were lucky beyond words to have at their disposal the wonderful Bermuda cedar. Not only was it everywhere plentiful; more important, it provided one of the finest boat-building materials the world has ever known. The wood is not as soft as our American white cedar; nor is it as glassy hard as eastern red cedar. And it is not as coarse-grained as the wood of the gigantic red cedars that grow on America's West Coast.

When it is planed, Bermuda cedar somehow gives the impression of softness; when it is seasoned, however, it becomes usefully hard. It is a delight to work. At the same time it has a close-grained strength and toughness that is surprising. Because of Bermuda's relative flatness, these cedars never grow to great heights. Their tops are gracefully swept to leeward by the prevailing winds. Cedar branches—and, even more important, cedar roots—make excellent natural crooks for boat frames and knees. The trunks, although comparatively short, grow thick with age, often attaining a diameter of two to three feet. These big boles make sound keel stock and excellent planking.

Bermuda cedar is faithfully durable. Not only does it tolerate water, it appears to thrive in elemental conditions. Its beautiful, soft reddish brown color is streaked at times with lighter shades. Left in the open, without paint or oil, it weathers to a silver gray. No other wood on earth is more pleasantly aromatic.

This species of cedar grows only in Bermuda. How it came there no one seems to know. I am told that it closely resembles what the Bible calls the Cedars of Lebanon. Perhaps it does. I have not been to Lebanon to compare species. But I do know that one of nature's great tragedies is that most of these useful and beautiful trees are now gone, perhaps forever.

The loss is the more cruelly ironic since from the early days the cedars were treasured and not wastefully squandered. The export of the wood itself was frowned upon. It was used very selectively in house building, the smaller pieces being saved for special furniture and decoration. In spite of this conservation philosophy, much of the native stands had, by the 1820s, been cut off through necessity, for use in shipbuilding. However, a second growth was progressing well, when, in 1943-1944, the trees were struck by a lethal blight. Although a few small cedars seem to be trying to make a comeback, it appears doubtful that the Bermuda cedar will ever be plentiful again.

To take the place of the cedar as a shade tree, casuarinas have been imported. Often called Australian pines, these evergreens grow well and do their job. Unfortunately, their wood is of little value except for the family fireplace on a chilly day (for even Bermuda occasionally has brisk weather).

Bermuda's unique multi-island composition, her widespread settlements, and her special location within a great ocean all kept her very much boat-oriented long after her seaborne trading operations gave way to the tourist industry that has been her chief source of income for nearly a century. By steamer more and more tourists came each year to enjoy the delightful island life and rewarding ocean climate. Although donkey carts and bicycles flocked onto Hamilton's busy Front Street on steamer days, still, a majority of the inter-island transportation was carried on by boats of one sort and another.

For a short run (such as back and forth across Hamilton Harbor), a fleet of rowing ferryboats stood by at all times. These 12- to 14-foot pulling boats were of excellent shape with slightly hollow bows, a moderate sheer, and wineglass sterns. They were strongly built of cedar, with natural crook frames and smooth planking. The ferryman rowed from a thwart some one-third of the way aft, where he had good control of his boat and practical boat width for his long oars. Aft, the seats extended along each side and in a curve across the stern. An additional forward and midships thwart gave space for six or seven passengers or an equal weight of cargo. With a high-crowned sternboard, a fluttering flag on a proper staff, several neat buttoned seat cushions, and a shipshape boatman at the oars, these ferries represented transportation of the finest kind. In the vibrant darkness of a late evening, with only the starlight above and small yellow harbor lights below, a Bermuda pulling boat gave a happy passenger the delightful sensation of gliding weightlessly through the air. And except for the slight rhythmic clunk of the oars in the locks and the whisper of a phosphorescent bow wave, the boat made its way without a sound.

Until the advent of the gasoline engine, sailing sloops of 20 to 35 feet handled most of the freight and passenger service between Hamilton or St. George's and the outlying parish settlements. These same boats also served fishermen and pilots who worked the barrier reefs and the surrounding open waters. Handled by one or two men, the boats had a deceptively simple jib and mainsail rig. They were not all alike, but in general were short-ended, broad- and deep-hulled. Like their narrower English counterparts they had a very sharp deadrise and considerable drag to the keel. As with most good work boats, their freeboard was average low. Their sheer rose gently to a modestly raked or clipper bow; it tended to flatten out as it approached a shallow transom or rounded stern.

The sloops were essentially flush deck, with two big hatch openings, the forward one being covered with a high, houselike hatch cover, the aft one usually left open to serve as a cockpit. These were day boats, and for the easy handling of cargo there were no permanent cabin arrangements or bulkheads, just a level, full-length floor.

Except for spruce or southern pine spars, the sloops were generally built entirely of cedar. Their frames were sawn from natural crooks; their smooth planking was light and fastened with copper nails. Being light, the hulls required quite a bit of inside ballast, which was in the form of iron pigs that could easily be shifted or removed to suit varying contingencies.

What interests most sailors about these sloops today is their so-called Bermuda rig. For unlike the established English gaff cutter, they were jib-headed. The term "Bermuda rig" retains its currency even now; it makes far more sense than the term "marconi," which, of course, is derived from the radio poles used by Marconi in his early wireless transmissions. The Bermudian rig did not, however, originate in Bermuda. Jib-headed mainsails had previously been used on small boats of many nations. In England, the rig was called "a shoulder of mutton." In New England, the rig was "leg-o'-mutton."

I have never heard or read a convincing account of how or why this jib-headed type of sail became *the* rig of Bermuda, but I feel that the common sense of the eventual detail was a matter of evolution from local to general use. We have seen how the great clipper ships became bigger and bigger and set more and more square sails in order to make fast downwind passages, during long voyages. Local Bermuda runs were entirely different in character, being short, often through narrow passages, and frequently to windward. Speed was not essential. (What difference an hour or two in a single day?) Ease and quickness of handling by a one-man crew were essential. Who would work, day after day, year after year, to load and stow cargo, then hoist a swinging gaff and its gear, then struggle to tack clear of the dock merely to sail a few hundred yards or a few miles—and then reverse and repeat the process? Simple efficiency was the virtue sought. In the Bermuda rig, it was the virtue gained.

There is much more that should be told about Bermuda's work sloops and her later class-racing boats, and in due course I hope to tell it. In 1932, however, my interest was only passively engaged by these little vessels, for better and worse.

ii

The year 1932 was a trying one nationally, as well as internationally. Americans were still suffering from the disruptions of the great 1929 market crash. Under prolonged adverse conditions of this sort, it seems surprising at first mention that there would have been any interest at all in a Bermuda Race, let alone an enthusiastic sign-up of some 27 exceptionally fine participants. Indeed, the overall seagoing quality of the boats and crews alike was uniquely high. My sense is, therefore, that the Depression years created an irresistible boat-building opportunity for those who had the courage—and, of course, the cash—to take advantage of the situation. There were in those days some of the finest yacht-building yards that our country has ever seen, many owned by yachtsmen who had a loyal determination and desire to keep their skilled and willing crews together and working. The farsighted and dedicated sailor could rationalize—and quite rightly, too—that the Depression was a once-in-a-lifetime opportunity to build the boat of his dreams. This is exactly what some of them did.

The following list reveals some interesting specifics and allows me to make some generalizations about the entries in the 1932 Bermuda Race. First, a majority of the fleet—18 out of 27 boats—were built during the Depression. Class A boasted 10 notably fine new schooners: the brand-new *Brilliant*, *Mandoo*, and *Barlovento*; the one- or two-year-old *Water Gypsy*, *Mistress*, *Teragram*, and *Grenadier*, each of which had previous successes in ocean races; the recently built Malabar types *Vamare* and *Discovery*. And, while *Jolie Brise*, among the cutters, was a pre-Depression boat, she had certainly shown herself to be competitive with *Highland Light* and *Lexia*. With such a strong gathering in Class A, it would have taken a brash odds-maker to pick a favorite.

The 12 boats in Class B were also impressive, albeit more varied in type. There were two early Malabars, *Twilight* and *Malabar V*, and two new schooners, *Sonny* and *Amberjack II*. The two cutters were both new, both designed by F. J. Wells. Two of the three ketches, *Dainty* and *Zena*, were Bermuda built and owned—small, old, and veteran ocean racers. The 47-foot ketch *Curlew* was the sport of Class B. She was one of Starling Burgess's early designs and had been built in his Marblehead yard back in 1906. The sole sloop, little *Duckling*, was in her third Bermuda Race. In the case of Class B, the seagoing bookmaker would have had a choice of two favorites: the yawl *Dorade* or the brand-new yawl *Ayesha*—a centerboarder designed by up-and-coming architect Philip Rhodes and built by a top yard.

Another obvious generalization is that John Alden, with 10 entries to his design, continued to dominate the Bermuda Race. Yet another is that Boston designers tended to work with New England builders, while New Yorkers favored the City Island yards of Nevins, Jacobs, and Minneford. Then, too, one

THE 1932 BERMUDA RACE CHART

Boat	Owner	Designer	Builder	Location	Year	LWL	LOA	Rig	Elapsed Time hrs-min	Corrected Time hrs-min
Class A										
Malabar X	J. Alden	Boston	Alden	Hodgdon	1930	44-3	58	Sch	75-42	69-45
Grenadier	H.A. & S. Morss	Boston	Alden	Lawley	1931	43-1	59	Sch	76-47	69-52
Water Gypsy	Wm. McMillan	Baltimore	Alden	Hodgdon	1931	43-2	59	Sch	76-57	70-57
Teragram	Geo. Mixter	New York	Alden	Dauntless	1929	43-2	58	Sch	76-13	71-33
Highland Light	Frank Paine	Boston	Paine	Lawley	1931	50	68	Cutter	71-35	71-35
Brilliant	W. Barnum	New York	S. & S.	Nevins	1932	49	61	Sch	76-42	71-37
Mistress	G. Roosevelt	New York	S. Hoyt	E. Ship N.S.	1930	50	60	Sch	75-10	72-10
Barlovento	P. duPont	Wilmington	Cox & Stevens	Pendleton	1932	50	64	Sch	75-47	72-15
Lexia	T.P. Rose-Richards	England	Shepherd	Lymington	1931	50	60	Cutter	80-08	76-14
Vamare	V. Makaroff	New York	Alden	Reed Cook	1930	37-11	55	Sch	89-28	77-31
Discovery	J. Nichols	Boston	Alden	Reed Cook	1928	43-2	57	Sch	98-37	91-43
Mandoo	S. Berger	New Haven	Alden	Lawley	1932	44-3	62	Sch	97-10	92-13
Sea Witch	E.S. Parsons	Providence	Alden	Reed Cook	1930	37-11	55	Yawl	123-35	116-01
Jolie Brise	R. Somerset	England	Paumelle	Paumelle	1913	48	56	Cutter	Withdrew, saving life at sea	
Class B										
Dorade	Rod Stephens	New York	S. & S.	Nevins	1930	37	52	Yawl	81-33	72-11
Twilight	E.S. Bradford Jr.	Springfield	Alden	Gamage	1926	32-6	43	Sch	98-09	80-36
Ayesha	J. Hogan	Philadelphia	Rhodes	Nevins	1932	32-1	46	Yawl	97-56	82-10
Sonny	A.D. Phelps	New York	Sweisguth	Jacob	1932	35	49	Sch	95-08	82-11
Viking	P. LeBoutillier	New York	F.J. Wells	R. Heisler	1930	40	49	Cutter	91-24	82-15
Malabar V	E.C. Parsons	New York	Alden	C.A. Morse	1924	36-9	49	Sch	94-53	82-56
Duckling	C. Atwater	New York	C.D. Mower	Portland	1925	29-6	37	Sloop	119-00	99-12
Zena	C.H. Masters	Bermuda	C.H. Masters			29-6	36	Ketch	127-31	105-22
Dainty (withdrew)	A.A. Darrell	Bermuda	C.H. Masters			30-9	37	Ketch	Withdrew	
Amberjack II	Paul Rust	Boston	Boston Yacht	Lawley	1931	34-6	45	Sch	Withdrew	
Cyclone	F.J. Wells	New York	F.J. Wells	R. Heisler	1932	35	47	Cutter	Withdrew	
Curlew	D. Rosenstein	New York	Burgess	Burgess	1906	39	47	Ketch	Withdrew	
Special Class										
Adriana	J. Ottley	New York	T.D. Bowes	Smith and Williams	1927	55	78	Sch	Abandoned at sea—fire	

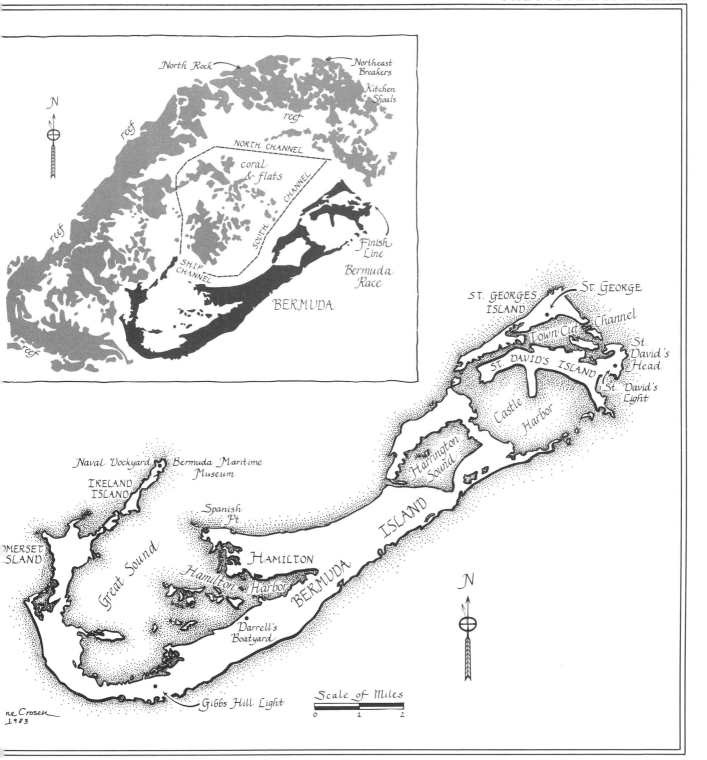

North Rock
Northeast Breakers
Kitchen Shoals
reef
reef
reef
reef
NORTH CHANNEL
coral & flats
NORTH CHANNEL
SOUTH CHANNEL
SHIP CHANNEL
Finish Line
Bermuda Race
BERMUDA

N

ST. GEORGES ISLAND
ST. GEORGE
Town Cut
Channel
St. David's Head
ST. DAVID'S ISLAND
St. David's Light
Castle Harbor
Harrington Sound

Naval Dockyard
Bermuda Maritime Museum
IRELAND ISLAND
Spanish Pt
SOMERSET ISLAND
Great Sound
HAMILTON
Hamilton Harbor
BERMUDA ISLAND
N
Darrell's Boatyard
Gibbs Hill Light

Scale of Miles
0   1   2

ne Crosen
1983

sees that the schooner rig, although it was still the favorite, especially in Class A, was losing ground to newer types and rigs. Finally, I can't help noting that five of the hottest boats in the fleet—*Highland Light, Cyclone, Dorade, Ayesha,* and *Malabar X*—had their designers aboard as skippers. Curiously enough, neither Frank Paine nor Phil Rhodes was very active in ocean racing in later years, although, of course they continued to design successful ocean racers.

When I reached New London the day before the start, it struck me right away that many of my young ocean sailing friends were missing from the scene. Could it be that keeping a job and economizing were more urgent than they had been in previous years? But not all had changed. Granted, older boats like *Flying Cloud III* and *Fearless* had been sold and had retired from racing, *Landfall* was in Europe, *Niña* laid up in City Island. Yet there was a solid foundation of familiar names among the many new ones. *Highland Light* was much in evidence, and I knew every one of her able crew: skipper and designer Frank Paine; John Parkinson, Sr., as first mate and port watch officer; Francis Stone (an old-time *Flying Cloud, Black Goose,* and *Rugosa II* pilot), navigator; young Jack and Nat Parkinson (who, by the way, asked to be assigned to Paine's watch), Gordon Prince, Pat Outerbridge, Oliver Ames, and Arthur Shuman as crew. I also had connections aboard the grand English *Jolie Brise:* her skipper and owner, Captain "Bobby" Somerset; Paul Hammond and Sherman Hoyt; and David Robertson, who, I later learned, had been the fearless acrobat chosen by Captain Martin to crawl along the main boom of *Patience* during those astonishing final minutes of the 1931 Fastnet Race and shake out the reefs.

When in due course I finally climbed aboard *Lexia,* I did so cold turkey. I had never seen the ship before, nor did I know her skipper or her crew. Knowing, however, who had made the arrangements for my berth, I expected the best and found just that.

Major T. P. Rose-Richards was a seaman of considerable experience, and a fine man. He had crewed for Bobby Somerset on three Fastnet races, first on the old cutter *Penboch,* then twice aboard *Jolie Brise* (1928 and 1930). Having by this time made up his mind that he favored an English cutter type for his long-term boat, he had commissioned Frederick Shepherd to work out the plans for him. Shepherd was one of England's ablest designers and was especially noted for his excellent cruising boats. *Lexia* was built during the winter of 1931 at the first-class Lymington Shipyard, across the Solent from Cowes and not far from Rose-Richards's own home port of Chichester. She was completed in time to enter, and fare well, in that tough Fastnet Race. In the early winter of 1932, Rose-Richards cruised his new boat to America via the favored southern route, making stops at Madeira, Las Palmas, and Trinidad, then working his way up through the Caribbean to Florida, Norfolk, and finally to Long Island Sound and New London. She had been as well tested and shaken down as any new boat could be for the upcoming race.

Cyril G. Holland-Martin was *Lexia*'s first mate. He had sailed in the 1926 Bermuda Race with George Martin, then owner of *Jolie Brise*. In the 1931 Fastnet, the two men were crewmates on *Patience*. Cyril was a quiet, capable sailorman and gave me the peaceful confidence to sleep well when we of the skipper's watch were below. To complete the English crew, there was young Hugh Eaton and A. Rosling—the latter doing most of our cooking. Fenton Trimingham—"Jerry," as he is called—was up from Bermuda for his first ocean race. (Jerry's father was one of Bermuda's most respected sailors, Kenneth Trimingham.) Souther Whittelsey, a Long Islander who had been on the 1931 Transatlantic Race in *Lismore*, was a fourth deck hand. I was told that our navigator was to be "Mr. Stone." This confused me, as I had just seen my New Bedford friend Francis Stone on *Highland Light*. The mystery was soon solved when Herbert Stone, editor of *Yachting*, came aboard *Lexia*. I was fortunate indeed to be sailing with such fine shipmates: two of them able watch officers familiar with the ship, a top-notch navigator, an experienced cook, and three young crew members who could be counted on to do what they were told.

The 1932 Bermuda Race rules departed in some particulars from those of earlier years. One big change was the starting line, which was moved from Sarah's Ledge to a whistling buoy southeast of Montauk Point. (The aim here was to avoid the fluky local winds and currents of Long Island Sound.) This change had the effect of shortening the actual race course from 660 miles to 628 miles. There was also a new restriction on the number of light sails allowable: under the rule, each boat could have but one spinnaker, one ballooner, one fisherman staysail, etc. The idea of Everett Morss's race committee was to save the owner some money in these hard times. As things evolved in the future, however, neither the Montauk start nor the special sail restriction was repeated.

A rule change that did have continuing important bearing on future Cruising Club sponsored races involved what is known as the "ballast ratio." The rule stated that yachts whose ballast equaled more than 46 percent of their displacement would be excluded from regular cruising classes. The purpose, a good one, was to eliminate boats that were considered too lightly built for practical ocean work. Henceforth racing yachts such as the New York Forties *Memory* and *Rugosa II* came under this ballast ratio ban. Herreshoff was a past master at engineering a strong, light hull that could support a heavy outside keel and thereby remain more nearly upright on her fine lines and carry sail longer as the wind increased. Such a feature helps win races. In a heavy sea, however, too much keel weight can unmercifully punish a hull and her crew, and eventually become dangerous.

In addition to news of the rules changes, I learned from my fellow crewmen

147

LEXIA

A study of *Lexia*'s plans and pictures reveals that she represents a fine combination of the new and the old. In many ways she is a typical old English cutter. She is on the narrow and deep side, with a shortish bow and a longish stern. Her mast is set well aft, and she carries a gaff rig with topmast and long bowsprit. She has a handsome sheer and flush decks with good rails.

In other ways *Lexia* shows many of the newer trends. She is not as deep and sharp as some of the older cutters. She is wider in the garboards and has a flatter deadrise that results in firmer bilges. Her counter is deeper and more V-shaped than the usual. The rig in overall dimensions is short, but the details are worked out to carry a variety of extra sails. The mast is a specially made one-piece pole mast, not the conventional separate topmast arrangement. The masthead is strongly stayed for a big light-weather genoa or ballooner. The working jib sets on a roller furling headstay and sheets well outboard. The forestay sets well aft of the stem. The mainsail is equipped with roller reefing, and the topsail sets without yard or club and can be simply handled from on deck. The gear is carefully thought out for ocean cruising and at the same time is adaptable to ocean racing.

All in all, she is a fine and strongly built little vessel and, with her excellent accommodations for owner and crew, she is the kind of yacht that it is a pride and joy to be aboard, whether in port or at sea.

The 64' cutter *Lexia* provided a berth for my third Bermuda Race in 1932. Her owner, Major Rose-Richards, was a real seaman of considerable ocean racing experience and, with a good boat like *Lexia* under him, made the race a memorable affair for all of us. Besides the owner, there were seven of us in *Lexia*'s crew. From left to right are the author, F. Trimingham, C.G. Holland-Martin, H. Eaton, S. Whittelsey, H. Stone, Major Rose-Richards, A. Rosling.

on *Lexia* that a late entry in the form of the schooner *Adriana* was being allowed to race against the best corrected time in the fleet, even though she was too big for Class A. And I learned that the old Burgess-designed ketch *Curlew* had been accepted for the race, in spite of some reservations the race committee had about the seagoing qualifications of her crew. In hindsight it would have been most fortunate if neither of these boats had started at all.

On the morning of Saturday, June 25, I fell heir to the usual prerace queasiness, so similar in its manifestations to the feeling I used to have before the start of an important football game or as I waited to take a critical exam at college. There was no rain or fog to worry about, but even at daybreak a fair breeze was already making up—not strong, yet too early to be normal. Our actual start was not scheduled until mid-afternoon. There were, however, 30 miles between us and the starting line. By midday most of us found ourselves tacking and slatting impatiently back and forth by the Montauk Point whistler, in a strong tide. I believe this was the occasion when serious talk about a Newport starting location began to circulate.

At the appointed time of 3:10 P.M., the fleet eagerly squared away on the southeast-by-south course for Bermuda. The breeze had backed a few degrees to the south, and the sky was taking on that brassy look that usually portends a bit of weather. *Highland Light* gained an early lead, followed closely by *Brilliant* and some of the other big schooners. *Lexia* wasn't going too well in the light chop until we shifted from the three working headsails to the more powerful genoa. It soon became a parade, most boats sailing full and by, with the faster ones gradually pulling ahead. Only *Ayesha*, with her shoal draft, figured to gain some speed by easing sheets and setting a ballooner. In doing this she sagged off a little to leeward while her chief competitor, *Dorade*, with her narrow hull and deep keel, sharpened up slightly above the rhumb line and still kept going in good shape.

As the afternoon wore on, the general picture took on an increasingly somber and lonesome aspect. The sky grew darker overhead and harder looking. There were fewer boats in sight. By nightfall the wind was definitely picking up. We hung on to our light sails—a big genoa—for another hour or so. Then a heavy squall put an abrupt end to the easy sailing. Although the squall passed quickly enough, the true wind now took on in earnest; even under working sails, we had all the air we wanted. And so we settled in as best we could for a spell of rough going.

For the next three days the occasional squalls and rain showers came and passed, but the wind never relented—a southwesterly wind that averaged 20 to 30 m.p.h, but was higher in gusts. I was mighty happy to be aboard a big, able boat. It had to be a punishing experience for those aboard the smaller, lighter racers. As we entered the Gulf Stream, the rough seas became even more confused. Never in any other race have I experienced such a continuous and prolonged stretch of hard going.

On one tack for the whole race and consistently making better than eight knots close-hauled, *Lexia* socked along in good shape, showing no signs of suffering. Because she was on the narrow side and deep, with a good forefoot, she had no flat spots to pound on. (She was, however, very wet and uncomfortable on deck.) Under these sailing conditions, the crew of *Lexia* had very little to do. Light sails were out of the question. Our loose-footed fore-staysail, tacked as it was well aft of the stem, was easy to lower and hoist as needed. The big mainsail could without serious problems be rolled up on its heavy boom by means of the well-tested roller reefing gear. There wasn't even much worry about chafe in our close-hauled situation. At the wheel, it was mostly heed the next oncoming sea and do your best to ease the ship through. For the rest of your watch, it was brace yourself in the cockpit and hang on.

Below, life was quieter—almost restful. But with the hatches closed, dampness everywhere, and a strong motion, it was no happy refuge for any worried stomach. Under these most difficult conditions, Rosling did a masterful job of keeping hot food on simmer for those who wanted it. I relish particularly the memory of his seagoing stews topped with substantial old-fashioned dumplings. The white biscuit batter gently cooked itself in the flavorful steam from the gravy beneath. Good solid fare, this was—bread, meat, and vegetables all in one big covered iron pot securely lashed to the railings of the galley stove. Another Rosling specialty was his own version of a plum duff. In a cloth bag, the flour and raisins steamed themselves without confusion or danger, creating a duff that could easily be eaten with a minimum of cutlery or crockery. Rosling, a quiet but friendly man who was the only professional on *Lexia*, earned a place right up with Major Rose-Richards and Herbert Stone for his ability to function effectively under the most adverse circumstances.

One food problem we did experience could have been serious had the race not been the fastest and shortest ever sailed to Bermuda. Somehow salt water found its way into our main watertanks. We soon found ourselves eating saltier food and drinking more bottled liquids. The location of the tank fill was at fault. I was to remember this predicament in later years, when considering the location and type of tank fills for other boats.

During an ocean race no one ever really knows how the other fellows are faring until all the action is over. In 1932 even the Bermuda Race Committee was taken completely by surprise. The members had only just reached their high lookout post on St. David's Head that Tuesday, June 28, and were beginning to settle in for the usual long watch when they saw, off to the northeast, a big cutter beating up for a finish line which as yet was not even in place. The Committee tugboat barely reached her official assigned position off

St. David's when *Highland Light* surged by at 3:45.* The next big excitement began shortly after 7:00 P.M., when seven of the A Class schooners led by *Mistress* came across the line in close succession and within an hour and a quarter of each other. We missed this history-making parade because we failed to get in until just after midnight. In B Class *Dorade* was barely an hour and a half behind us, but the others didn't start coming across the line until late the following morning and into that afternoon. The wind had been slacking off ever since Tuesday noon, and several of the smaller boats and one in A Class failed to arrive until Friday.

The committee and the rest of us to a lesser degree became very impatient and concerned for news of the six boats that never did finish at all. Then we learned that *Adriana* had burned and sunk at sea before daylight Sunday morning. *Jolie Brise* had picked up all the crew but one, presumed drowned, and had returned with them to Newport. *Amberjack II* and *Cyclone* had likewise gone back because of leaks and rigging troubles. *Dainty* made it to Bermuda, but just barely and under power. She had a serious through-hull-fitting leak. *Curlew*, the last to be accounted for, was found after much Coast Guard expense and a great deal of newspaper notoriety sailing somewhat aimlessly in the area of Nantucket Shoals. This is the sort of occurrence that race committees work hard to avoid, and generally do so successfully.

In deference to the *Adriana* tragedy and the loss of the much respected Clarence Kozlay (the first Bermuda Race fatality), the customary festive race dinner was canceled. Prizes were given out at The Steps, then a landing place across from the old Royal Bermuda Yacht Club on Front Street.

I have indicated final corrected times and positions for the fleet on pages 144-145. Although *Highland Light* was not among the winners on corrected time, she set a record that no other displacement boat of 50-foot waterline length is likely to equal: 71 hours, 35 minutes, for the shortened 628-mile Bermuda course. Had parts of the race been dead to windward or to leeward, she most likely would have saved her time. As it turned out, she was pushed to her limits by a determined and brilliant skipper and a strong and skillful crew. *Highland Light*'s average speed for the whole race was eight and three-fourths knots, which means she had to be sailing over nine knots for much of the time. During two separate 24-hour periods she made over 210 miles. None of the schooners did this well, although four of them with shorter waterlines had two days of 200-mile runs; others exceeded 200 miles for a single day's run. This is unbelievable going. There may never be a faster Bermuda Race.

As for *Lexia*'s ninth place finish, I recall no feeling that we had failed her or she us. But none of us failed to notice that *Dorade* had saved her time on

*The official finish line is located one and a half miles southeast (146 degrees to be precise) off St. David's.

us—and finished eight hours ahead of the second boat in Class B. Clearly her modified Six Meter type hull had fulfilled once more its great promise for ocean racing.

iii

Rereading the 1932 Bermuda Race tally, I'm struck by the great proportion of entrants that have proved to be exceptionally long-lived. Like the old yacht *America*, each has in her own way represented a quality of design and construction that has helped keep her sound, useful, and practical for many diverse assignments.

For nearly 10 years, owner Dudley Wolfe continued to race *Highland Light* often and hard. At his untimely death in a daring mountain-climbing attempt, she passed under his will (along with a handsome $100,000 endowment fund) to the U. S. Naval Academy in Annapolis, whence she sailed to compete in many blue-water events, including the next 10 Bermuda races. With her big cutter rig, no one would ever call her a family cruising boat. But the Navy had the needed extra manpower and was able to make good use of this finely built and powerful vessel. More recently, *Highland Light* has seen use in southern California waters. She is once more privately owned.

George Mixter, an important early member of the Cruising Club and the author of the highly respected and popular *Primer of Navigation*, enjoyed his *Teragram* for another 10 or more years, entering her in numerous short races, as well as five to Bermuda. For a number of years after the war, this sound little schooner sailed out of New London as a U. S. Coast Guard Academy training vessel. During this time she raced to Bermuda five more times, giving her a grand total of 10 Bermuda races. In 1967 *Teragram* was bought by F. L. Anderson of Long Beach, California. At last report she is still sailing out of Long Beach. Major Smyth and his Dauntless Shipyard in Essex, Connecticut, had built this schooner to be shipshape in every respect and to last a lifetime.

After her two Bermuda triumphs, *Malabar X* was bought by John Wilson and taken to Grand Haven, Michigan. She sailed in the Great Lakes for a decade. Then, in 1953, Bob and Edie Jo Chamberlain acquired her as a charter boat, working out of Essex, Connecticut, in the summer and Nassau, Bahamas, in the winter. This partnership lasted some 12 years, after which Edie Jo kept her in the charter business for another eight years, sailing *Malabar X* for her own account. In 1973 the good ship was bought by James Wright, who sailed her down to St. Thomas, in the Virgin Islands. Now at age 50 *Malabar X* is back again on the Great Lakes. Race winner, commercial charter boat, yacht, she has throughout the years remained active, useful, decorative.

Walter Barnum, an influential member of the Larchmont Yacht Club, the Cruising Club, and other yachting organizations owned *Brilliant* for nearly a decade, racing her three times to Bermuda. Briggs Cunningham, her third owner, sailed *Brilliant* out of Southport, Connecticut, for seven years, racing her to Bermuda in 1946. In 1953 he presented her to Mystic Seaport Museum, together with the endowment necessary to retain her in an annual Youth Training Program—a program that became an immediate and outstanding success. It was a wonderful thing for Briggs to have done, and now, a half a century old, *Brilliant* is still in the finest of condition and still training new groups of enthusiastic young sailors under the command of her long-time master, Francis Bowker.

After Spencer Berger sold *Mandoo*, this schooner changed hands several times, going first to Maine, then to Long Island Sound and the Great Lakes, and, finally, to the Virgin Islands in 1957. Except for three years in the Chesapeake, she has been a fixture in the Virgin Islands for 25 years.

Mistress must represent some special sort of record. Over a span of three and a half decades and without any auxiliary power, she safely sailed George Roosevelt to most corners of the yachting world, both here and abroad. No important racing or cruising event was considered complete without the welcome presence of George and his beautiful *Mistress*. For eight years she served as flagship of a top yacht club: in 1935-1936, it was the Cruising Club of America; in 1942-1945, the New York Yacht Club; and in 1949-1951, her home port club, the Seawanhaka Corinthian. Nine times she raced to Bermuda, never a winner, always a serious competitor. After Commodore Roosevelt's death in 1964, his lifetime ship first became a training vessel for the New York Maritime College at Fort Schuyler, New York. She moved under new ownership to the Chesapeake in the early 1970s.

Barlovento remained with her original owner, Pierre S. duPont III, for some 30 years, racing to Bermuda three times. In the late 1950s, when Pete duPont built a new *Barlovento* of motorsailer type, he gave the schooner to the University of Miami for oceanographic work. She was later owned in the Virgin Islands. More recently she has moved to California.

I could go on and on with further examples, but I hope I've made—perhaps I have overmade— the point that many of these "dream yachts" of the Depression years did in a very positive way show their enduring worth, proving the sound thinking and ability of the men (designers, builders, and owners) who created them. One of the original intents of the Cruising Club was, as it has always been for serious deep water sailors, to promote better boats and better boatsmen. It then follows that for the thoughtful seaman, an ocean race is not really the proper place to try out extreme experiments. I cannot emphasize too strongly this philosophy or praise more enthusiastically the boats that it tends to produce. The thinking that a race is something to be won, whatever the means, may be appropriate for round-the-buoys sailing, for *America*'s Cup or Olympic competition. But for ocean racing, victory can take many forms—just as, in the 1932 Bermuda Race, the real victory belonged to *Jolie Brise*, her captain, and her crew.

iv

Lexia remained in Hamilton only long enough to reprovision for the return sail to England. This meant that I had to get back to New England by steamer, in the *Monarch of Bermuda*, as it turned out.

My ticket on a first-class ship was a piece of good fortune for me. (I was certainly more fortunate than my parents had been a few months earlier, when the steamer *Prince David* was wrecked on Bermuda's outer reefs.) Even more fortunate was the fact that *Lexia*'s navigator, Herbert Stone, was also booked on this passage. Because of Stone's prominent position in the yachting world, his reservations assigned him to the finest and grandest of the *Monarch*'s upper deck staterooms. My own lack of status and last-minute application consigned me to a small, shared double in a far less favorable location. Herb was having none of that. He immediately arranged to have my sea bag moved up to his palatial quarters, where I felt very grand indeed. He then explained to me that he had been plagued with the gout and that his doctor had advised him to refrain from drinking. This might have been tolerable to him except for the fact that he really enjoyed the ship's bar and the convivial conversation to be found there. His suggested solution to this dilemma was simple enough and quite satisfactory to me. He and I would proceed to the bar. He would order and pay for the drinks. I would drink them. In this way, everyone could swap yarns and be happy. It was an unusual plan, but, then, Herb was a man who could make unusual things work.

I never thought of Herb as being old or close to it. In fact, however, he was born almost 10 years before my father, which made Herb 61 in 1932. For a short time in the 1870s he had lived in Charleston, South Carolina. But he was raised in New York, where he lived and worked the balance of his long life. Herb first started sailing during the summers he spent at Plymouth, Massachusetts. In various small boats he learned the tricks and fascinations of Plymouth's big shallow harbor and, soon enough, of the open and shoal Cape Cod Bay. When Herb developed a suspected lung condition (tuberculosis was, of course, a much dreaded malady in those years), his family sent him off on several West Indian trading voyages aboard the coasting schooner *Hattie Weston*, which was owned by a Plymouth friend of the Stones, Captain Josiah Morton.

The first formal job Herb had was with the New York Central Railroad. His position as paymaster involved him in a great deal of interesting travel, but still allowed him time to row on the New York Athletic Club eight-oared crew, to do his share of sailing, and then to write articles about his experiences.

In 1908 Herb was asked by a former schoolmate and friend, publisher Robert McBride, to take over the editorship of *Yachting*, which had been founded the year before. This arrangement was working out beautifully for all concerned when World War I intervened. New owners acquired the magazine and continued its publication under the able editorship of naval architect-writer William "Billy" Atkin and Charles Hall. Herb himself became Lt. Herbert Stone, U.S.N.R. (I never heard him talk about his war experiences myself. But he did become Commander of Submarine Chaser Squadron One, which operated out of Hampton Roads. In connection with this duty he was awarded the Distinguished Service Cross.)

At war's end, Herb endeavored for a short time to operate a small fleet of cargo schooners. The glut in postwar shipping soon put an end to the operation. Herb decided to return to writing and editing. When *Yachting* once more came up for sale, he organized Yachting Publishing Company, which raised the needed capital to buy the whole business. Herb himself became president and publisher, as well as editor and part owner. Hendon Chubb later told me a good deal about this fortunate venture. Mr. Chubb and others vitally involved in the sport of yachting fully realized the importance of a good yachting magazine. They all had admiration for, and faith in, Herbert Stone, which they demonstrated by buying shares in his company. Herb lived up to their expectations and even surprised the shareholders by making a financial success of a notoriously difficult enterprise. Under his leadership, which lasted until his retirement in 1952, *Yachting* became a veritable Bible for its countless readers and had a profound and healthy influence on the sport of yachting as a whole.

Herbert Stone's actions spoke as loud as his words. With a high degree of ability, sportsmanship, and, I am sure, pleasure, he owned, sailed, and raced his own boats. He was a leading spirit in organizing the Cruising Club of America, of which he was both a charter member and second commodore. Unquestionably he was *the* leading spirit in reviving and organizing the second (post-Thomas Fleming Day) series of Bermuda races and making them a success. As navigator on different boats (*Sunbeam*, 1923; *Lloyd W. Berry*, 1924; *Jolie Brise*, 1926; *Malabar VIII*, 1928; *Lexia*, 1932), he raced to Bermuda at least six times. At his death in 1955, the Royal Bermuda Yacht Club flew their flag at half-staff—the first time they had ever done so in honor of a nonmember.

Herbert Stone was a splendid and lovable seaman. Like *Lexia*, he made his mark by the soundness of his character. To compete against such a presence was an honor; to compete *with* such a one was a delight.

For those interested in old-time sailing craft, the working sloops of Bermuda offer an interesting study. Their hulls were built entirely of Bermuda cedar, copper fastened, and their rigs were utterly simple, yet effective. Sloops like *Queen of May*, shown here, delivered cargo to various parts of the island from early times up through the beginning of the twentieth century.

8
1933:
Winter Passage, *Niña*

i

After a triumphant victory in the 1928 race to Spain, *Niña* might have passed out of the limelight forever. Happily for all, she did nothing of the sort. Commodore De Coursey Fales chose to buy her in 1935 and then spend the remainder of his long boating life developing her sailing prowess into a living legend. By many she is now held second only to the yacht *America* as a racing schooner—the rig for which early American yachting is most famous.

It was not until 1933 that *Niña* came to be more than a name to me. This occurred shortly after she had been bought by that best known of English racing skippers, Bobby Somerset. In addition to the fact that she was built for Paul Hammond, there are some details about her designer, builder, and second owner that are worth a brief review.

I had learned from my *Landfall* associations that Paul was a man of action (not to say impulsiveness). No sooner had the King and Queen of Spain offered a King's and Queen's cup for an ocean race from Sandy Hook, New York Harbor, to Santander, Spain, than Paul, with the enthusiastic cooperation of Elihu Root, Jr., made up his mind to build a new boat for himself and enter her in this royal renewal of transatlantic racing—the first such race since 1906. He had but a few, very few, weeks to execute his ambitious plan. The event was announced in the fall of 1927, with the start to take place the following spring.

For the designer of his new boat, he chose W. Starling Burgess, a son of Edward Burgess, the creator of the three Cup defenders *Puritan*, *Mayflower*, and *Volunteer*. Starling had been a student at Milton Academy during my father's time there, and Father and Starling therefore saw quite a bit of each other. As a matter of fact, Father found his schoolmate right eccentric. Among Starling's

Our planned February sail in *Niña* from New York to Nassau, offshore, was interrupted when she started leaking badly in heavy Gulf Stream seas. A stop in Bermuda cured the leak, but for me it marked the end of that voyage.

scientific adventures at Milton Academy were several he thought might be useful in the then-infant field of aeronautics. To toughen himself up for flying trials, Father recalled, Burgess would run along the dormitory landings and hurl himself down the stairs, to land (generally in a heap) as far along as possible. Then he had an umbrella routine that involved jumping out of high windows with his makeshift parachutes. These exploratory maneuvers were not always successful by any means, but they were all grist for the mill of this genius spirit.

In due course Burgess went on to Harvard (with time out to spend a year in Paris, publish a book of poetry, invent a machine gun, marry, and become a widower). Next, in about 1906, he moved from Boston to Marblehead and there set up a boatyard near the old town power plant well up the harbor on the north side. Here he worked with M.I.T.- and Herreshoff-trained naval architect Alpheus Packard, as well as carrying on a general storage and repair business. In addition, he designed and built several of those ultralight-displacement sloops known as Sonder boats. Given the right breeze, these scowlike craft came close to flying. (Achieving long waterlines when heeled, being so light in displacement, and having plenty of sail area, they had little to stop them.) For a short period Burgess served as measurer for the Eastern Yacht Club in Marblehead. This job is valuable if you want to study the results of rules; but Burgess had to relinquish the assignment when his own design work placed him in a potential conflict-of-interest situation. Following Burgess by a few years, Professor Evers Burtner was designated measurer for the Club and held that important post continuously for half a century.

The Burgess and Packard partnership gradually came to an end (as most of Starling's partnerships had a way of doing), and Burgess shifted his operations slightly eastward to Little Harbor at Marblehead, just about where the Hood sailmaking firm now operates. Here, with his older brother, Charles, Starling went seriously into the business of designing and building aircraft, a high-risk undertaking that held his full attention until the end of World War I. (Charles remained an aeronautical engineer and, at a later date, designed the revolutionary Duralumin mast for the J boat *Enterprise*. It had always been Starling's dream to produce as many Cup defenders as his illustrious father had, and the metal spar helped him realize that ambition.)

After World War I, Starling and his protégé Frank Paine, along with A. Loring Swasey, Norman Skene, and L. Francis Herreshoff, worked together in the firm of Burgess, Swasey, and Paine. But this arrangement did not last long, either. Burgess became involved in marital problems and other difficulties, and left Boston, spending some months on Cape Cod. For the balance of his rich and productive career, New York was his home base.

Paul Hammond found Starling imaginative, progressive, and always ready

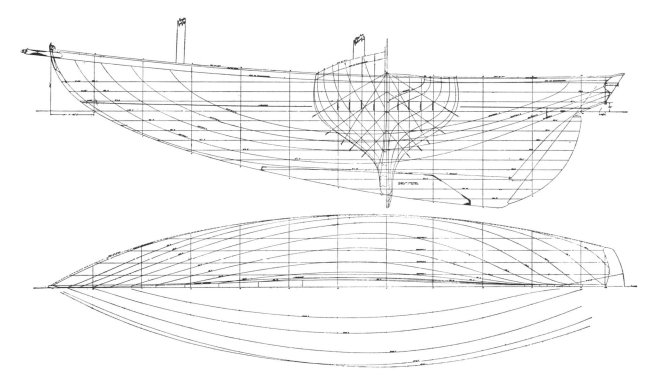

to try new techniques. He was also much aware of the breakthrough in schooner rig design that Starling had achieved in the form of John Lawrence's staysail schooner *Advance*, which had won so many important races in her first year or two of operation. And, also, though Burgess and Hammond were New York residents, they shared New England roots.

There has long been speculation as to why Paul chose Reuben Bigelow's little yard in Buzzards Bay to build *Niña*, and some have questioned the quality of the work that Bigelow put into her. But the fact is, Starling Burgess had had several good boats built by Bigelow. And while cost, privacy, and the top priority the Bigelow yard could give Paul were surely factors in his decision to have *Niña* built there, my strong sense is that Paul and Burgess both believed, and with good reason, that Bigelow was up to the job. Paul did have a builder of his own choosing go to the Bigelow yard to supervise, expedite, and advise. But Bigelow was undoubtedly grateful for the help: *Niña*'s keel was laid on January 16, the boat was in frame three weeks later, fully planked by the first of March. On June 1, she was prophetically christened by Admiral Susie Hammond: "May the elements be kind to her and man think well of her." Soon thereafter *Niña* was in full commission and out on trial runs with her racing crew, many of whom were Buzzards Bay sailors (and hence men I knew at least by reputation).

Her appearance alone would have made the beautiful schooner *Niña* a classic, but her racing record made her legendary as well.

161

W. Starling Burgess, circa 1940

Looking back now at Paul's royal victory in the Spanish race, I get the feeling that this was his greatest sailing achievement. There is no doubt that *Niña* was a special wizard on the wind, and it was a last glorious thrash to windward that brought her in ahead of all the Class A boats (which had started a week earlier), as well as of her own two smaller class rivals, *Pinta* and *Mohawk*. Overnight *Niña*, Paul Hammond, and Starling Burgess became world famous. The sport of transatlantic racing had, by this victory, been changed from one of big gaff schooners with professional crews to one of smaller boats with modern rigs and largely amateur crews.

Important victories continued to come *Niña*'s way over the next few months. Paul himself had to return home immediately after the lavish celebrations surrounding the Spanish race came to an end, but Sherman Hoyt took over, and in a tough race he sailed *Niña* to the first American win in the Fastnet. My friend Art Shuman was on *Niña* in 1929, when, against strong competition, Paul won that year's Gibson Island Race.

Then followed several years of great activity for Paul himself, and for *Landfall* and the J boat *Whirlwind*, of which he was syndicate manager—but years of sad inactivity for *Niña*, laid up for sale at City Island awaiting a new owner. *Niña* was still unsold when Paul, Sherman Hoyt, and David Robertson signed on for the 1932 Bermuda Race aboard Somerset's *Jolie Brise*. The Somerset – *Jolie Brise* combination was the most notable in English ocean racing of this period. But having raced against *Niña* and also sailed with many of her crew, it is understandable why Somerset was persuaded to sell *Jolie Brise* and try his luck in *Niña*. This trade, which he made in the fall of 1932, might not have been such a dramatic mistake were it not for the fateful winter cruise of *Niña* that I will now try to describe as best I can.

ii

My invitation was to join *Niña* for a trip to the West Indies with a first stop at Nassau. The crew was to consist of Somerset as skipper, Paul Hammond, Sherman Hoyt, a young former shipmate of Sherman's by the name of Edward ("Pluggety") Foster, a paid hand named Ted (he was aboard as a professional cook), and myself.

I have recently made a point of reading Sherman Hoyt's account of the trip, as well as the log kept by Somerset on the voyage. Their version of events differs from mine in some respects; I make no claim that my version is the only correct one. I was, after all, young then, and there were much better seamen than I aboard to do the worrying.

Before leaving, on February 11, 1933, we all had a fine meal at the River Club in New York, and as we ate we watched the never-ending traffic plowing up and down the East River. Going aboard *Niña* I did wonder a little how things would work with three captains in command. As matters actually turned out, however, there was no problem in this area. I should have known. With good sailors there is always one captain—and only one at a time. Somerset was able and respected. The ship was his. He was captain. If attitudes had been otherwise, this voyage could have been a most unhappy one.

In any event, all of us, big brass and small, did what we were asked to do without question. The professional cook asked no questions either. In fact, the first afternoon he murmured something about bad ham and then said not another word and moved not another muscle for the next five days. (For all I knew—or at times, even cared—he might have been dead. He simply lay in his oilskins, curled up in the doghouse, oblivious to people, sails, or even the buckets that banged against his inert body.)

For the first couple of days the cold was intense. But we had little time to sit still and freeze, and a strong northwester drove us on our way in good shape. Icicles to me are normally beautiful objects—thin, tapered, transparent jewels hanging vertically in the brilliant sunshine, from the eaves of Poland Spring House. The ones on *Niña* were opaque at best and only a dark shadow at night. They streamed in horizontally from the lifelines. Ice collected everywhere, looking most unnatural, even formed stiff little collars around our necks.

We detected some leaking the first night out. The leak began to take on serious proportions during the second day. To be sure, this was *Niña*'s first trip offshore after being laid up for several years. She was being subjected to some heavy strains. Yet we all wondered what was causing the problem and whether it was really serious.

A known leak you can fight; an unknown leak under your bilge tanks you can only pump out and worry about. Both of these things we did. I was put in charge of the pump. It was situated on deck just forward of the doghouse—a two-cylinder double-action affair. It was a good pump, but up against tough conditions. With all the rolling about and all the extra water, not to mention shavings and other bilge matter, the pump clogged frequently. In a boatyard, in daylight, it would not have been a difficult job to take the pump apart for clearing. In the dark, wearing frozen mittens, and with a lashing around me to keep me in some proximity to the task, the situation was difficult to the extreme. And after I had taken the pump apart a few times, the nuts on the bolts became a bit rounded and developed a will of their own to wander away from me. And so, I learned about pumps. Forever after, when working on boat plans, I have kept in mind the pumper as well as the pump.

Conditions in the Gulf Stream are never very good for any length of time. In February I learned that they could be god-awful. As we got into the Stream the third day out, the weather became less cold, but the leaking appeared to get worse. The seas peaked up steeper, and *Niña* seemed to labor heavily as she plunged into them. On the fourth morning the wind really came on to blow, and we lowered and secured all sail. *Niña* then proved to us that she could heave herself to under bare poles. She lay easily in the trough of the seas, rolling down as the squalls hit her. And thus I found out that there are times when a good ship can do more for a crew than they can do for themselves. This is important and comforting to know.

The leaking remained constant, but was less severe. The pump was free of ice and was working better. Although the drinking of spirits was not part of the daily routine, which was doubtless a good thing, Sherman felt that with matters under control for the moment and no sails set, it would be good for his morale and for that of the two younger crew members to have "just one." And so the three of us enjoyed just that—and no more. At about the same time Somerset made the decision to alter plans and course and to steer for Bermuda. Once underway again we experienced two more days of good but rough sailing before we sighted Gibbs Hill dead ahead.

When we reached Bermuda, Paul did the impossible and, through a well-placed contact in the British Admiralty in London, worked out an arrangement that permitted *Niña* and her crew to berth at the Royal Naval Dockyard in Somerset, and have access to the dockyard facilities, including the huge crane, if necessary. We still did not know what caused the continuing leak, and another telephone call to New York brought *Niña*'s designer to Bermuda in quick time to assist in determining what the problem was.

Starling Burgess was then in his early fifties. He came aboard at the dockyard, listened to the theories of the three captains, and forthwith stripped off his city clothes right down to his birthday suit and mustache, and jumped over the side. He disappeared under water and stayed down so long that I thought he must have drowned. But no, up he came for air, then down again for an equally long interval. After several such dives, he climbed back aboard and reported that he could find no obvious structural weakness.

Starling was certainly an amazing individual. By now he was the top U. S. yacht designer, having taken over the designing of Cup defenders from the great Captain Nat Herreshoff. It was he, more than any other individual, who was responsible for mechanizing yacht racing and yacht equipment. It was a rewarding experience just to meet this remarkable man. But what most amazed me about him was his straightforward approach to the investigation of *Niña*'s problem—and his physical ability to do the job himself.

Sherman Hoyt made the next move as a hull damage inspector. He called on his friend Bert Darrell, the operator of the local boatyard that was—and still is—located over on the Warwick shore just west of the Paget line. Bert was a member of the ocean-racingest family in Bermuda. His father had started the boatyard in 1920, but soon left its management to several of his five sons. The family owned a little native sloop, *Dainty*, which was designed by Henry C. Masters, a good sailor and one of Bermuda's few well-known yacht designers. In this sloop, later converted to a ketch, the Darrells took in most of the early Bermuda races and acquired thereby countless American friends and admirers. Different brothers often crewed on American boats, when they were not aboard *Dainty*.

Bert, who ran the family yard until his death in 1983, came right over to the dockyard and with Sherman removed *Niña*'s tanks from the bilge and exposed a small geyser. This proved to have been the cause of all our problems. As Bert later explained to me, there was a loose, knotlike condition that came diagonally up through the keel. It was a fault in the oak that was easily repaired by boring a one-inch hole in the area and plugging the hole with a soft wood plug. Apparently the fault in the keel was frozen up when we left New York, but thawed out gradually and let the floodwaters in.

Before the tanks were replaced, Bobby Somerset had the keel bolts all checked and tightened up, and then had *Niña* further strengthened in the deck area by the installation of some beautiful Bermuda cedar knees. (At a later date these were replaced by metal knees that the experts felt would be stiffer and lighter. Perhaps they were.) With *Niña* back in commission, Somerset and Sherman Hoyt, accompanied by a new crew, went forward with their cruise to the Caribbean. No other serious trouble developed. But instead of continuing on to England as planned, Somerset sailed *Niña* back to New York, listed her for sale, and laid her up at Nevins's yard. After his steady old *Jolie Brise*, he never adjusted to *Niña*'s quicker motion and tendency to plunge; nor was her rig really handy for a small crew. Bobby Somerset was a good seaman, a good navigator, and a fine skipper to sail with. It was not perhaps the best introduction to *Niña* that I could have wished. But if all is well that ends well, this is a story with a happy ending, indeed.

During our stay in Bermuda we were invited to several very pleasant parties. I especially remember when Kenneth Trimingham invited us to dinner. We left the dockyard in the late afternoon by horse and carriage, and drove slowly down the length of Ireland and Boaz islands and into Somerset village during the course of a superlative sunset. Thence we steamed by the all-too-short-lived new railway into Hamilton to meet our host at the old Front Street clubhouse.

As might be expected at that time of evening, there was a gathering of convivial souls in the vicinity of the yacht club's great cedar bar. Mr. Trimingham asked if we would care to join the group for a few minutes before driving along to his house. Drinks were offered, and I was tempted. However, I knew that Paul never drank. To keep him company, I demurred. (This was not as big a sacrifice as it may appear, because I realized I would have another chance at the Triminghams'.) Next a great box of sweet-smelling cigars was passed around. Paul accepted one without hesitation, and stuck a second one in his pocket. But my own distaste for cigars prompted me once more to demur. At this point a grand-looking, white-haired old gentleman rose from his seat and signaled for silence.

"Young man," he said. "Come here. Stand up in this chair."

I did as he bid me do.

He paused a moment and then asked in a serious voice: "You don't drink and you don't smoke?"

I was getting flustered by then. The assembled company had stopped their yarning and were looking at me. "No, sir," I said.

"Well, then," said my tormentor, "do you like straw?"

Once more I was forced to say that I did not. At which point the old gentleman waggled an accusing finger at me and gave forth the ultimatum. "You don't drink, you don't smoke, and you don't like straw? Well, then, you're not fit company for man or beast."

I searched my confused mind for what Uffa Fox might say under these awkward circumstances, and was prompted to say, "I know I don't drink and don't smoke and have no liking for straw, but I'm really fond of nice flowers."

For this touch of inspiration I received a rousing, "Hear, hear," and the old gentleman said, "Fair enough. You can come in." And so I was, in the end, gracefully accepted by the Royal Bermuda Yacht Club.

The rest of the evening at the Triminghams' house was happy and interesting, one of those special occasions when one doesn't have enough ears or memory to absorb all that is said. The Royal Bermuda Yacht Club was a very old one. That I learned. Indeed, it was founded in 1849. A group of British army men stationed on the island seems to have been the prime mover. And I learned that the Triminghams had been in the very center of Bermuda's yachting activities since the early 1900s. Starting with punts and 14-foot dinghies and all sorts of larger craft, the family was instrumental in starting the famous Bermuda One Design Class. This was in 1926, and these 29-footers, I was surprised to learn, had been designed by Starling Burgess and built by Abeking and Rasmussen, Lemwerder, Germany. About this time, some wise and affluent folks from Long Island Sound formed the pleasant habit of shipping their Sound Interclubs down to Bermuda to enjoy the keen winter racing. These American Interclub One Designs were very similar in size and shape to the Bermuda One Designs, although they had been designed by Charles Mower.

The Triminghams branched out in 1930 and imported from Norway several Six Meter boats; they thereby helped to put in motion an era of international racing that has seldom been equaled for fun and fame.*

Hamilton's sheltered harbor offers good day racing and has long been the scene of both local and interclub contests. The 28′ Bermuda One Designs, shown in this 1926 photo, were a creation of W. Starling Burgess, designed especially for Bermuda waters.

*Bjarne Aas of Norway did a superb job of designing these Trimingham Sixes and as a result soon received a commission to design the now-famous International One Design Class, which still flourishes today.

Yes, it was a rich and delightful evening, and if wishes were money, boats, and skill, I would have been tempted to lay over in Bermuda indefinitely to try my hand at Six Meter racing. As it was, I was all too soon homeward bound by steamer and the start of a new career.

In 1935, two years after our winter passage, De Coursey Fales became *Niña*'s owner and gave her a new lease on a racing life that continued— most actively and most successfully—for three decades.

iii

After De Coursey Fales bought *Niña* in 1935, he tempted me with many kind invitations to sail or race with him. But I found it hard to work and play at the same time. I did, however, go along on a rough Cape May race early on, when the Commodore was just getting to know his boat. Then after the war I joined *Niña* for segments of several New York Yacht Club cruises. This was during the years 1946-1948 when *Niña* was NYYC flagship. Especially I remember the last day of the last cruise on which Fales was Commodore. Having this position of command and responsibility is no easy or restful task. At the end of this final race, the Commodore requested, "Now, Waldo, you take charge of me for the evening." This project was an honor and a pleasure, and on this occasion (unlike others) did not keep me up until all hours of the night.

Niña has had a remarkable history. Among many another prize, she won the Astor Cup twice, competed in a succession of Bermuda races (culminating with a resounding and very popular win in 1962), and was first to finish in dozens of offshore races. She was an entirely successful transitional design, combining much of the best in both traditional and modern thinking about fast cruising auxiliaries. She was blest by having only one owner for over 30 years, under whose inspired management she grew more, not less, competitive in racing carried out under the Cruising Club Rule.

Niña represents outstanding and living proof that if you start with a good boat, you can, with intelligent and continuing effort, genuinely improve her sailing ability, handling, and overall performance. And strangely enough, the closer she comes to perfection, the finer she looks. I like to think of this as a kind of evolution: evolution that occurs within the structure of a single boat, rather than with a series of boats.

For example, one of the early problems with *Nina* was the uncomfortable plunging that Somerset noticed. Sherman Hoyt thought that *Niña*'s bow needed a bit more buoyancy, and when he designed *Mistress* for George Roosevelt he added a bit of flare to her bow. In fact, I believe that *Niña*'s problem was partly due to an original mislocation, later corrected, of some of her fore and aft weights. As time went on her motion in a seaway improved.

It is not enough that a vessel trim fore and aft correctly on her lines; the weights have to be distributed correctly to suit the hull's shape. Too much weight amidships is bad, but too much weight in the bow and stern is worse. In the old sawn frame vessels it seemed as if the standard structural members in themselves distributed the weights very well. In a lighter hull with outside ballast and stowage spaces in the ends, weights can very easily work out wrong.

On *Niña* fine adjustments were made not only in hull weight distributions, but also in mast heights and weights, rigging and winch weights and locations, sail shapes, sail sizes and weights, until Mr. Fales and his right-hand man,

Captain Thorson, got old *Niña* tuned up as few yachts have ever been tuned. With a ship in this condition and with a good regular crew, *Niña* was a constant and deserving winner. Some of my few regrets about being in the boat business occurred in Newport before the start of several Bermuda races. In spite of friendly, even urgent invitations to sign on as crew, my conscience drove me to wave good luck to *Niña* and return to boatyard business. I often wish it hadn't.

Many folks, myself included, have wondered what happened to *Niña* after the death of Commodore Fales in 1966. I found out quite by chance in 1979, when I asked myself aboard as she lay moored right off the New Bedford-Fairhaven bridge. The first thing I noticed was that her old cylinder bilge pump was gone. It had been replaced by a fine Edson diaphragm pump.

Briefly, I learned that she had first been given to the U.S. Merchant Marine Academy at Kings Point on Long Island. I think this was in 1965. Shortly thereafter she was sold to two professors from Huntington, Long Island. A storm that caught them off Norfolk on the way down to the Caribbean discouraged them from their planned chartering venture. (I, for one, can understand how they felt.) Next she fell in to the hands of a company that had a plan to charter to individual club organizations. Financial difficulties put an end to this ownership and eventuated in an auction sale at Stamford, Connecticut.

Finally in 1973, Hans Van Ness of Yonkers, New York, bought her, and he continues to enjoy her as a private yacht for summer cruising. *Niña* never was what one would call a family cruiser. However, Mr. Van Ness seems to find enough young folks to help him cruise and sail in shipshape fashion. From the ferry dock in New Bedford, I have watched *Niña* as she charges in through the opening in the harbor's hurricane dike with all sails set. I cannot take my eyes off her until she has executed her sail-lowering routine and, as of old, has rounded up smartly to her mooring.

In 1962, the 34-year-old *Niña* delighted the yachting fraternity with a Bermuda Race win. She still sails, although under other ownership, today.

Part III:

CONCORDIA'S EARLY YEARS

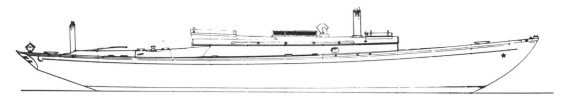

Escape, *the first Concordia Yawl.*

9
50 State Street:
Escape and
Fishers Island Sound
Thirty-ones

i

It was time and then some for me to depart the fancy-free life of ocean racing and get on to the serious task of trying to earn a living. The year 1930 had brought about a big change in the lives of most Americans. For me the big turnaround came at the end of four years of college that had been generously financed by my family but carelessly handled by me. Even to achieve a bachelor's degree I still required one more complete course in American history.

Luck was with me. It turned out that Milton Academy was in need of a new assistant athletic coach for the 1930-1931 school year, as well as a floor master. The school agreed to hire me; the winter became a pleasant case of having my cake and eating it too.

The autumn of 1931, however, took on a less providential appearance. With considerable reluctance I had decided not to remain a schoolteacher. The move had the immediate result of saddling my parents with an unemployed son. I did help with the shopping and cooking. I tended the old coal furnaces (there were two of them, as well as a coal-fired hot-water heater, in our Brookline house) and undertook other household chores as well. At the same time, but without benefit of a fixed goal, I attempted to locate a job.

Father found me a chair in Ellis and Lane, a small Boston brokerage firm, where, as I remember, I read the *Wall Street Journal* and watched the clock. As the days dragged on, I found myself spending more and more time in Frank Paine's office, and thereby became better acquainted with E. Arthur Shuman

The 39′ Norwegian-built Colin Archer-designed double-ender *Escape* came into my life in 1933. Here she is shown preparing for a sail from her Padanaram mooring. A Herreshoff Fish Class sloop is in the background.

and C. Raymond Hunt. They talked boats and were avid and successful Marblehead racing celebrities. Although the connection between my operations and theirs was rather sketchy, Arthur and I were able to do a bit of boat brokerage business together.

At the time, there seemed to be a surprising number of old but good schooner yachts laid up at Lawley's Neponset yard. Most of them were for sale. Concurrently, there were a number of nameless buyers who discovered a lucrative occupation for these very yachts. For these were opportune Prohibition days as well as depressed business days. One of the most amicable negotiations I recall took place in the winter kitchen of a summer hotel down near Stonington, Connecticut. At the sale closing, tea was served with all due ceremony (including the presence of the local minister and his wife). If we had been in the used car business we could probably have moved a few Pierce-Arrow limousines as well as the schooner. From these activities Arthur and I acquired a sufficient finder's commission to enjoy several noon meals at Boston's famous Thompson's Spa, rather than our usual economy joint in Faneuil Hall. Even at Thompson's, however, the pinch was on and they were cutting their delicious pies into five pieces instead of the pre-Depression four.

Ray Hunt's interests tended more toward design than brokerage, and while the exact sequence of events now eludes me, I do know that he and I ended up together in a small—very small—office on an upper floor at 50 State Street, Boston. The building on the corner directly north of us had been torn down, so that, with only a rutty parking lot below us, Ray had a beautiful north light for his newly acquired drafting table.

With unexpected ease we hired a very handsome lady to be our secretary. She took shorthand, typed beautifully, answered the phone, and handled our few customers most graciously. The mystery of why she was willing to do so much for us for so little pay was solved in melodramatic fashion. One noon we heard all the newsboys hawking an extra. It meant nothing to us until our Miss Burns excused herself and left the office, only to return a few minutes later with a copy of the extra, which told how a man—an anarchist—had thrown a stink bomb in the heating duct of the Stock Exchange. Miss Burns sadly advised us that the culprit was her husband and that she was duty bound to leave us and take care of him. As a replacement, Miss Burns sent us her younger sister, also a Miss Burns. But this arrangement didn't work out. The new secretary was too young and too attractive. We gained many visitors, but no customers; and our bookkeeping fell by the wayside.

It was at this stage that Miss Shine came to our rescue. This wonderful little lady, no bigger than a minute and a severe asthmatic, stayed right with the company all through the thirties in Boston, and then moved down to Padanaram with Concordia, when World War II and other circumstances changed all our plans. As late as 1965, long after she had retired, we were still hiding our postage stamps in the "Shine" file—*s* for "safekeeping."

Just how Ray and I became Concordia was really my father's doing. He chose the name from a famous Howland whaling vessel. By the time Ray and I went into business together, Concordia Company, Inc., had been an existing legal entity for several years. Father had used it mainly to hold and manage certain investments both sound and speculative. I remember Ballard Oil, Birdseye, and several gold-mining ventures. But no doubt the oddest asset listed was Howland Island, that tiny pile of rat-infested sand situated in the Pacific, about on the equator, and perhaps 1,000 miles east of Australia. Right of discovery by a Howland whaleship was the basis of claim; but as England had at one time worked the island's guano deposits and as Father was reluctant to declare war on England to regain possession, Concordia's claim on the island was academic. In a word, Concordia Company, Inc., had a very liberal charter, and we worked along with it as it was for a number of years, until finally my lawyer friend John Noble redrew the terms to make the corporation more closely fit the boat business. The revised corporate instrument left me the basic owner of Concordia stock. Father had one share as a director. Our legal clerk had another. For practical purposes, however, Ray and I worked as partners, sharing equally in income and expenses.

As we commenced brokerage operations in earnest we found that there was a plethora of boats for sale at giveaway prices, but few buyers to pick up the bargains. For six months I struggled to sell a beautiful Ten Meter boat for $2,500. She was as good as new, designed by Burgess and built by Abeking and Rasmussen to top specifications. Dr. Philemon Truesdale, the Fall River doctor who became famous for his successful operations on upside-down stomachs, was my best prospect. He must have enjoyed talking boats and details because we had endless appointments.

The best sale I made during those early years was a beautiful New York Forty built in 1926 for the meat-packer E. I. Cudahy. Mr. Cudahy died not long after the boat was delivered and *Marilee* went on the market. I told my friend Spencer Borden about *Marilee*, since Mr. Borden owned the older New York Forty *Sally Ann*. Mr. Borden told his brother-in-law Brooks Stevens, and in due course Mr. Stevens became the happy owner of *Marilee* for $7,500.

Ray Hunt's most engrossing brokerage project was to sell the 46-foot Rhodes-designed yawl *Ayesha*. He thought a lot of that boat, and she especially appealed to him as a promising new type of shoal draft centerboarder. I don't know how many months that sale took to accomplish, but Ray finally did sell *Ayesha* to Charles H. "Pete" Jones of Cohasset, who raced the boat with conspicuous success for many years.

In those days it wasn't just a matter of selling a boat. We brokers became very

much involved in each transaction, learning all about the boat in question and often making a lasting connection with both seller and buyer. The work was frustrating, of course, and none of us made any money to speak of; but it was instructive and always interesting, and a majority of the sales stuck not just for a few months, but often for the sailing lifetime of the new owner.

One sale of lasting importance to my father and me might well have endured the sailing lifetime of the new owner had not the boat come to a premature and tragic end.

ii

In the spring of 1933, not long after the cruise of *Niña* to the Caribbean, Paul Hammond invited me to come to New York to look at a 40-foot boat that was for sale. A young Englishman had just sailed her over from England, taking advantage of the winter northeasterlies across the South Atlantic to the Windward, Leeward, and Bahama islands, and thence outside and up the coast to New York.

It was raining when we showed up at City Island, a raw day that was just right for a critical boat inspection. All the shipyards were filled with stored boats still shivering under their winter covers and looking very dreary. And it was not hard to remember that many of the boats in storage were urgently for sale, that now, if ever, a buyer's market prevailed.

It was Uku Walter, the one-man crew, who rowed us out to *Escape*, where we were cordially greeted by David Robertson,* her owner. Paul had told me that David had sailed across the Atlantic single-handed on one or two previous occasions. And I soon learned that Uku Walter was an Estonian. What I did not learn about Uku that day was that he was a seaman of extraordinary ability, courage, and intelligence. Nor did I yet know that Uku had three brothers of equal ability, all of whom had already made, or would make, their presence felt on the Seven Seas. (For a good introduction to the Walter family saga, see Ahto Walter's *Racing the Seas* [New York, 1935].)

As for *Escape* herself, it was obvious that many years of experience and thought had gone into her design and construction. Even to a comparative novice, this fact shone forth in a forceful and captivating light. The words "genuine," "functional," "shipshape," "handsome," and "purposeful" all applied to her in equal measure. She was a true Colin Archer double-ender, broad of beam, full in the ends on deck, but quite fine on the waterline. She was rigged like an English cutter with stout lower mast and tall topmast. She had laid decks, a low capped rail, and a short, paneled teak house. In sum, she was a magnificent little ship.

Escape was a wonderful sea boat, as might be imagined, but she was also exceptionally well built and was outfitted with features so good and so practical that a number of them were later worked into our various Concordia designs.

---

*Although I didn't know it at the time this was the sailor I mentioned earlier in connection with shaking out the reef on *Patience* near the end of a Fastnet race.

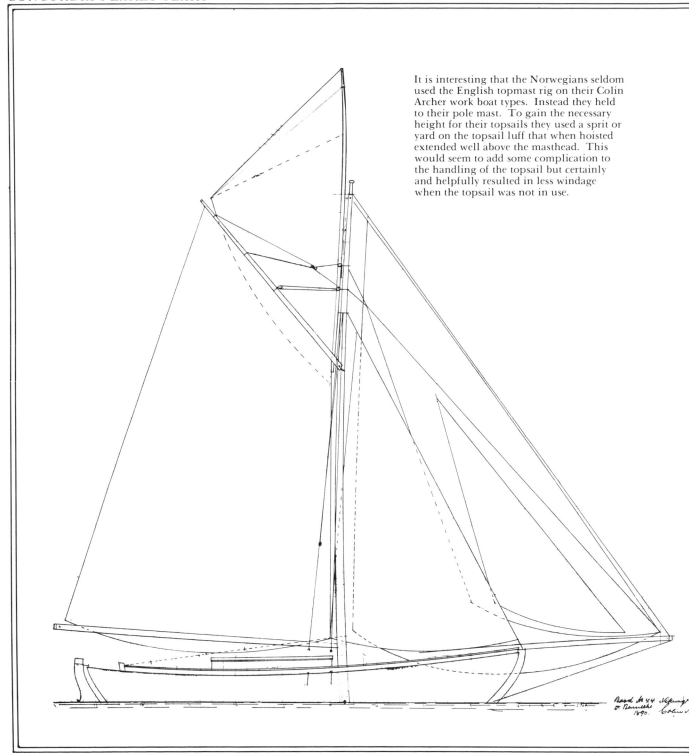

It is interesting that the Norwegians seldom used the English topmast rig on their Colin Archer work boat types. Instead they held to their pole mast. To gain the necessary height for their topsails they used a sprit or yard on the topsail luff that when hoisted extended well above the masthead. This would seem to add some complication to the handling of the topsail but certainly and helpfully resulted in less windage when the topsail was not in use.

ESCAPE'S RIG

The overall proportions of *Escape*'s rig were really quite high and narrow. The mainmast was of moderate height—some 34′ above the deck—strongly stayed, and set well aft (or about two-fifths of her overall length from the bow). This allowed for a well-proportioned staysail and a stem-head forestay. The topmast was tall, extending about 17′ above the head of the mainmast. Relatively light, it was grand for moderate-weather sails, but expendable in a calamity situation.

The mainsail was vertically cut and loose-footed, which had a number of advantages. The vertical seams made for a strong sail. I've seen many a native Bahamian sloop sailing happily along with ripped and patched vertical-seam sails, but I've never seen anyone making such progress with a ripped crosscut sail. The loose-footed feature made for a nice-setting sail and one that was easy to reef. Just set up on the topping lift, ease away on the halyards, set up on the tack reefing line, next the clew reefing line, and then tie in the fixed reefing pennants around the skirt of the sail only. The detail and location of the halyard blocks on mast and gaff were such that the gaff on *Escape* tended to hang in, and not sag off. In set position the blocks on the gaff were higher than their mates on the mast. Of course in a strong blow and under reefed conditions the gaff did fall off, but this tended automatically to release the wind pressure in the right area and at the time such was most needed.

The long-footed staysail was sheeted on a traveler or horse, as they call it, which extended completely across the deck from rail to rail. There was a bull's-eye in an iron strap shackled to the clew of the sail. On the traveler there was a fitting that included in essence a ring around the traveler plus a band around a wooden bull's-eye plus a becket.* The sheet itself was a relatively short line that dead-ended in the becket, went up through the bull's-eye cringle in the sail's clew, down through the bull's-eye on the traveler and then up again to be fastened to itself with a rolling hitch.

The final direction of pull being straight up made it possible for one to exert quite a bit of tension on the sheet with a minimum of effort.

The jib was set flying. The halyard went from a jig in the starboard rigging up to a single block, down through a block at the head of the sail, up to a single on the port side of the mast, then down to the pinrail near the base of the mast. The tack of the jib was attached to a sliding ring on the bowsprit by means of a pigtail hook. The ring was hauled in and out on the bowsprit by means of an endless line controlled from the deck. This system permitted the sail to be handled from the foredeck and in the lee of the staysail. Also it reduced the need for manpower or winch to get a taut luff.

A topsail at first seems like a complicated sail, but if the detail is well worked out, and the sailor is sympathetic, this sail can be most useful and practical. It requires no winches or complicated gear and can be handled in the lee of the mainsail and from the deck. *Escape*'s topsail halyard was a single part leading from the head of the sail through a sheave at the head of the topmast and down to the pinrail. The tack arrangement was most interesting to me. The luff of the topsail was set flying from its head down to the miter seam opposite the peak of the gaff. From there down the luff was threaded on to a luff wire at intervals of about 4′. This luff wire started as a loose padded eye splice around the topmast, extended down to and around an iron hook in the deck just forward of the mast, and ended in another eye splice at about pinrail height. Into this eye a light tackle was shackled, and the upper end of the tackle was then shackled to the tack of the topsail. With this rig, it was a simple non-straining matter to hoist the topsail to the peak of the topmast, flatten in the sheet to bring the clew to the end of the gaff, and then set the whole sail taut by setting up on the light tackle or jig. Thus, the topsail was a one-man job both to set and take in.

* See sail plan for *Prospector*, page 282.

Now I was, at this time and for quite a while thereafter, a distinctly struggling yacht broker, and the intention was that I collect all the necessary information on *Escape* in order to be able to present it to prospective customers. And this information David Robertson helped me gain, between sips of hot coffee from white mugs decorated with green trim and the name *Skarp*. (I still have a number of these mugs, and some plates and soup bowls to match.)

Escape was designed by Colin Archer. If I remember correctly, David told me that she had been built as a work boat and later converted to a yacht for a Norwegian naval officer. In any case, she was built in 1896 at Archer's own yard in Larvik, the port below Oslo on the southern coast of Norway where so many of Archer's other double-enders were built. She was in overall length 39 feet, on the waterline 34 feet. Her beam was 12 feet; her draft was 6 feet.

So far so good. But the next step did not work out quite as planned. Major Smyth, my father's friend and mine, was working at City Island and looked *Escape* over for me. With his encouragement I decided to buy the boat myself. This decision came quite naturally and spontaneously. I just had to do it. Producing the purchase price of $1,500 was a little more difficult; but with three enthusiastic friends, as well as a sympathetic father, as partners, the deal was closed. David sailed *Escape* to Padanaram for our syndicate, and Padanaram remained *Escape*'s home port for her next—and her last—five years.

We knew that *Escape* needed a variety of repairs and replacements. But it was pure good luck (and, I suspect, Father's friendship with Gene Ashley, a

For convenience it was Colin Archer's practice to draw his plans on a kind of graph paper. These lines of *Escape* show a beautiful symmetry of form; she can't help but be a buoyant, dry, and sea-kindly boat.

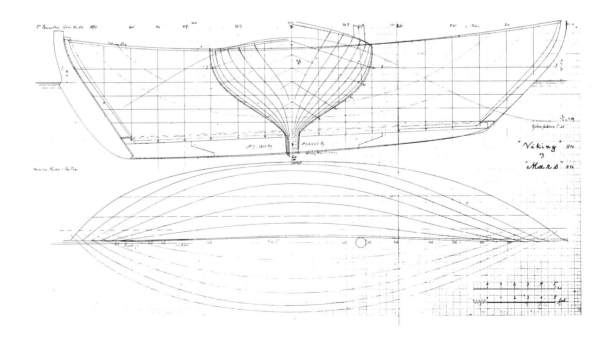

director of the Peirce and Kilburn Shipyard) that, in due course, Major Smyth moved to the P. & K. yard at Fairhaven and thus continued to be involved with Howland boat pleasures, as well as the problems that went with them.

Escape's bottom was made of reasonably wide oak planks, and to prevent their drying out and checking, she had to be kept in the water at all times, except when she was hauled out for painting. When we hauled her the first time we found that the anti-fouling paint had been applied on top of a base coat of asphalt or tar. (The Major told me this material was known in Europe as "black varnish.") The anti-fouling copper tended to wear and in some places to flake off, but the tar remained solidly in place to the very end; the oak beneath remained smooth and without checks. Coating with tar is a simple and quite inexpensive procedure; almost any boat that I later became involved with was a candidate for a black bottom. Unfortunately this material can't be used on topsides, because it "bleeds" through oil paint. Copper bottom paints, however, just love it and stick to it in good shape.

I'm not sure what *Escape*'s original mast was made of—presumably Norwegian fir—but we found it was rotten in some pretty vital places, and Major Smyth got hold of a good piece of Douglas fir for us and had it worked up with saw and adze into a new one. I was never more impressed with this new stick than when, at a certain stage in its shaping, the Major had it propped up on a sawhorse at one end (the other end remained on the ground) and proceeded to bore a one-inch hole a few inches into the higher end, then caused a steady trickle of kerosene (or paraffin, as the Major called it) to drip into the hole. I may be exaggerating, but I think it was only a day later when the kerosene started showing at the lower end. I now could understand why my great-grandfather warned his whaleship captains to keep the mastheads salted. Wood, after all, is full of small tubes. In the growth of a tree, sap has got to go up and down. Once when I was watching steam-bent frames going into a 30-footer, I was encouraged to take a three-foot sawed-off piece of discarded red oak, one inch square in section, place one end in a bucket of water, and blow on the other end. It was a shocking surprise to see bubbles coming up from the submerged end of that oak. White oak will not do this so easily; its tubes contain obstructions called tyloses. Nevertheless, if you want to give your wood a fair chance, fill or pickle the tubes or the grain with oil or salt water only. Don't just paint or treat the outside, and then complain when rot develops.

A few other areas of *Escape* needed attention. The covering boards and rails were in bad shape, and Major Smyth replaced them.* *Escape*'s skylight leaked,

---

* Because of the roundness of the deck fore and aft, the covering boards had to be carved out of wide pieces of teak, leaving many good scraps of 1³/₄" stock. The shape of these leftovers was such that they cried out to be made into tavern table legs, feet, and bearers. I heeded the cry, and we still have at home the two tables made at the time. The many smaller tavern-type tables we later made for sale through Concordia have legs that bear a striking resemblance to the originals. Design can develop in devious ways.

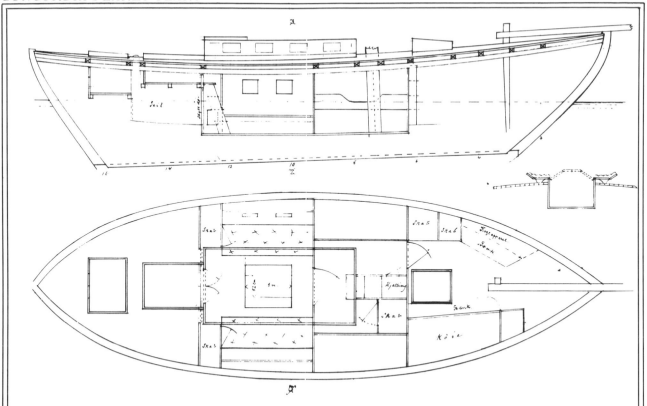

ESCAPE'S ACCOMMODATIONS

Escape had a steering well and a short main cockpit that was open and deep, with the only seat aft and athwartship. There were gear lockers on each side. Beautiful paneled teak doors opened into the cabin, with just three steps to bring one down to the cabin sole.

No one could ask for a more inviting or charming cabin. All the joiner work was varnished teak, in color a golden brown. At each side of the companionway were hanging lockers; then generous transom seats with upholstered and hinged-down backs; lockers and shelves outboard. Lockers aft facing inboard completed the restful symmetry of the cabin.

A door to the sleeping cabin was placed just off center to port, and a double-walled coal heating stove stood just off center to starboard. Above this was a circular-wick center-draft brass kerosene lamp. In the center of the cabin was a big rectangular water tank, topped by a wooden cover with hinged leaves to form a table. Above this was a large skylight.

Forward of the main cabin was an adequate, but not luxurious, sleeping cabin, the aft part of which had full headroom under the cabin house. There was a built-in berth on each side. The headroom in the forward third of this cabin was only deck height, and it was in this area that the throne sat in its open glory, alongside a fold-down wash basin attached to the bulkhead. A doorway to starboard led into the fo'c's'le where the floor was narrow, but the space above was amply wide for an athwartship pipe berth forward, and galley areas both port and starboard, aft. (This layout was clearly designed with a paid hand in mind; it was not intended for use by the owner or his wife or even by an honored guest.)

so Major Smyth designed and made a new one for us. Granted, any skylight is inclined to leak, but while a bit of leaking in a boat's bottom can be tolerated, a leak from overhead never can. In the case of *Escape*'s skylight, its two lights were solidly framed with proper drains at the bottom. Deep, wide gutters were provided under the top center and sides of each frame. Brass drip strips were also installed on the underside of each frame. For it is a fact that water can never entirely be kept out of an open joint, but can be gently led away. This new skylight for *Escape* was later installed on the first Concordia yawl and copied again on at least 100 others to provide light and ventilation without leakage.

In the days when *Escape* was built, most boats were designed for a special job, such as fishing, cargo carrying, or rescue work. The details of design and equipment developed by evolution; they were not dreamed up by one man or controlled by any set of man-made rules or theories. Either the details worked and were retained—or they did not work and were given up in short order. Since Norway, where Colin Archer was born, is separated from Scotland, where his father was born, only by the North Sea, it is not surprising that Scandinavian work boats should be quite similar to Scottish work boats. The best details of hull form and rig were adopted by both nations. What I am trying to say is that *Escape*'s hull and rig were developed by fine seamen over a period of many years. For what she was built to do, she and her like were hard to improve upon.

The gaff cutter rig has been a faithful servant to generations of sailors. *Escape*'s was an English version of the rig and worthy of close consideration by the serious sailor. Simple and functional, it featured no mechanical gear to break or malfunction. Indeed, we never found the need to make any changes in the rig. The details had all been worked out years before by sailors whose lives and livelihoods depended on its safe performance.

Over my bureau at home there hangs a beautiful half model of *Escape*. Major Smyth made it for me, using white pine for the underbody and Honduras mahogany for the topsides. Gazing at it, I have savored time and time again the many features of a true Colin Archer design. The hull is relatively easy to build: just a long straight keel with a simple stem and sternpost; no deadwood, no rudderpost, no transom. With fine underwater lines and balanced ends she is bound to be a fine sea boat and to handle well under power. With propeller on center and placed down low, she would even make a good towboat. Certainly the shape of the stern sections seems ideally designed for auxiliary power: the engine fitting well aft and low, and needing only a short, straight propeller shaft.

The hull itself has sufficient lateral plane fore and aft so that no great depth of draft is needed. The straight keel with modest rake makes it an easy matter to haul the boat on a railway or to save money by grounding her out on the beach for painting or repairs. (She has sufficient freeboard and a suitable deck arrangement to survive an unintentional stranding on a falling tide—provided, of course, she does not ground on rocks in a gale or hurricane.) The ample beam and long, low bilge lend themselves to the finest of accommodations in the shortest of hulls. The deck shape and the outboard rudder make for good working space forward and an out-of-the-way location for the helmsman aft.

Considering all the good qualities of the Colin Archer type, it is not surprising that knowledgeable yacht designers like Bill Atkin and John Hanna designed a number of very popular double-enders with many Archer features. And, of course, the Archer model has always had a strong following among blue-water sailors.

Escape was the first boat in which I was financially involved in any substantial way. And I soon learned that the first, or purchase, cost is never the last, when you own a boat. Repairs, a new mast, new sails from Ratsey, a new Buda gas engine, regular maintenance and winter storage, insurance, provisions...on and on expenses continued. In the fullness of time, it was Father, not my syndicate (Andrew Oliver, Westcote Herreshoff Chesebrough, and Thomas Whitney), who really owned *Escape*. This new arrangement had its good side for the upkeep of the boat, but its bad side in light of the expectations of the syndicate. Nonetheless, I want to believe these kind friends had a few happy memories of *Escape*. And have them still.

Escape was certainly not designed as a racing machine; but whenever Father sailed in any boat he was wont to trim his sheets quite carefully, especially if any other boat was going his way. In 1935 we entered *Escape* in the Whaler's Race, which was then a fairly new overnight affair, run by the New Bedford Yacht Club. For us it turned out to be a match race. Public enemy number one, as it evolved, was a practically new Sparkman & Stephens 38-footer with a 26-foot waterline. This boat was on the narrow side and somewhat on the lines of the famous Stephens ocean racer *Dorade*. She was marconi-cutter-rigged with single mast set well aft, and double head-rig but no bowsprit.

Our start was from anchor and off Padanaram breakwater. The time was mid-morning. The breeze was from the southwest, already strong enough for reefed sails. Our first leg out around Dumpling Rock was a close reach and in the lee of the Nonquitt shore. In this smooth water, *Escape* with her long waterline slipped along in good shape and gradually left her rival *Balkis* astern.

Close on the wind, however, and out in the open rip off Sand Spit, old *Escape* slowed right down. With her great beam and flaring ends, she tended to bob up and down very aggressively. She had all the sail she could carry, but this was not enough to push her bulk through the rough, short seas. The conditions were just what she didn't like. *Balkis*, on the other hand, heeled evenly to the breeze, gained waterline length, and sliced nicely if wetly through the chop. She was a grand sight, but a disheartening one for us. Fortunately a thick fog soon hid her from view and we could at least imagine we were doing better than we actually were. Conditions were a lot easier for us after we weathered South West buoy off Sow and Pigs lightship and could slack sheets for No Mans Land.

On the leg to Block Island the wind gradually slacked off and we shook out the reef and set the topsail again. The fog cleared, but at first there was no sign of *Balkis*. With a dying wind we slowly worked our way south about, around the western end of Block Island. What breeze there was now came from our port quarter off the mainland shore. The sun and the sea went down, and the moon and our balloon jib came up. This big sail, hoisted to the topmast head, was tacked out to the end of the bowsprit and sheeted to the end of the main boom. *Escape* liked these conditions, as did we. She slipped along silently and very fast in the modest breeze. She must have made a beautiful sight (from a purely pictorial standpoint) from the deck of *Balkis* as we slowly but steadily caught up with and passed her. We now had the greater waterline length, a big sail area, and fine lines as well.

I learned that weekend that *Escape* was a passage maker, but that she could proceed against short head seas and a strong wind only at a slow pace. In later day races under the fairly simple New Bedford Yacht Club rules, *Escape* surprised quite a few people and even brought tears of rage to the eyes of one gentleman. He had ordered and had built by Casey Boatbuilding Company in Fairhaven a new 42-foot ketch similar in design to Demarest Lloyd's very successful *Musketeer*. He explained to Major Casey in no uncertain terms that there was something wrong when a 40-year-old boat could beat his new one.

Always, I have admired and loved *Escape* for what she was and for what she could do superbly well, and have forgiven her for any shortcomings. As the old fellow defined it so aptly, "A real friend is someone you know all about and still

Although built in 1896 as a boat for the Norwegian pilot boat service where speed was a less-than-primary goal, *Escape* could—and did— prove fast against other boats if conditions were right. Both she and the 38' *Balkis* are reefed down here, near the start of the New Bedford Yacht Club's 1935 Whaler's Race, an overnight affair. Although *Balkis* had the better of it at first, later on, as the wind eased and came fair on the return leg, *Escape* became the leader.

185

like." Fenwick Williams put it another way. He said: "Some people like to race—I like my boat." Fair enough. As a matter of record, *Escape* did beat *Balkis* back to Padanaram; but I must admit that a change of conditions could have meant a change in results.

The 1938 hurricane drove *Escape* against the stone causeway that forms the westerly end of the Padanaram bridge. Such was the nature of the storm that the old boat was quite literally divided in two. The starboard side was ground to pieces. But by one of those strange flukes that seem to attend hurricanes and other great natural disasters, *Escape*'s port side remained largely intact—dishes in the pantry locker and all. There was much gear left to be salvaged, and we had to get about it quickly before the "heartless people" beat us to it. In this salvage attempt we were largely successful. But the loss of *Escape* was very hard for Father to accept. That he did, in time, adjust to the loss was the reason the Concordia yawl was born.

In the mid-thirties Concordia's brokerage business took a very rewarding spurt. This was directly due to the Herreshoff-designed class of Fishers Island Sound (F. I. S.) Thirty-one Footers. I have always felt that these were the boats that finally hooked me for keeps on the boat business. They happened to be a type that was right down my alley, and circumstances played them right into my hands.

First I had occasion to see some of the F. I. S. Thirty-ones under construction and to talk to Sidney Herreshoff, Captain Nat's oldest son, who was mainly responsible for their final form and layout. This came about partly because I had a longtime school and college friendship with Westcote Herreshoff Chesebrough, whose grandmother was Captain Nat's sister. Early on, Herry (or "Cheese," as many called him) had the misfortune to lose his mother and then his naval architect father, with the result that he was brought up by his Herreshoff grandmother and then a Herreshoff cousin Julia, both of whom lived in a fine old house close to the Herreshoff Manufacturing Company yard. This gave me the valuable opportunity to visit Bristol and see a bit more of the famous shipyard than would otherwise have been possible.

By the thirties, the Herreshoff family no longer had any financial interest in the yard. (It had been acquired in World War I by a group of businessmen looking for wartime profits. However, the group lacked the experience and qualities that would have made such a venture viable in peacetime. Boatyards seem to take a very special type of management that often is a mystery to the conventional business brain.) As of 1924, Herreshoff Manufacturing Company went into liquidation and most of its assets were acquired at auction by the Haffenreffer brewing family. It was during the Haffenreffer period (Carl Haffenreffer in charge) that the dozen or so F. I. S. Thirty-ones were built.

The F. I. S. Thirty-ones were worthy grown-up sisters of the Newport

Twenty-nine Footers and of Captain Nat's own 26-foot centerboard sloop *Alerion*; something of the Herreshoff 12½ and Fish Class showed in them as well. Most of all, they resembled the Newport Twenty-nine Footers, of which Horatio Hathaway's *Mischief* of Padanaram was such an influential example during my upbringing. The F. I. S. Thirty-ones were just enough longer than the Newport Twenty-nines to include the luxury of a really comfortable main cabin with full headroom. Their bow and stern had slightly more overhang and their sternpost was more raked, giving the F. I. S. Thirty-one proportionately longer ends. For the most part, these refinements in model were to the good and seemed to give the boats improved possibilities for competitive racing performance.

I came to admire the boats of N. G. Herreshoff largely through my early exposure to the Newport Twenty-nine Footer *Mischief* (35′ overall), which sailed from Padanaram under Horatio Hathaway's ownership.

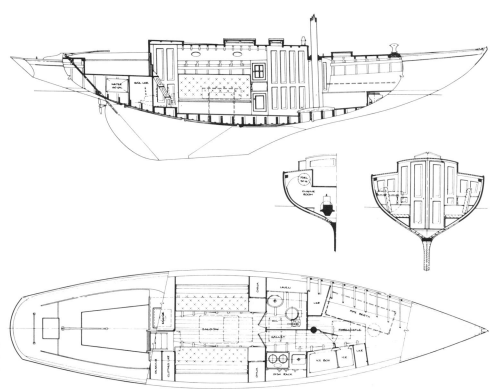

Interior arrangement for the Fishers Island Sound Thirty-one Footer.

The first F. I. S. Thirty-one was built in 1926, when many yacht owners still required or employed a paid hand. This was a time when good professionals were available—and in most cases eager—for yachting jobs. Fine schoonermen came up from Maine as the coasting trade dwindled. Able seamen from the Scandinavian countries learned that American yachting was more pleasant and profitable than North Sea fishing. Even English sailors who had been trained as professional yacht hands from boyhood found New York and New England yachting jobs attractive: good pay and working conditions; a short season; and American citizenship as perhaps the ultimate lure.

It is axiomatic that yachts are mirrors of their owners' aspirations or expectations, as well as of the economic and social climate in which the yachts and their owners live. So it is quite understandable why the F. I. S. Thirty-ones were laid out with space for a one-man crew forward, and with galley and toilet space amidships. The comfortable owner's cabin was aft, with uppers and lowers for sleeping and with suitable locker space. The enclosed engine room occupied the aft port portion of this master cabin.

With the 1929 stock market crash and all that followed, a number of Fishers

The Herreshoff Fishers Island
Sound Thirty-one Footers
were really enlarged Newport
Twenty-nines (like *Mischief*).
Concordia's first big broker-
age project was in selling a
number of them to Buzzards
Bay owners.

For their new use as family cruisers in Buzzards Bay, several of the F.I.S. sloops were rearranged below deck: galleys were moved aft, enclosed engine rooms were eliminated, fold-down Concordia-type berths were added, etc. These alterations were all supervised by Concordia.

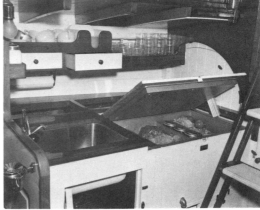

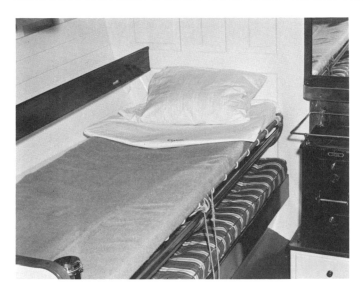

Island Sound owners gave up their paid hands and F. I. S. Thirty-ones and bought smaller One Design boats. After all, they used their boats mainly for day sailing and afternoon racing, neither of which required much cabin space, never mind full-time professional help. However, the situation was different in Buzzards Bay. There yacht owners found cruising to be their most enticing weekend occupation. But there, too, the big schooners and ketches and such like that had made sense in affluent times suddenly seemed larger than necessary. So for Buzzards Bay yachtsmen, the F. I. S. Thirty-ones were an ideal compromise. In the mid-1930s I found little difficulty and much satisfaction in transferring about one-half the fleet of F. I. S. Thirty-ones from Fishers Island Sound to our home waters.

Through these sales I established a number of new and very important connections that were to stand me and our boat business in good stead. John Parkinson, Sr., bought *Praxilla*, and his family, especially Jack, Jr., became very good friends and customers. Hendon Chubb bought *Savage*, and I came to know and value his friendship, as I have his son Percy's. In the same way, I got to know well John Stedman, Sr. (who bought *Amaranth*), and Joe Knowles (who bought *Azura*). A bit later I sold two other Thirty-ones—one to Brooks Stevens, Jr., and one to Fred Levasseur in Marblehead. In both these Thirty-ones we rebuilt the cabins to include a forward stateroom for two and a galley aft by the companionway. With their 31-foot waterline length, this then-new, but now conventional, cabin arrangement was really luxurious: fold-down Concordia berths and all.

Although there was plenty of cruising activity, the Saturday F. I. S. racing out of Padanaram was very keen for several seasons. Mr. Chubb was no doubt the most experienced of the owners, and had as a professional Swedish-born Walter Jackson, a brother of Martin, my father's professional on *Escape*, who was to play such a central role in the future history of Concordia Company. Mr. Stedman's professional was Uku Walter, whom I had first met that rainy day at City Island when Paul Hammond and I inspected *Escape*; Mr. Stedman himself, a senior executive of Prudential Life, was intensely competitive. Joe Knowles was more easygoing, as was his professional, a local man whom I remember only as "Andy."

Although our Thirty-one class usually consisted of only three boats, the occasional special race attracted other competition, and old Jack Parkinson sometimes sailed *Praxilla* up from the head of the Bay with an all-amateur crew to liven things up. I ended up cruising with old Jack a number of times, and even with just two of us aboard, *Praxilla* was a joy to handle. No less joyful were Jack's endless stories about bygone times and big yacht racing, in which he had played such a large and happy part. My one complaint about him was his ability to snore. Not even Gene Ashley could beat him in that department.

One other F. I. S. Thirty-one that came over to race with us was *Skidoo.* She was one of the newer boats and was owned by Pete Haffenreffer, an older brother of Carl. She had a taller, narrower rig than our boats did, which in theory should have made her faster. Perhaps it did make her a more efficient racing boat. However, on our triangular courses and with limited light sails, we usually beat her. For day sailing and weekend cruising an owner is apt to use working sails primarily or even exclusively, and I expect that the old rig under these circumstances kept the boats going faster on the average than the "modern" one. The same seems to be true with the Herreshoff 12½-Footers, which, on average, seem to do as well or better on most points of sailing with the original gaff rig, instead of the later marconi rig.

Newest, in a word, is not always best.

10
Ray Hunt
and His Concordia Designs

i

Ray Hunt's main interest was, as I have said, in design work. He had no
formal design training (though, to be sure, I had less than none) and was
up against many able yacht designers who had this schooling, as well as years of
active experience and great native ability. However, during the Depression,
even some of the most gifted designers found it difficult or impossible to obtain
design commissions. For example, Frederic "Fritz" Fenger did hours of work
for my father for a mere pittance. Then when I stirred up a bit of interest in
building Colin Archer type boats for pleasure use in New England, Howard I.
Chapelle spent a great deal of effort preparing sketches for me to use as bait. For
this work he received nothing except a hope that some buyer might bite. In
Boston, Alden and Eldredge-McInnis were reasonably busy, as was Hand in
New Bedford; but many another good architect was living on a starvation diet.

The production of a few frostbite dinghies turned the tide for Ray and me at
Concordia. This experiment in winter racing originated on Long Island
Sound, among some of the Sound's best sailors. Ernest Ratsey and Bill Swan
were right in there with the promotion. Very rapidly frostbiting became an
important off-season yachting activity, and winter regattas sprang up in
numerous harbors between Larchmont and Greenwich. Among the first
dinghies were the Ratsey Internationals, known in England, where they originated, as Lymington Scows. Over here they were classified as A boats. They
were lug-rigged with a short deck forward; as an extra, they sported a white,
canvas-covered kapok fender. All were of cedar lapstrake construction with a
mahogany transom, sheer strake, and rudder. The English Ratsey sails were red
with white stitching, and the whole boat looked exceedingly smart. Among the
early owners were some really topflight sailors. The New York owners included

Queen of the Concordia
designs was Hendon Chubb's
62′ schooner *Victoria*. She
was Concordia's largest
design, she was beautiful, and
she won the New York Yacht
Club's prestigious Astor Cup
for schooners during her first
season—in 1938. Ray Hunt
drew her lines, Bill Harris
worked up her construction
drawings, and Lawley's built
her.

After they were introduced to this country in 1930, the English-built Lymington Scow sailing dinghies, shown here with Arthur Shuman at the tiller of the leading boat, became the inspiration for several classes of frostbite dinghies. Class B was an open class in which Ray Hunt and I competed with Concordia's very first designs—*Plover I* and *Plover II*.

Sherman Hoyt, Robert Bavier, Ernest Ratsey, Henry S. Morgan, Jerry Bliss, and Briggs Cunningham. Corny Shields, too, was an original owner, and he was very influential in working out class rules and regulations. The names of the first Boston owners were no less impressive: Jerry Lambert, Chandler Hovey, Morgan Harris, Fred Goeller, John Alden, and Art Shuman (who first brought the Ratsey Lymington A boats to Boston and who has furnished me with much of the information about them).

Little by little new dinghy classes were developed. Alden promoted a One Design class of his own. Then there was an open B class, in which, subject to certain restrictions, you could work up your own design. This was the class that Ray and I were interested in. Unfortunately, however, we could find no buyers willing to take a chance on Ray's design ability. So in a very small way we

decided to go it alone. Ray drew up the lines. I put up the money. Pat O'Connell, a former Lawley employee, eagerly took on the job of building a prototype—and did so at a very favorable price. A Boston piano factory had an excess supply of fine Honduras mahogany they were glad to get off their hands. Away we went.

The first design was on the narrow side, but performed well. We trailed her down to Mason's Island off Mystic, Connecticut, to enter a frostbite regatta being held there. *Plover* was the trade name I picked for our boat, and she was a great success, winning four out of five races. The planned strategy for our spectacular victories was just about perfect. I was to sail the first race and, if I won, was to continue as skipper. If I failed, Ray would take over as helmsman, and I would be the crew. The expected happened. I lost the first race. But with Ray sailing the boat, we were unbeatable. *Plover* found a customer for herself before the day was out.

With the money from *Plover*, Ray designed a slightly wider dinghy, and Pat O'Connell repeated his wonderful building job for us. (Really beautiful, she was, with lapstrake construction, matched mahogany planking, white oak frames, copper rivets, and the whole boat finished bright. As I remember, Pat charged $180 for the work.) *Plover II* we took to a big regatta in Essex, Connecticut. It was a glorious two-day affair, and Father saved all the clippings about our overwhelming success in two days of big B class racing. It was champion Howland this and that. First prize. First prize. First prize. Very impressive and rewarding. But no matter who was holding the tiller, it was really Ray Hunt who was sailing the boat, as it was certainly he who designed her. Thus did Concordia Company become officially recognized as being in the design business.

ii

Ray had an interesting approach to handling a boat. He once said to me in so many words that anyone could sail a boat to windward, that the *real* skill came in sailing downwind. Running before it, he would sometimes give me the helm and rely on me to steer a certain steady course. He himself would devote his entire concentration to playing the spinnaker, holding sheet in one hand, guy in the other. Or, in different conditions, he would adjust the trim of the main and spinnaker to his satisfaction, then take the helm and follow the course of fickle, light breezes as they eddied in from changing directions. Sailing on the wind, Ray didn't immediately make a lot of adjustments to the sail trim. He always let the boat settle down and get going. Then and only then would he concentrate on the fine tuning for which he became so famous.

A few weeks before his death in 1978, Ray and I had a fine last reunion and a leisurely opportunity to talk about worthwhile matters, past and present. Ray's family came from Duxbury, Massachusetts. His grandfather founded—and literally built—the original Duxbury Yacht Club in the 1870s. Constructed on piles, it eventually became Ray's garage—and the building in which he created the first 110, that revolutionary and successful plywood double-ender. Ray's father was also a boat-minded individual, and was co-sponsor of the New Duxbury Yacht Club. Officially in the fish business, he headed a syndicate that built the great fishing schooner *Mayflower* at Essex, Massachusetts, to designs by Burgess, Swasey, and Paine. Ray himself made a trip to the Grand Banks in the schooner *Lark* while he was still a schoolboy. He went off in a fishing dory—the whole drill.

Duxbury is a very social community that has long been known for its active boat racing programs. In starting his racing career at a very young age, Ray was following in his father's footsteps. For his father had not only designed successful boats, he had won a New England championship in the old I class (a long-ended, shoal-bodied type much in fashion at the turn of the century).

I didn't know Ray in the early days, when he was winning races and then junior championships. However, his success in Mallory Cup racing, in Marblehead regattas, in J boat competition, and on New York Yacht Club cruises soon established him as a top helmsman. And we were close enough in age to sail with or against each other, in boats large or small, for nearly 50 years.

Ray attributed his success largely to the fact that he learned sailing in Duxbury. Here the shoal water, the tidal currents, and the shifting winds made him acutely conscious of the elements. Throughout his sailing career he had the uncanny ability to anticipate favorable or contrary breezes or tidal factors. In boats like the Duxbury Ducks he learned all the tricks of sailing shoal draft boats—how they would behave with various amounts of centerboard up or down, under varying conditions of wind or tide. All this involved considerations of wetted surface, of centerboard streamlining, and of the movement of live ballast forward and aft. Ray learned his boats in a way that cannot be taught in books or from sailing conventional keel boats in waters of more normal depth.

Certainly sailing with Ray was always an education for me. As with many strong, athletic men, he could handle sails and do heavy work with a minimum of motion or weight shifting. There were no panic parties with Ray. He thought his moves out and studied them well ahead of time. He talked little. He never shouted. If he were inwardly upset with some move I made, he kept it to himself and spent his effort getting us back in the groove again. I know he was not relaxed, but he appeared to be. The appearance was enough to give confidence to his crew or helmsman.

I don't mean to suggest that Ray and I were frequent shipmates. Ray had his own readily available sailing friends. And as time went on he depended more and more on his children and near relatives for serious campaigning. Regular crews have always been a great advantage for racing success, as Ray knew so well. (Ray was also well aware that a badly tuned boat or a boat with a foul bottom would be at a disadvantage, no matter how well she was sailed. He was meticulous in his own racing preparations.) But our sailing careers intersected at so many different points there is no question that he was a central figure in my professional development, as, indeed, I may have been in his.

C. Raymond Hunt and his wife, Barbara, in 1962 while at Lallow's yard in England.

199

iii

We had built the first *Plover*s on speculation. Concordia's first design commission was for a small fleet of One Design sloops destined for summer residents of Dublin, New Hampshire. The boats were 11½ feet, a cheaper version of the *Plover*s and built smooth-sided with a hard chine and sawn frames. Even for me it is hard to believe that the boats were priced at $200, delivered. For many years these little sloops saw plenty of real hot racing—competition made the more exciting by the contrary and often puffy lake breezes that came down off the New Hampshire hills. Simple and small as they were, the boats suited the requirements very well and remained a One Design class that could be handed down from father to son.

By 1934 Concordia's horizons commenced to open up a bit more and in several new directions. Thanks to my uncle Edward, Father's younger and only brother, Concordia was introduced to Joseph Plumb of the Plumb Tool family. Mr. Plumb had exciting and ambitious plans to build a proper boat for cruising and ocean racing, not only for his own pleasure, but as an interest for his only son, young Joe, then in his twenties. The whole project was quite beyond our qualifications. Father, Ray, and Mr. Plumb therefore turned to Frank Paine, who not only cooperated wholeheartedly, but included us, especially Ray, in many of the design decisions. What was ultimately worked out was a new version of *Highland Light*. She had the same 50-foot waterline, with a foot less beam. Slightly deeper than *Highland Light*, she retained her older sister's displacement. The recent successes of the meter boats and of ocean racers like *Dorade* no doubt influenced the design.

Nam Sang was the name Mr. Plumb chose for his new boat, and Ray worked out a building contract for her with James E. Graves, Inc., of Marblehead. This was a good yard and had been managed by three generations of the Graves family. The shop was located on Front Street in an area where boats had been built since the seventeenth century. Ray had already done, and was later to do, a good volume of mutually satisfactory work with Graves.

Rightly or wrongly, *Nam Sang*'s specifications called for extra-large steam-bent frames—3 x 3 inches, as I remember. These dimensions are at the upper limits of what oak and man can bend and expect to stay bent and not to straighten out subsequently. I suspect that, because her frames did in fact straighten slightly during construction, *Nam Sang* must have lost a little of her shape. Nevertheless, she proved a good if not spectacular ocean racer and a very satisfactory all-around cruising boat. The last I saw of her was in the 1960s. She was then owned out on the West Coast. She looked well and was still being raced. With her ketch rig she was probably less efficient than *Highland Light*, but she was easier to handle—and to me a much prettier boat.

On her first ocean race (the 1934 Bermuda Race) she showed all the weak-

With the exception of the little Dublin sloops, the 61′ ketch *Nam Sang* was Concordia's first commissioned design, although, in truth, Frank Paine should have most of the credit. *Nam Sang* was much like Paine's cutter *Highland Light* in shape, although somewhat narrower and deeper. She was built by Graves of Marblehead, Massachusetts, for Joseph Plumb.

nesses of a new boat with a new crew. Ray was aboard as sailing master, but it was not a good trip for the home team. Rigging failures occurred. Dispositions got rumpled. Rudie Schaefer's Sparkman & Stephens sloop *Edlu* captured first in Class A and had the best corrected time overall. *Nam Sang* finished far down the list, fifteenth in a class of 32 boats.

Concordia had another entry in the 1934 Bermuda Race in which we all had considerable interest. I had sold the old Herreshoff cutter *Doris* to our young friend Lawrence L. Reeve. At 76 feet length overall, *Doris* was too big for Class A and had to sail in a special class all by herself. She did not do well on elapsed time, let alone corrected time, but, still, she was beautiful to look at, even though we had converted her to a ketch.*

With changes in rigging and other details, *Nam Sang* took another go at the Bermuda Race in 1936. On this occasion Ray Hunt stayed home on the job and I joined the ship. In many ways it really was unfortunate that *Nam Sang* didn't have an experienced racing skipper and top crew, because she was a fast boat. As it was, young Joe Plumb generously invited some of his own young friends along, and we all just did the best we could.

The race turned into a very tough one, rougher than any previous Bermuda Race. Out of some 44 boats, 10 were disabled or dropped out. The winds were mostly ahead and often of gale force, which created good cause for many of the crew to be pretty groggy for most of the trip. There is nothing, absolutely nothing, like seasickness to take the will-to-do out of a fellow.

This 1936 race was one to remember and talk about, not one to enjoy at the time. *Stormy Weather*, a Sparkman & Stephens yawl and a repeater, won handily in Class A, in spite of competing against half a fleet that looked very much like her. *Kirawan*, a new cutter, made a name for herself and her designer, Phil Rhodes, by taking Class B and overall honors. There were two Frank Paine 36-foot cutters in the race. *Actaea* (later *Auk III*) owned by Harry Sears was second in Class B, and Frank Paine's own *Gypsy* was sixth. I was happy to see the old *Brilliant* come in a good second in Class A, *Teragram* a worthy fourth. Schooners were fast losing ground in popularity, but the good ones continued to show their merit. Pushed skillfully to her limits, *Nam Sang* might well have been in the running. As it was, we ended up above the middle in our class.

---

*Built by Herreshoff in 1905 *Doris* was 56' LWL with a 15' beam and 9'4" draft. Her butternut-finished interior was perfection itself. We found her available for a song at Lawley's, and we had Lawley's perform the work necessary to convert her from a gold-plater handled by a crew of paid hands to a cruising boat for young amateurs. I remember we called on Father's classmate and long-time Howland friend Captain Rodman Swift to oversee the alterations. This conversion gave us a wonderful opportunity to get acquainted with many of the top Lawley workmen. We especially enjoyed discussing details with Bror Tamm, who was deservedly considered the very best at rigging and spar-making. In later years we called many times on Tammy for guidance.

iv

The year after *Nam Sang* was built we got our first commission to design a cruising boat that came within our abilities to create without Frank Paine's help. Again the order was from a friend of Father's, James H. Perkins, a highly respected New York banker and the laird of Mishaum Point. This was the first in a series of boats the lines of which were drawn by Ray Hunt for Howland friends. My own main responsibility was to work out the details of the arrangement and then plan for the building of the boat.

What Mr. Perkins had in mind was a 30-foot sloop with overnight accommodations for two. We began our thinking by carefully studying Uffa Fox's book *Sailing, Seamanship and Yacht Construction* (New York, 1934). Having sailed aboard the Shepherd-designed *Lexia*, I took a fancy to a little Shepherd sloop named *Crystal* that Uffa had illustrated in the book. Ray approved of this boat in general, but favored a slightly deeper stern and transom, rounder sections in the bow, and fractionally harder bilges. Thus the boat's shape was developed in part on a successful existing craft, in part on Ray's theories and hoped-for improvements. My contributions were to the general layout and cabin plan.

The Perkins sloop, named *Weepecket* after the least of the Elizabeth Islands, was built by Casey of Fairhaven. As to why we chose Casey's, I can only say that through storage contacts we had become used to them, knew what they could do, and trusted them. Mr. Casey himself often seemed like an odd duck to those who didn't know him. He was not much of a man for talking to customers. But his right-hand man, George Brodeur, was an agreeable sort, and with George we got along just fine.

Casey's first name was Major, which my sons tell me was also the given name of the fictitious Army major in Heller's *Catch-22*: Major Major Major. Originally from New Brunswick, Canada, the Casey family came to this country sometime in the 1880s, Casey being the anglicized version of the French name Caissie. Major Casey was one of a large family, seven in fact. Five of them were boys—and so there were always numerous Caseys and Casey relatives employed at the yard. Charlie Westgate, a Casey nephew, was in charge of the lumber and milling. He knew his business, and while some of the yard's workmanship was a bit rough compared with that of builders like Herreshoff and Lawley, the materials used on the Casey jobs were generally good, and his boats tended to last a long time.

Major came by his boating interests quite naturally. His father not only sailed coasting schooners, but built them as well. Major's first boat job in New Bedford was with the same Charles Beetle yard that built whaleboats (and where my father earned his first paycheck). The first Casey yard commenced operations about the year I was born. It later moved from the original small shed on

WEEPECKET

Feeling that the crew of any smallish boat spends most of its time in the cockpit, my aim was to keep the cockpit on the large side. There was no bridge deck. The seats were wide and positioned slightly below deck level, to allow the coaming to be high enough for a comfortable backrest.

The cabin layout was conventional, except for my own early version of fold-down berths. On Father's sloop *Java* the seat backs were solid and high, making the cabin seem narrower. I worked out a shaped metal bracket and framework for canvas-bottomed berths; there were three brackets per berth, and they curved slightly outboard at the top, so that when used as a backrest the unit would be narrower in height, and more comfortable, but was positioned to allow it, when folded out horizontally, to retain the same wide sleeping surface of *Java*'s bunks. This first attempt at what came to be known as a Concordia berth was crude to a degree. But it worked.

Another *Java* feature incorporated into the Perkins boat was the outboard cant of the seat faces. This arrangement made for greater seating comfort, allowing one to pull his heels in, as under a chair. It also gave more foot room— adding some six inches of usable width to a cabin sole that perforce must be of limited area in a small boat. (The cant was especially useful when the boat was heeled over. The exposed sheathing below the seat became a semi-flat area on which to take a step or brace a foot. This seat front slant did make the under-seat locker less capacious on its inboard side, but the loss of volume was negligible.)

Because of the scant headroom, the main hatch was designed especially wide: it made for easier access and helped provide headroom for the cook.

All these features were retained in one form or another on later Concordia boats, so I conclude there is virtue in them. In any case, our first design as completed worked out to be all we had hoped for.

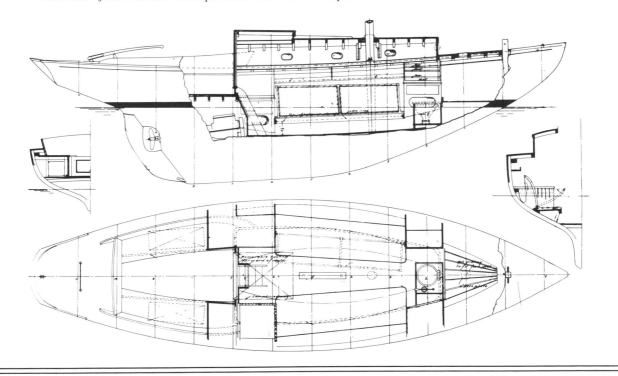

Bridge Street to larger—and larger—quarters on Fairhaven's town wharf. Before I knew him, Major had built a fair number of sturdy fishermen, as well as several out-and-out rum runners. During World War II he turned out his share of wooden craft for the government. But through the years of the 1930s he concentrated on the production of family cruising boats.

Among Casey's early yacht commissions were a number of cutters and yawls for Alden. Then he came out with a line of auxiliaries of his own (which, I must say, were quite similar to the Alden yachts that had preceded them). It was at this time that first Walter Cross and later Bill Harris came into the Concordia picture. Cross, a naval architect who had once been chief draftsman for Lawley, helped Casey (as well as Bill Hand) with the design work. Harris, after a stint with the Alden office and Boston Yacht Sales, came to Fairhaven in 1933 and went to work for Charlie Furnans. While working for the Furnans Yacht Agency, Bill designed at least two very fine cruising boats: *Quisset*, a 43-foot yawl for our neighbor Henry Holcomb, and *Musketeer*, a 45-foot ketch for Demarest Lloyd. Both were fine looking and successful boats. Both were built by Casey.

For Mr. Perkins's *Weepecket*, Ray drew up a complete set of lines and offsets and a dimensional sail plan. I outlined in a very crude way the cabin and arrangement plan we wanted. Neither of us, however, had the training or experience to draw up a proper construction plan. Major Casey wisely suggested that Walter Cross could and would do this for us, and it turned out to be a first-class arrangement for all concerned. Walter, who was a thin little man (probably he was bigger than I, but he didn't seem so), had the patience and ability to grasp what we wanted in the way of detail. The result was that the construction went very smoothly and economically, in spite of my hovering around with suggestions and questions.

Weepecket turned out to be a handy little vessel, and, judging from Mr. Perkins's comments, she seemed to fit the bill. He used her mainly for day sailing, and soon found that she could handle the rough Buzzards Bay conditions well enough so that his older friends enjoyed going out with him. That, I now realize, is an excellent test of a boat.

v

At about the same time that work was proceeding on *Weepecket*, my *Landfall* shipmate Kim Norton came forward with enthusiastic ideas for a good-performing 35-footer. Ray drew up the lines of a handsome little sloop that showed the *Dorade* meter boat influence. No great accommodations were required, and the new boat was on the narrow side. She was meant to be a fast sailer. In finished form, she most definitely was.

While working on *Weepecket* at Casey's we had come to see more and more of Wilder Braley ("Bill") Harris. Bill was supervising the building of several boats, and his draftsmanship as well as his own design skill was very impressive. We were delighted when he was willing to help us out on small matters, and by degrees he came to work for Concordia full-time. We might well have stuck with Walter Cross had Casey remained our only builder. But with Norton's boat we shifted over to another Fairhaven yard. For at about this time (as previously mentioned) Major Smyth left Minneford's Yard in City Island and joined the staff at Peirce and Kilburn. Here he instigated a small boatbuilding program with the idea of keeping the crew busy during the slack winter months. Even more than Mr. Major Casey, Major William Smyth loved to build good boats. *Cinderella* was a fine example of his best work.

Kim Norton, God bless him, had given us every opportunity to work out a boat that we could—and would—be proud of. He sailed *Cinderella* until

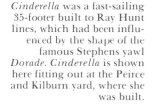

Cinderella was a fast-sailing 35-footer built to Ray Hunt lines, which had been influenced by the shape of the famous Stephens yawl *Dorade. Cinderella* is shown here fitting out at the Peirce and Kilburn yard, where she was built.

CINDERELLA

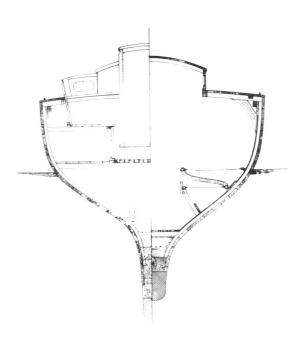

*C*inderella's accommodations were spartan as called for: the simplest galley possible with shelf for small stove to starboard and counter with slide-out basin to port; early versions of our folding Concordia berths to sleep on; and an open fo'c's'le forward for the throne. Special patterns were made in order to cast the special deck fittings wanted. A small Gray Sea Scout engine drove an off-center propeller, to avoid an aperture in the sternpost. As on *Weepecket*, the watertight cockpit seats were low to allow for comfortable seat backs. (This arrangement accomplished its aims, but gradually I could see that it complicated good construction and had some other disadvantages, too. For one thing, it was time-consuming to shape the deck framing and fit the curved seat backs. For a second, both backs and seats were wide flat surfaces and tended to shrink, causing leaks. And finally, with the boat heeled, the leeward seat naturally pocketed water and, thus, had to be carefully scuppered by pipes into the cockpit well. In later boats I modified the detail with no great loss of amenity.)

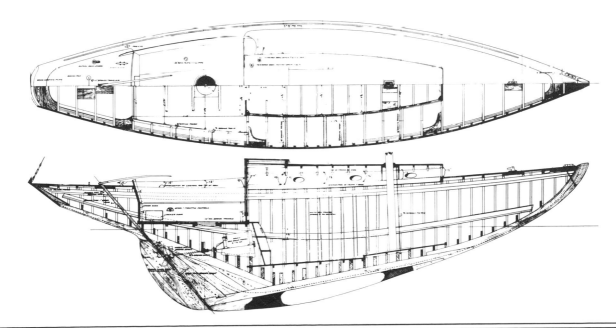

Concordia Yawls came into being. Under the ownership of Thomas Card, a Fairhaven resident and good friend, *Cinderella* continued to fare well, until, during the 1954 hurricane, one whole side of her was badly damaged. Fortunately a neighbor thought well enough of her to buy the wreck and rebuild. At this point I don't know where *Cinderella* is. Still giving good service, I hope.

vi

The winter of 1936-1937 was a banner season for Concordia's design department, which had commissions for two fair-sized and challenging auxiliaries. The lines of both were drawn by Ray, the drafting work was shared by Walter Cross and Bill Harris, and the various other details fell to me to oversee.

Hostess III was a 43-foot yawl. Although basically similar in hull form to the two earlier Hunt boats, she did display a number of distinctive features. She was ordered by Philip P. Chase, a long-time Howland friend who had previously been owner of one of the many 35-foot Maine-built Alden yawls. Philip Chase wintered in Milton, Massachusetts, but sailed first out of Manchester, Massachusetts, and later from Horseshoe Cove, Maine, where he built a new summer home. With an 11-foot beam and a 30-foot waterline, *Hostess III* was big enough to provide very suitable cruising accommodations for four boatwise adults.

We had *Hostess III* built at Peirce and Kilburn's, where a special joy and satisfaction from the project came through my ever constant association with Major Smyth. He not only oversaw every detail of the boat's construction, but spent hour after hour discussing relevant considerations with me. Smyth lived in one of the fine old Fairhaven waterfront houses just a few hundred yards north of the yard. There I enjoyed many a noon or evening meal with the Smyths. Mrs. Smyth was patient beyond words with our never-ending boat talk, and the three children, two boys and a girl, all had their talents and were a pleasure to be with.

For several years, in fact, the Fairhaven waterfront was really home base for me. With Mother's financial help I had a little house built on an empty Fort Street lot between Peirce and Kilburn and the Major's house. I called it the tax assessor's despair, as it had three stories on the water side and only one that faced the street. Stonemason Elmer Pierce and my neighbor Wilton Gifford built the house with full-time assistance from Major Smyth's brother Hugh, a real artisan and a lovely man. The living room and kitchen were actually a part of the stone basement and looked out over the embankment to New Bedford Harbor and its constant traffic. Later we built a simple 20- by 30-foot shingled shed in the front yard close by the street. This became Bill Harris's office, the one in which he drew and filed his plans for many of our best designs. The shed was forehandedly mounted on two heavy hard-pine timbers. When the time

Another Concordia/Peirce and Kilburn collaboration resulted in the distinctive 43' double-ended yawl *Hostess III*, which came out in 1938 for Philip Chase. She remained in the Chase family for over 40 years.

208

HOSTESS III

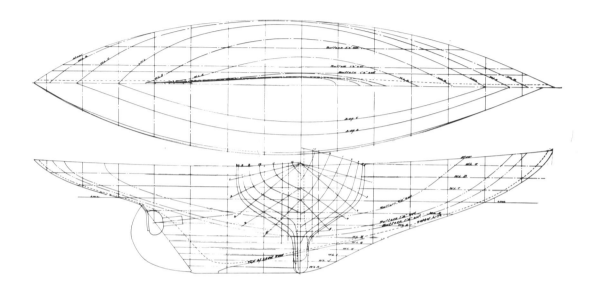

While working out details for *Hostess III*, I was very conscious of the features that I enjoyed aboard *Escape*. This is how *Hostess III* acquired a canoe stern in place of a conventional transom. To me, the canoe stern was both striking and good looking. In addition, it did away with the need for the then ubiquitous mizzen sheet boomkin on yawl-rigged boats. *Escape* also influenced the boat's deck and cabin arrangement. Starting aft there was a helmsman's cockpit with wheel steering, then a narrow bridge deck that took care of the compass and main sheet. Next came a deep, but watertight cockpit with an athwartship seat aft. The gas tank was located under the seat so that any leaks or spillage would drain down the cockpit scuppers, not into the bilge. Passengers sat comfortably facing forward, just below the helmsman's line of sight.

Access below was over a raised sill and thence down a two-step ladder into the main cabin. Here on the starboard side was a fixed berth with narrow seat inboard and always available as a settee, even with both main cabin berths in use. To port was a fold-down Concordia-type berth. The galley was amidships—unusual today, commonplace then, and affording the cook a space out of the way of companionway traffic and free from spray or drip. The forward cabin was conventional, with two built-in berths.

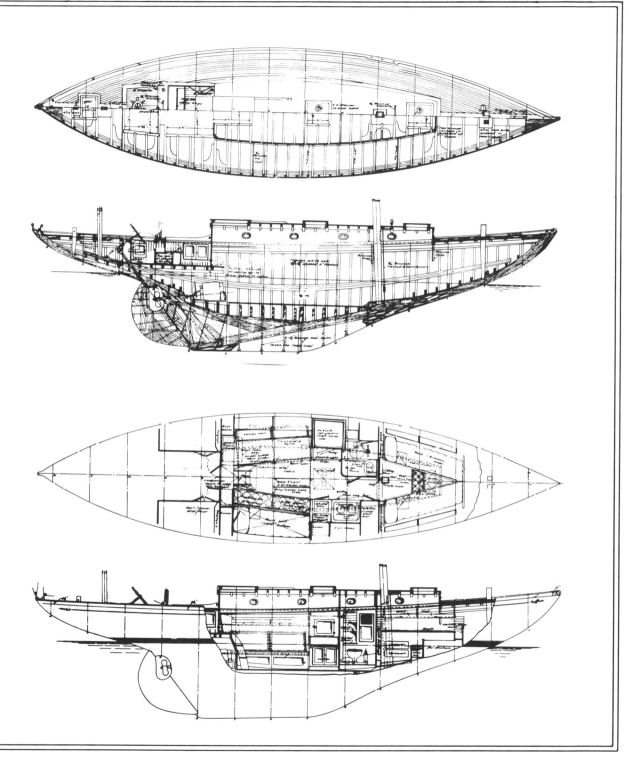

came, we had no difficulty moving the shed to Concordia's Padanaram yard, where it remains in modified form, right by the front gate, today.

Hostess III sailed and handled well. There is little doubt that the Chases enjoyed her. For over 40 years the family—mother, father, three sons, two daughters, and grandchildren in due time—kept the boat roaming the incomparable bays and harbors of the Maine coast. A worthy member of the Cruising Club, Mr. Chase was well into his nineties before he gave up active boating.

The other major yacht commission Concordia undertook in 1936-1937 was a 62-footer. She was ordered quite out of the blue by Hendon Chubb, a great benefactor and friend. Mr. Chubb's basic request was that we design and build for him a schooner with which he could once again win the Astor Cup for schooners. This is an historic race sponsored annually by the New York Yacht Club, and was first run in 1899. As owner of the beautiful 77-foot Herreshoff schooner *Queen Mab* (ex-*Vagrant*), Mr. Chubb had, in 1915, won the cup. He now wished to repeat the achievement. His order was the finest compliment that young Concordia could ever hope to receive. Ray rose to the challenge and proved once and for all that he had a genius for design.

The new boat when finished looked very similar indeed to her younger sisters, the Concordia Yawls, which were designed two years later. She was beautifully built by Lawley's. And with her graceful sheer, balanced ends, and a carefully worked out schooner rig, she caught everyone's eye. There was no mistaking her for any other boat.

The new schooner was christened *Victoria*, a time-honored name that for many years had been associated with Chubb-owned yachts. And she was immediately entered with the New York Yacht Club for the 1938 Astor Cup race. Without time for a real shakedown she appeared on the appointed day at the starting line in Newport. Mr. Chubb was in command, Walter Jackson was the professional skipper, Ray Hunt was sail trimmer. Several other guests and I were along to do what we were told. At the start there was one of those big old seas running; the breeze, however, was fine. *Niña* was our chief rival, but on that day she could not hold us. And so *Victoria* won the prize that Mr. Chubb had set his heart on.

It was too good to be true. Commodore W.A.W. Stewart, who had won the two previous Astor Cup races with *Queen Mab*, and De Coursey Fales, who was to win the next two with *Niña*, joined with others in urging Mr. Chubb to continue on with the annual cruise then underway. As his home port was Padanaram, and the next cruise port was Vineyard Haven—both to the eastward—he agreed to one more race. The day was perfect and blest with a sou'west breeze as clear and clean as you could ask for. With her huge balloon topmast staysail and big reaching jib, *Victoria* was unbeatable. She not only won her own class, but was best in fleet.

Victoria could really go when the wind breezed up. Sadly, she was never campaigned to show her long-term racing potential; happily, many of her features were incorporated into the later—and supremely successful—Concordia Yawls.

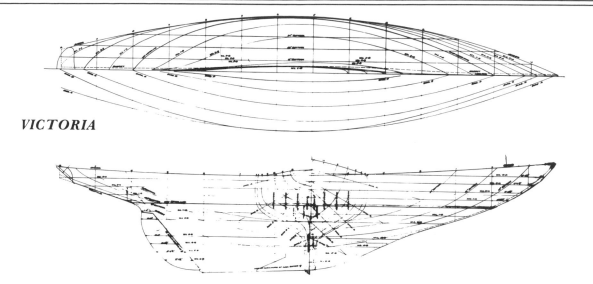

VICTORIA

Bill Harris's construction plans fit well with Lawley practices, and the building proceeded smoothly and quickly. There was nothing unusual about the basic cabin arrangement. Starting aft there was our usual Concordia cockpit with comfortable seat backs; then an easy three-step ladder into a lovely aft owner's stateroom. Next came washroom to port and enclosed engine room to starboard. The main saloon was large (you entered it by a curved stairway) and had a washroom of its own. A good full width galley and then a three man fo'c's'le completed the accommodations.

Considering that the boat had been intended for some serious racing, I had, in my ignorance, omitted one very important detail: I made no adequate provision for the stowage of light sails. This meant engine room, main cabin, fo'c's'le, and deck suffered their share of clutter. Percy Chubb tells me that this omission was partially corrected later on by the installation of a removable platform over part of the engine room.

Much study went into the exact measurements of the rig, but the general sail plan was conventional and workable: marconi main, gaff foresail, stemhead staysail, and jib on a short bowsprit.

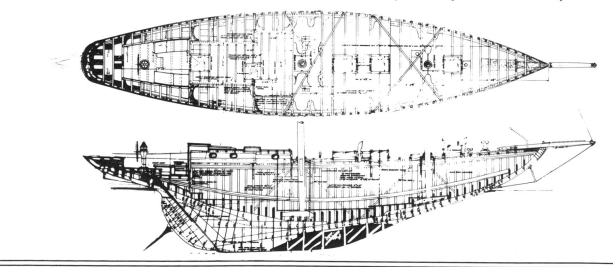

This was *Victoria*'s last race. The Chubbs enjoyed her for summer day sailing and cruising until the war loomed. Uncle Sam then took her over and converted her for inshore patrol work. My Marion friend Sam Register was placed in command of her, and she patrolled the New York and New England coast winter and summer for several years. It was rough duty, most of it spent under sail. Sam said he couldn't have wished for a better boat.

After the war, the Chubb family chose not to take *Victoria* back and refit her for yachting. Under new ownership she found her way down to the Virgin Islands, where she served for many years as a charter boat. More recent reports bring sad news about her condition, although I believe she is still afloat.

It is impossible for me not to wish that *Victoria*, like *Niña*, had been campaigned hard and faithfully by a single owner over many years. For as must be obvious from my account of her, I regard her design as inspired by any measure, and I do feel that she would have been a boat for all seasons. But considering how much in her design was to be reflected in the Concordia Yawl, I like to think that something of her spirit will endure long after she herself has perished in the Caribbean sun.

In the mid-1930s, Peirce and Kilburn's management team consisted of (back row, left to right) William G. MacDougal, Albert E. Davis, Chester E. Petty, (front row, left to right) Major William Smyth, L. Edgar Smith, and Clifford S. Kilburn.

11
Concordia Moves toward South Dartmouth

i

Along with his boat design work, Ray Hunt developed about this time a deep interest in the construction of sailcloth. Ratsey at City Island had, as I recall, access to the very excellent Egyptian cotton duck of English manufacture. Ray wished to make improvements in American sailcloth. Through Father's good offices, Ray met Charles Broughton, president of the New Bedford-based Wamsutta Mills, who proved willing to cooperate in the venture. For the balance of the prewar years Ray spent most of his time working with Wamsutta's Mr. Kenworthy and others at the Mills. They tried different weaves and different yarns, both cotton and synthetic. Ray had special sails made by several sailmakers, especially Wilson and Silsby. These he tested on a variety of racing boats. At times the experiments looked most promising. We and the Wamsutta sales agents, Howe and Bainbridge, were enthusiastically encouraged. But the experiments became expensive, and for a big mill the volume of sailcloth produced was small in proportion to its main line of work. Ray did learn much of value about the requirements for good sailcloth. As a commercial venture, however, the project was not successful. It came to an end shortly before the war.

Ray next experimented with light spinnakers—big parachute types, in contrast to the old-fashioned flat, triangular models. In this work, Ray recalled, he attracted the attention of the then very young Ted Hood and his father Stedman Hood. In the fullness of time, sailor Ted and his very capable engineer father brought sail design and sailcloth manufacture to a peak of art and science that has made the Hood name world famous.

Almost every suitable morning, summer and fall, Father and Martin Jackson set forth for a long day's sail. They are shown here leaving the New Bedford Yacht Club in our Chaisson-built Swampscott dory. Concordia's wharf and a glimpse of its basin show in the background.

During these final prewar years while Bill Harris was working for Concordia, I, like Ray, tried out several tentative business ventures on the side. Since I spent so much of my time in Padanaram, both winter and summer, the idea came to me and my designer friend (and neighbor) Bruce Williams to open up a boating store on the north side of Bridge Street, right in Padanaram village. Our plan was to sell our own special boat equipment both over the counter and by mail order. The project was probably doomed from the start, but it did have the important result of gettting Concordia into the manufacturing business on a modest basis—with equipment to our own design such as smokeheads, cabin heaters, lamps, and berths. Some of these products are still being made and sold today.

My brokerage efforts also took a new twist. Working alone, I found myself quite limited as to used-boat listings, and gradually I drifted more and more to Hasket Derby's door for help. This descendant of the famous Salem mercantile family was operating the Boston branch office of Sparkman & Stephens, which gave him access to a much greater range of boats being offered for sale. Furthermore, Hasket's office was just a few doors below Concordia's on State Street. It was all very convenient and turned out to be a most helpful and pleasant—if short—association. Indeed, although I had forgotten about it until Percy Chubb recently reminded me, my name even appeared for a spell on the Sparkman & Stephens letterhead. As an extra dividend, I also came to know and enjoy the company of John Leavitt, who was another temporary member of Hasket's office at this time. Thirty years later at Mystic Seaport I was to see a great deal more of this fine seaman, artist, and author.

Another of my sideline activities of the late thirties turned out to have a critically important influence on Concordia's later history. The owners of several boats that I had sold, new or second-hand, commissioned me to look out for the boats during the winter months. I made arrangements with both Peirce and Kilburn and Casey whereby they took work orders from me, permitted my supervision, and then paid me a small fee for bringing in the business. In those days yards were really looking for customers. Some professional skippers even got into questionable relationships with the yards—involving kickbacks and the like. My own program, on the other hand, seemed to work well for all parties. At least it kept growing from year to year.

In fact, it was not too long before the operation expanded to the point where I needed help. I found it in the person of Father's professional skipper, Martin Jackson.

By nature, background, and experience, Martin was exactly the right man for the task. His folks belonged to that old southern part of Scandinavia where the Norsemen and Vikings had settled. Their homeland had at one time been part of Norway, but was then Swedish territory. For generations, Martin's

218

family had owned and lived on one of those many small islands that dot the coast north from Göteborg to Halden, and it was there that Martin grew up, surrounded by the sea and boats. All communications were of necessity by water. Even school could be reached only by rowboat.

Following family custom, Martin's father owned a fish business, as well as a small trading schooner. As his sons came along, they each became at an early age a part of it all, learning respect for seamen and the sea alike. Home life likewise followed a strict routine and discipline.

Martin recalls that his mother opposed all card playing. This meant that when Martin played cards, he had to do so under cover (often under bedcovers). Now I don't approve of disobeying your mother, but it is a fact that when you play cards—especially for money—you must learn to guess well and to keep facts and figures in your head. No school can teach basic arithmetic more effectively. Martin was, and is, a very good poker player. More important, he early became an excellent judge of what would work in the boat business and what would not.

After World War I there was a period when the Scandinavian fishing

Martin Jackson at Concordia after World War II.

grounds were alive with cod, mackerel, and herring. But in the best of times a fisherman's life is a hard one, even aboard an able Brixham trawler. One by one, Martin and his three brothers—all ambitious and able—came to America. (A fifth brother had been lost overboard on a trading trip at the age of 15.) The family name in Sweden was Isakson, but the boys anglicized this to Jackson when they emigrated. Thus, Ivor Isakson became Martin Jackson.

Martin's oldest brother, Herby, was the first to arrive in the United States. This was in the early 1920s. After a brief stint on a commercial schooner, he switched over to yachting aboard Harold Vanderbilt's schooner *Vagrant* (later *Queen Mab*). By 1926 he was skipper on Vanderbilt's *Prestige*, an M boat designed by Starling Burgess and built by Herreshoff. For crew aboard this brilliant 80-foot racing sloop he hired at one time or another all three of his younger brothers. Then in 1929 he went with Walter K. Shaw on the New York Fifty *Andiamo* (ex-*Virginia*), and it was at this point that my father met Herby and learned about Martin. During World War II, Herby served as boss painter at Lawley's. After the war, he stayed on with Frank Paine, Lawley's chief stockholder, as skipper of Paine's last and most famous *Gypsy*.

Walter Jackson is my age and came to this country with Martin, his slightly older brother, in 1927. His prewar list of employers included Walter Shaw, W. Cameron Forbes, Jack Parkinson, Sr., and Hendon Chubb. After the war he turned to running big power yachts, starting with Emily C. Strawbridge's *Maintenon*.

Nils, the youngest Jackson, followed a similar pattern. First he worked for Shaw and Forbes. Then he was skipper on the Q boat *Hornet* and the Eight Meter *Ellen*, both from Marblehead. During the war he was with the Coast Guard, following which, and until his retirement, he was captain aboard Pierre duPont's several fine *Barlovento*s.

Martin tells me that in order to enter this country legally, he had to do so as a farmer and that he actually did work for a few months with an uncle who had a farm in the States. The first seagoing job he had was aboard the four-masted schooner *Astoria*, but this experience was short-lived. (It was a lash-up of some sort that ended with a strange grounding and a questionable insurance claim.) During the winter of 1928 he was at Lawley's. That summer and part of the summer of 1929 he was a crew member on Vanderbilt's Class M sloop *Prestige*.

It was in the fall of 1929 that Father had the good fortune to sign Martin on as a boat man aboard *Java*. (The term "boat man" deserves to be defined. And in essence it describes a professional who is paid to maintain a yacht and serve as crew; but who is considered the sailing master of the yacht only in the absence of the owner. The term, as applied to Martin, is nominally correct. But only nominally. Martin is a leader, not a follower, by temperament and ability. That we all realized early on.) For several years this job with Father was for the

Martin Jackson had served, as had his three brothers, aboard Harold Vanderbilt's lovely M-class sloop *Prestige* before he came to work for the Howlands in 1929. He had also worked at the Lawley yard and had grown up with small boats in his native Sweden.

summer only; during the winter months Martin and his brother Walter would go commercial fishing off No Mans Land in their own small powerboat. However, winter fishing was cold, rough work, and not at all profitable. Martin was more than pleased when Father bought *Balek* in 1933 and employed him year-round. From that time until Concordia Company was sold in the early 1970s, Martin remained a vital part of the Howland boat operations—or, as some have suggested, the Howlands remained an important part of Martin's boating operations.

I wish there were space for me to describe some of the many fine and memorable sails and cruises that Father, my brother, and I (and a succession of friends) have had with Martin, first aboard *Java* and *Balek*, then aboard *Escape*. And I vividly recall the routine that Martin followed on *Escape*, whereby every good, or merely bad, morning in season he would board the boat promptly at seven o'clock, chamois off the brightwork, polish the brass, and set mainsail and topsail in anticipation of Father's usual nine-o'clock arrival. Thus rigged, with the main sheet flattened down, *Escape* was a study in gracious self-composure, a reliably lovely sight for anyone stirring in Padanaram Harbor at that hour.

Until 1934, Martin worked for Concordia Company only sporadically. Gradually, however, he and I worked out arrangements with Palmer Scott to use space in one of Scott's sheds in an old shut-down New Bedford cotton mill. These mill sheds were finest kind for the job. They had windowed, sawtoothed roofs that made for good natural lighting, as well as beautiful hardwood floors that would tolerate tupelo rollers or heavy automobile-type jacks on casters. At the time, Palmer was building boats as well as storing them, which meant he had machinery, lumber, and extra hands that we could call on when we needed them. The Scott yard made a fine base from which Martin and I could carry on a winter business of storing and servicing a few good boats of our own choosing.

During the summer Martin continued to work for Father, and not only was he able to keep this exacting owner happy, he also found time to sail for his own pleasure. For a number of years the racing program at the New Bedford Yacht Club included a Herreshoff 12½-Footer class. Martin became much involved in the Wednesday 12½-Footer series, crewing for an independent young lady named Evelyn Jean. Martin had the knowhow, Evelyn had the boat, and they both had the enthusiasm. Indeed, in one race, they were apparently too enthusiastic for the wind conditions, as Evelyn's boat, *Plaben*, swamped in the midst of a too-quick tack and then sank stern first. Evelyn and Martin were soon rescued, but not before Martin had taken several quick bearings. After reaching shore and changing into some dry clothes, Martin returned to the scene of the mishap, bringing with him a kedge anchor suitably rigged with line and marker buoy. This he set where his bearings indicated.

The next day Martin was back with a small grapnel, and he began dragging in the area of his marker, being very careful not to work too closely to it and risk displacing it. He dragged in ever-widening circles. Still no *Plaben*. Finally, in frustration, he stationed his boat right over the marker buoy and sent down his anchor once more. It came up with a bit of sailcloth, and the search was over. Mr. Taylor, the Fairhaven marine contractor, came over with his barge and a diver. When the diver went down, he found the original marking kedge in *Plaben*'s cockpit. (*Plaben*'s sinking was not the first among the Padanaram 12½-Footer fleet. Thereafter, the boats were fitted with copper flotation tanks in bow and stern, replacing the sometimes fallible watertight bulkheads that resulted in several sinkings.)

Martin has an unusual way of winning when he is losing. In one race, *Plaben* clearly fouled another 12½-Footer, and the owner of the fouled boat filed a protest the minute he got ashore after the race. The protest meeting was about to declare *Plaben* disqualified when Martin brought up the case of *Endeavour* vs. *Rainbow*, during which T. O. M. Sopwith claimed a foul, but Sherman Hoyt claimed that the protest flag had not been set immediately following the foul in question. Sopwith's protest, had it been upheld, could well have resulted in our having to go to Cowes instead of Newport to see future Cup races. Martin's successful pleading had no international repercussions. It did put a bit of spice into Padanaram's 12½-Footer racing program.

There really is no end to the stories I could tell about Martin Jackson. None of them does justice, however, to the mixture of brawn and brain, earthy humor and basic kindness, force of character and astute and subtle intelligence that long ago made Martin a legend among the Buzzards Bay watermen of my generation.

Any boat with Martin Jackson aboard would sail faster and look smarter. He was regularly in demand as crew for the Herreshoff 12½-Footer *Plaben*, shown here.

12
Bill Harris
and His
Concordia Designs

i

In spite of Concordia's many sidelines, our basic design department continued to operate out of the Fairhaven shed drafting room. Here Bill Harris began his own stint of designing boats for Concordia customers. Bill was an easy, pleasant, patient, and meticulous fellow to work with. Older than me by a few years, he was slight of build and was of average height. With brown hair neatly parted, a small well-trimmed mustache, a white shirt and bow tie, he could easily have been mistaken for a city man. However, he lived very simply in an old-fashioned rented Fairhaven house, and he rode to work on an old second-hand blue bicycle.

Bill's childhood years had been spent in Melrose, Massachusetts, but being "hooked" on boats at an early age, he went to work for the Morse boatbuilding family in Thomaston, Maine, after attending that state's university. His first-hand knowledge of boatbuilding and his proficiency at designing (his father was a professional draftsman) soon caught the attention of John Alden, who in 1928 offered him a job in his Boston office.

Before coming with Concordia, Bill Harris had accumulated a good deal of experience, having served as a yacht designer for Alden, Eldredge-McInnis, Boston Yacht Sales, Furnans Yacht Agency, and Casey's. His wonderful eye and exacting hand created many a fine drawing for the Concordia files and, of

Plans for the 40′ motorsailer *Hurricane* were drawn for Concordia by Wilder B. (Bill) Harris in 1939.

Bill Harris had a natural eye for a good-looking boat, which, coupled with his superb ability as a draftsman, resulted in some of Concordia's finest designs. This photo shows Bill in 1983.

course, many a fine boat for the owners who commissioned them built.

The Fairhaven shed that was Concordia's design office had a northeast door that opened straight into the drafting room. This section was sheathed with insulation board and occupied the eastern two-thirds of the building. The west end, unsheathed, was just storage space, with big double doors for an entrance. During the winter months Bill's first project each morning was to fire up the pot-bellied stove and get things warmed up enough to make drafting possible. There was no pretense of big business here, but the room had a glancing southerly view of the water and good north light. It was very quiet and altogether a suitable and pleasant place for working in.

Except for *Prospector* (see Chapter 14) Bill's first Concordia design was a 35-foot auxiliary drawn up for William G. Saltonstall. This was during the winter of 1937-1938, and the commission was for a good-performing but simple family cruising boat for Buzzards Bay. She was to have plenty of strings on her, to keep Bill's growing family busy. (A double-head-rig yawl fulfilled this laudable aim, and we settled on it.)

Bill Saltonstall was at the time headmaster of Phillips Exeter Academy, and Exeter is not far distant from Dover, New Hampshire. Here at Dover Point, D. C. "Bud" McIntosh operated his two-man boatbuilding shop, and a major consideration of Bill's plans was that his friend Bud build the boat. I had never met McIntosh. But my very first visit to Dover marked the beginning of my enduring respect and friendship for Bud and his brother, Ned, and all their works.

The McIntosh yard nestled securely in a little marshy hollow tucked away below Dover on the west bank of the Piscataqua River. Entrance from the main road was gained through a farmyard gate, thence down a steep winding track (which first snaked along open fields, then meandered through a stand of trees), and finally fetching up on a small uneven shoulder of land that could accommodate a car or two and a small truck. Bud's house was across a narrow marshy area that supported a light marine railway extending up from the river to two modest boat sheds.

At first glance the setup seemed rather more picturesque than efficient, but even a brief tour and talk convinced me that our new boat would be in the very best of hands. Small stacks of lumber, mostly native pine and oak, were of excellent quality. The building shed had a dirt floor that sloped slightly downward toward the big doors, and was just right to fit the raking keel of a normal auxiliary. No high staging or extra blocking would be needed. The structure of the roof was low and sturdy enough to accommodate the many braces that are needed to hold firmly the molds and framing of a boat under construction. The mill shed had the band saw, jointer, and planer that are the most essential machine tools of the boatbuilder's trade. Hand tools were there

The skill of the builders, coupled with a low-overhead shop, made the yard of Bud McIntosh a most practical place to produce a number of the boats that Concordia designed. It was (and still is) situated at Dover Point, New Hampshire, on the west bank of the Piscataqua River. Bud's own boat, *Bufflehead*, is on the railway in this recent photo of his establishment.

Bud McIntosh in 1982.

aplenty, many of them homemade, all those with cutting edges being newly sharpened. I can't say the place looked neat to the amateur eye, but it had a natural orderliness well known and useful to Bud and Ned. Within Bud's house was a wood stove to keep things warm and dry, to cook its owner's meals, and to heat up the guest's coffee. The furniture was pine, made by Bud to suit his own needs—and included one table of a size and shape to hold and display sketch plans and blueprints. House and owner worked unobtrusively together to make the visitor confident and at ease.

Bud was and is a little older than I. Of medium height and muscular build, he moves slowly, with obvious decision. His voice is never loud, nor does he speak rapidly. But he is a fine conversationalist, as well as a witty one. If my memory serves, he was a Phi Beta Kappa man at college. Certainly his knowledge and experience spread over a wide and varied field.

One of my early visits to Bud's yard remains particularly vivid in my mind. Outside his house and partway around the short path to the privy, there was a narrow gully. The gully was bridged over with the butt end of a noble pine plank that was beautiful to behold. About an inch and a half thick, a strong 22 inches wide and 40 inches long, it was round-edged just as it had come from the sawmill. My obvious admiration prompted Bud to hoist it from the gully and deposit it in my car. For eight years, only shortened slightly, this lovely piece of pine served as the Howland dining table. When it became too small for our growing family, we moved it to the stove area in our kitchen. Here it still makes

ARBELLA

As originally designed and built, *Arbella* was arranged with galley aft, main cabin amidships with Concordia berths and lockers, fo'c's'le with Root berths and a toilet under a locker seat. The Underwoods changed things around a bit and ended up with an enclosed toilet room. An enclosed toilet certainly has many virtues, but it is sometimes awkward to attain in a 26-foot-waterline two-cabin boat. Here, as in so many things, intelligent compromise will help you achieve what you most want or require.

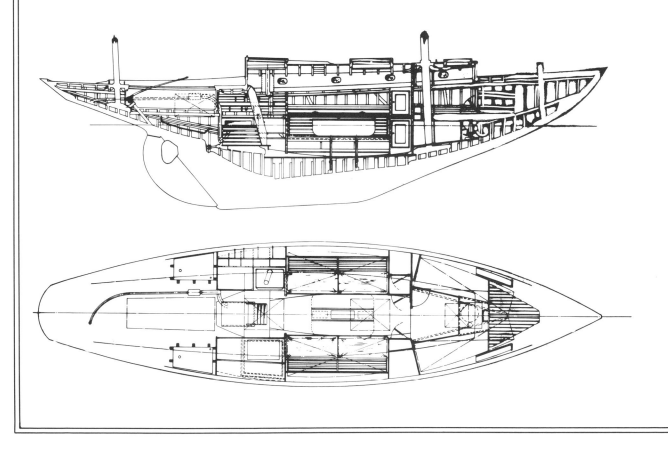

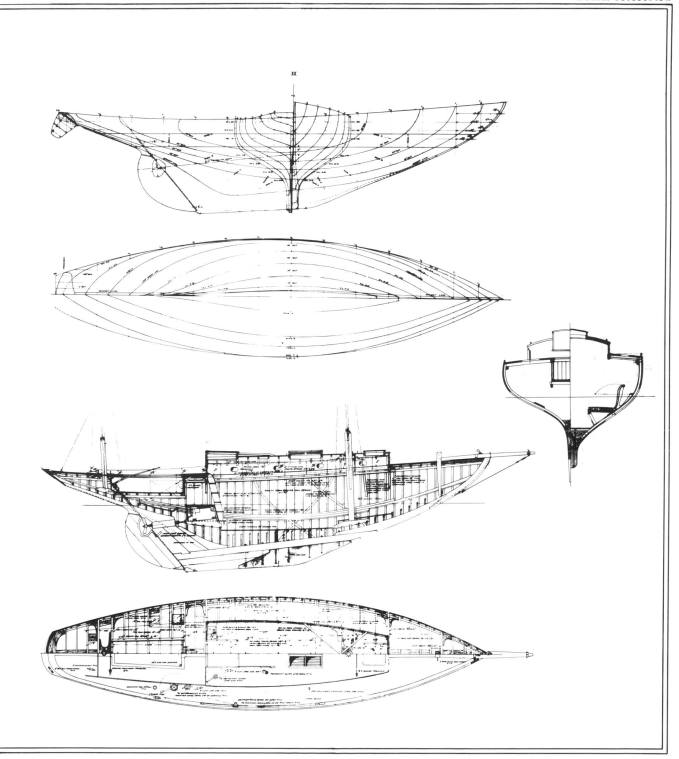

the perfect counter for all culinary endeavors, and constantly reminds us of the treasures to be seen and felt at the McIntosh boatshop.

Bud's partner and brother, Ned, was at the time living at his parents' home in Dover, so I saw less of him than I did of Bud. But I have since come to know him as a very special and capable gent in his own right. Not only is he a skillful boatbuilder, Ned also is an excellent mechanic, a cruising seaman of the finest kind, and a true friend.

Looking back now at the designing and building of Bill Saltonstall's boat, I am wondering why we at Concordia drew up so much detail and wrote such long and exacting specifications. I suppose it was just Bill Harris's training. For given the essentials, in lines, sail plan, and cabin arrangement, Bud and Ned could without a doubt have built a fine boat for Bill using their own construction detail—and thereby saving themselves the time and expense involved in following ours.

The finished *Arbella*, as she was named, proved a satisfactory, strong, and useful boat for Saltonstall cruising and racing. The family sailed and enjoyed her for some 25 years. For another 5 years she was owned by our Nonquitt friend Julian Underwood, who sailed her as *Ara*. Throughout these three decades she was stored at Concordia's yard in Padanaram.

Almost simultaneously with the order for *Arbella* we were asked to work out a little sloop for Arthur H. Morse of Boston. The basic conception of this sloop, to be christened *Shawnee II*, was Mr. Morse's. He had clearly in mind a big-little boat, one in which he could, with pride and pleasure, sail and cruise with his wife and teen-aged son, Fessenden. Good sailing qualities and seaworthiness, simplicity of handling, original price and future cost of maintenance were all important considerations.

Lines for the boat and proportions for the snug sloop rig were developed primarily by Bill Harris. The construction plan was likewise drawn up by Bill, but in this task he had the welcome advantage of working with Major Smyth, the man in charge of building the boat at Peirce and Kilburn. Details of the layout, rig, and equipment called for a meeting of the minds of the owner, designer, and builder, and in this process I took an active part.

Although she was designed in the fall of 1937, *Shawnee*'s actual construction didn't commence until March 1 of the following year. Bert Briggs, the salt of the earth and a long-time boatbuilder from nearby Westport, was selected to do the actual building for Peirce and Kilburn. In years past, and in his own shop, Bert had built boats for Bill Hand and many another satisfied customer. Essentially a one-man crew, he knew exactly how to make every move count. Watching him work, and I did a lot of this, was pleasure and education combined. With but occasional help from Al Alves, he completed *Shawnee* in good time for a June 15 launching. The choice of builder, the selection of

Arbella was one of Bill Harris's earliest designs for Concordia and resulted in our first association with Bud McIntosh, who built her in 1938.

materials, the design, and the construction details all had been well planned and carefully utilized. Mr. Morse certainly received top value for his $3,533 purchase price.

Home port for *Shawnee* was Falmouth, Massachusetts, but each summer the Morse family ventured forth on extended cruises that took them west to Long Island Sound or east as far as Roque Island in Maine. The boat lived up to her

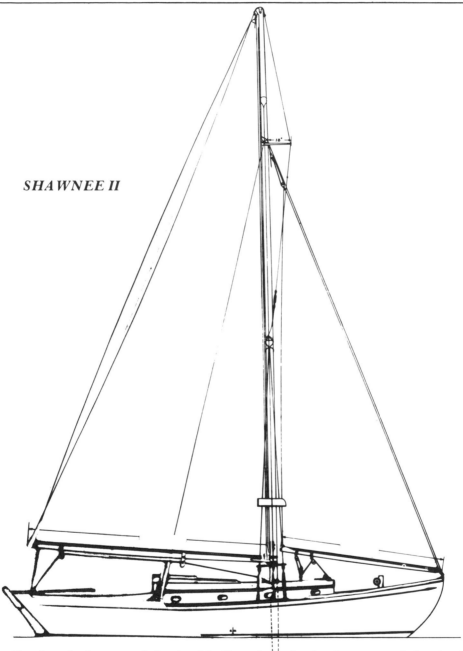

SHAWNEE II

Waterline length, beam, and depth of hull really determine the size of a boat. In order to attain a usable cockpit, a simple galley with quarter berth opposite, full-length berths for tall adults, plus a fo'c's'le for storage and the installa-tion of a head, we were led quite directly to a waterline length of 22½′ and a moderate beam of 8½′. By going to short ends for the design it is always easier to attain a little extra freeboard. On a long-ended boat higher than normal freeboard

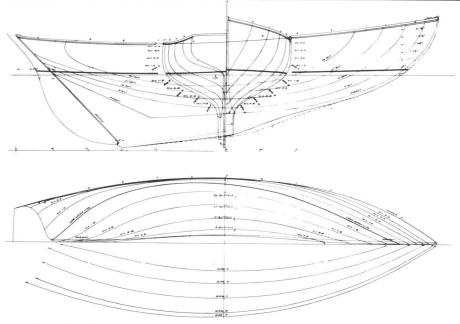

looks just terrible and with the extra windage usually acts that way, too. *Shawnee*'s freeboard was not excessive in any way, but did make it possible to sit below without discomfort.

As a rule of thumb it is a mistake in a small cruising boat to sacrifice needed deck width above for cabin space below. Thus we made no attempt to attain full standing headroom—which, given the small area of potential standing space, was not much of a compromise anyway. (A wide hatch and a seat opposite the galley made it quite tolerable for the cook to carry out operations either standing or sitting.) Being open from end to end, *Shawnee* gave an impression of having generous space below; excellent ventilation below was not an impression but a luxurious actuality. (Too much furniture, too many lockers, an over-abundance of shelves all tend to crowd living quarters and generate a clutter of nonessential gear, as well as blocking the free circulation of air.)

The specified flat transom stern with out-board rudder was strong, uncomplicated to build, easy to maintain. It balanced nicely with the short rounded bow. With fairly hard bilge and widish keel, *Shawnee*'s displacement came in at 9,900 lbs.—neither heavy nor light. Too much

displacement requires extra sail. Too little of it limits cabin space and the boat's ability to cope with added cruising gear and weight.

Shawnee's backbone and steam-bent frames were of carefully selected white oak. Her ballast keel was iron. For planking she had Port Orford cedar, a lovely clear Western wood that has a pleasant, lasting, and distinctive aroma. Plank fastenings were bronze screws. Deck and house-top were clear native white pine, canvas covered. House sides and cockpit were also pine. Shelf and bilge stringers were of close-grained Oregon fir.

For economy and by preference, Mr. Morse chose a shipshape and suitable paint schedule for his boat. Bottom was red, topsides a warm light gray. As a luxury, the sheer strake was varnished mahogany, which served to accentuate the boat's lovely sheer. (It also gave an illusive impression of a ship's rail, which made the boat look lower, hence longer.) The rails and trim were likewise varnished and stood out neatly against the buff deck and housetop.

The off-white or eggshell paint below made for a light cheery cabin, but without glare. Rails and moldings were varnished not only to smarten things up but to prevent finger and handprints from showing on frequently handled surfaces.

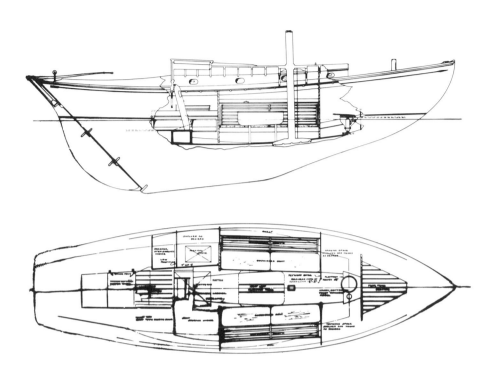

The fact that the Lawrences had three young daughters led to some interesting modifications to *Windsong* (ex-*Shawnee II*). Added was a Concordia forehatch, one of those made with two covers hinged on outboard edges. With the covers held in a vertical position by two crosswise brass rod brackets, the unit was equipped with a canvas cover that kept the rain out, but allowed a flow of air through the forward and aft openings. These openings were equipped with screens to keep mosquitoes out, as well as canvas flaps to lower as needed. With forward flap closed and rear one open an exhaust ventilator was created; with openings reversed, a wind sail of sorts materialized and blew fresh air into the cabin.

Below in the fo'c's'le two three-quarter-sized Root berths were arranged. These pulled out, as needed, over two small slatted and topless clothes bins, port and starboard. For two children, the area was then usefully transformed from a fo'c's'le to a splendid airy forward cabin, blest with full headroom under the opened canvas-topped hatch.

Aft, a conventional folding buggy top was fitted over the companion hatch. In the up position it seemed to increase greatly the usable main cabin space. When it was folded down, the helmsman had clear visibility forward—a distinct benefit not possible with a high fixed cabinhouse. Good sailing vision is really more useful than cabin headroom, if, in fact, your interest is sailing.

Charlie Lawrence had no difficulty installing a small engine. (The installation involved modifying the icebox arrangement by making a portable box that would fit on the forward end of the quarter berth. The wide cabin sole could always be used for sleeping, the pipe-leg table was removable, and a spare mattress was carried aboard.)

On deck Charlie added lifelines, stowage chocks for the extra anchor, shock cord furling gear, a Concordia ventilator, and a number of other little conveniences that neither cluttered up the decks nor obstructed normal easy handling of the ship's gear.

owner's expectations; no material changes were made in her, except for the addition of a bowsprit and the lengthening of her boom. Without an engine, the right amount of sail power was essential, and *Shawnee* was a stiff boat that could carry sail well.

Even the best of sailors have a way of getting older and in 1954 Arthur Morse decided to sell *Shawnee II* to Charles H. Lawrence III. However, she remained in Concordia's care and kept a mooring right off our dock in Padanaram. For a decade the Lawrences cruised the New England coast aboard the boat they renamed *Windsong*. Then due to family circumstances, they laid her up for what they hoped would be only a season or two. In fact, she lay idle for 11 years, in a storage shed at Concordia.

Among those who admired the sleeping beauty as she lay in the shed were two young fellows who worked at Concordia. During winter lunch hours they were wont to climb aboard and eat their sandwiches in *Windsong*'s cockpit, all the while dreaming dreams and talking boats. Fate decided to be kind to both of them. In 1973, John Garfield, the first admirer, bought her and changed her name to *Wynsum*. John, newly married, worked long hours with his wife to bring the boat back to perfect condition. After sailing her far and wide for some nine years, the Garfields sold the boat to John Anderson, the other admirer.

And so it is that *Windsong* (ex-*Wynsum* ex-*Windsong* ex-*Shawnee II*) has been in Concordia's care for 44 years. In all these years, she and her owners have been a source of pleasure and pride to the yard. I, for one, wouldn't know how to improve on her for a loner, for a couple, or for a small family. Still in excellent condition, she is a lasting tribute to Bill Harris, Bert Briggs, Major Smyth, and those many others who have been involved in her story down the years.

ii

In my continuing quest for brokerage customers I was constantly coming across the buyer who was searching for a four-berth family auxiliary, while at the same time clutching a pocketbook containing but $2,500. Little, low-priced cruising boats were on the market in the 1930s, to be sure, but they were too old and rundown, or lacked the necessary accommodations or equipment. A realistic and honest appraisal would always confirm that before the desired boat could be put into commission in decent condition, costs would be in the $3,500 range—or even higher. Bill Harris and I therefore put our heads together in an attempt to work out our best solution for those $2,500 dreamers.

Rebuilding or remodeling an old boat at home or in a shipyard is never as simple and cheap as one expects it to be. Old work has to be carefully removed before new work can be begun; the new work and old work have to be joined— often with untoward complications. Thus we concentrated our efforts on the

CONCORDIA 25

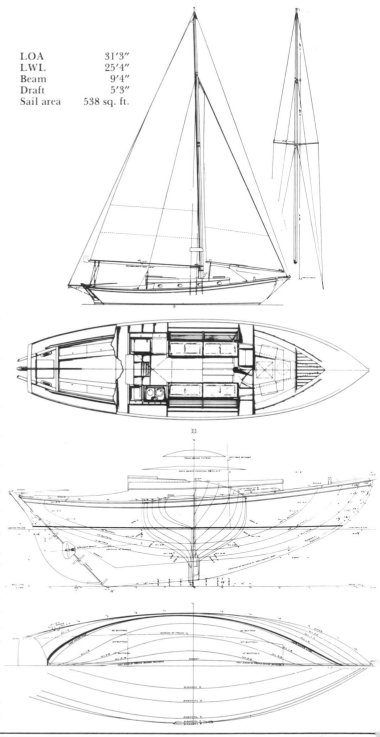

LOA	31'3"
LWL	25'4"
Beam	9'4"
Draft	5'3"
Sail area	538 sq. ft.

Wind, water, and basic boating considerations remain much the same even as the years pass and new fads develop. The thinking behind this design is as important and useful today as it was back in 1940, when I wrote the following for Yachting *magazine.*

From bitter experience I have determined that "modest comfort" on a coastal cruise cannot be obtained for four adults on a waterline length of less than 25'0". Such a boat should have good working deck space and a comfortable, watertight cockpit with seats below deck level. The fewer the deck fittings and gadgets, the better. More time can be spent sailing and cruising and less time in the repair shop, if all running and working parts are kept as simple as possible. In the long run, wooden cleats, no winches, halyards made up and hung on the mast, and manila sheets belayed within reach of the helmsman make for economy of cost and ease in handling.

The exact arrangement below is open to some variation, but every cabin should have air, light, and the greatest possible amount of useful working space. A really wide companionway hatch is a delight. If it is kept longer than it is wide, it will slide easily and not jam; if it is canvas covered, it will not leak. A forward hatch is an essential. Opening ports forward and, more important, an opening port in the forward end of the cockpit, are desirable, but opening ports in the side of the house add very little ventilation and are not worth the expense.

A coal stove is the most foolproof, serves for heating and drying as well as for cooking, and is best located aft on the starboard side under the companionway. Here there is air, light, and headroom. The working part of the galley is best located opposite the stove. Have a plain, flat dresser top to work on and a drawer underneath containing all the most constantly used foods such as sugar, salt, coffee, and small kitchen utensils, etc. Have an open space below that, in which to stow a good gurry bucket with a top on it. Between the dresser top and the drawer, have a flat pullout slide such as you have in an office desk. It will only take about 2″ of space, and if it has a hole in it of the proper size, you can set an ordinary enamel basin in it and have the most practical and easily cleaned sink possible on a little boat. A board fitting into the same basin hole makes a perfect place on which to cut meat or bread. Aft of the stove and aft of the working part of the galley is ample and handy room for food stowage. A portable ice box will hold enough food and ice, is far less expensive than a built-in one, and is easier to keep clean. Such things as sinks, pumps, Monel tops, etc., all add vastly to expense and clutter; they take up space for essentials and should be eliminated.

Comfortable seats to sit on and dry and comfortable bunks to sleep on are the most essential. To maintain floor space and to have a proper seat, the transoms should be normal seat depth of about 18″ and slanted outboard. On all our boats of this size we install special Concordia berths, which in the daytime form the backs for the seats and which at night fold down and form canvas berths 28″ wide and 6′6″ long. An inexpensive kapok pad is used in place of an ordinary mattress. Even eliminating the consideration of expense and the economy of space, a Concordia canvas berth with light mattress is the most comfortable bunk possible, since it does not accentuate the motion of the boat, as do springs. The tension on the canvas and the angle of the berth can be varied.

Root berths are also extremely comfortable canvas berths and make the most practical bunk for a small forward cabin, since they fold completely out of the way when not in use and are always dry when needed.

There is not space in a boat of this sort for a separate room for the toilet. The latter essential can best be located under a seat in the forward cabin, which is separated from the main living quarters by lockers on either side with a door between. A separate wash basin not unlike those used in every house a short time ago is a most suitable substitute for a lavatory.

In order that everything can be kept in its proper place, locker space should be planned very carefully. Two little transom seat lockers, one on each side, give stowage space for clothes belong-

Bill Harris drew the plans for the Concordia 25, including several interior renderings like this one.

ing to the two people in the forward cabin. Amidships, the locker to port has shelves for the two people using the main cabin. The full-length locker to starboard is for holding go-ashore clothes. At one side of the passageway is a bin-like dresser on top of which books can be set and in which linen and extra blankets can be stowed. Aft of the galley on the starboard side is space to hang waterproofs.

The finish below in the Concordia Twenty-five Footer is plain but neat and in keeping with the whole conception of the boat. All bulkheads are pine staving of random widths and oiled with a quick-drying oil. Other woodwork below is likewise pine oiled. The underside of the deck and house as well as the sides of the house is painted white. The floor is painted a dark color. With a minimum of work, this cabin can be kept clean and tidy and at the same time homelike and pleasant. The outside finish of the boat is almost entirely paint. There is no varnish whatsoever, as varnish requires frequent attention and is not in keeping with the idea of the whole. Certain of the members such as rails, rubbing strakes, etc., are left natural, wood-oiled, but the oil used is durable and does not require being removed or sanded down annually.

In general, the keynote of construction, finish, and equipment is simplicity, economy of upkeep, and resistance to the actions inherent in the elements of air and water.

creation of a new boat that could be built by a yard like McIntosh's both well and inexpensively. During the fall of 1938 two young brothers, Henry and Avery Sawyer, who lived near my parents in Brookline, gave us the opportunity to prove our contentions. We held more conferences, wrote and rewrote more letters, and sketched out more details than would be needed to construct an ocean liner. But in those days we had the time and the interest. And we urgently needed the business.

The Sawyers named their dream ship *Star Dust*. Bud McIntosh and his brother built her during the winter of 1938-1939, and when she was launched that spring she became the first Concordia Twenty-five. As customary back then, we used the waterline length as the designating figure. Later these same boats became known as Concordia Thirty-ones, which expresses their overall length.

From watching the building of *Arbella* we had gained complete faith in McIntosh's ability and integrity, and the specifications for *Star Dust* were quite brief. Paragraph one stated merely that the specs listed were "to cover the building and finishing of the hull, spars, rigging, deck fittings, and interior joiner work of a plain cruising sloop, sufficiently to show the buyer and builder the type of boat that is to be built and equipment which is to be supplied by the builder." Materials and workmanship were to conform to good commercial practice as followed in the usual type of small "fishing or work boat." A few specifics were noted: oak backbone and steam-bent frames, native white pine planking, clinched and bunged galvanized boat nail fastenings, iron keel, pine cabin sides and interior, hollow spruce spars, outside bronze chainplates, etc. Then there was a general paint schedule and a list of equipment. The plans that Bill drew up showed his usual skill and accuracy: fair lines, correct offsets, good basic construction detail, carefully worked out cabin and sail plan, as well as a number of sketches that were especially helpful to the owners as they visualized what they were going to get.

It was all very simple, and it left a good deal of leeway for the builder to do things his accustomed way. Bud said that much of the detail he played by ear, which at first mention sounds like a risky way to build a boat. With Bud, however, the end of a day's building was also the beginning of an evening of thinking and planning. The McIntosh approach meant that work went along quickly and well without time-consuming mistakes.

Later that winter, while *Star Dust* was still a-building, Dr. Harry Forbes of Milton and Naushon accompanied me on a weekend jaunt to Dover Point. This gave us a leisurely time to see and feel what the new boat looked like and how she was being built. What was to be observed sold itself, and the good doctor ordered a sistership, *Lauan*, to be started about April 1 and substantially finished by July 1. The only major difference in specifications between the

Conceived as a low-cost, four-berth family cruiser—a boat for the economically depressed 1930s—the Concordia Twenty-five, plans for which were drawn by Bill Harris, proved to be all we had hoped for. Bud McIntosh built the first two boats, *Star Dust* (shown here) and *Lauan*, before World War II. Seven more of this design, subsequently called the Concordia Thirty-one, were built afterwards—mostly by the Concordia Company's own South Dartmouth yard.

239

Sawyer and Forbes boats was the planking: the Forbes boat was to be planked in Philippine mahogany. (This was because of family connections. Cameron Forbes, King of Naushon Island, had been Governor of the Philippines, and one species of this country's wood that was readily available and inexpensive was mahogany-like and went by the name of Lauan.)

Dr. Harry's Concordia Twenty-five was actually built by Bud and Ned McIntosh in nine weeks, meaning that she was in full commission for the summer of 1939. All indications now seemed clear that the Concordia solution to the economical four-berth auxiliary had real merit. Indeed, I felt sure enough about the success of the venture to write an article on the Concordia for *Yachting.* I include an edited version of this piece on pages 236-237.

As of 1982 both of the first two Concordia Thirty-ones, or Twenty-fives, were in Concordia Company's care. After 44 years and the addition of seven sisterships, both are alive, lovingly cared for, and in absolutely beautiful condition. The design seems to be ageless, and the boats not only handle well, but sail far faster than the casual observer would expect. Many a sailor has swung off his course to take a closer look, only to find that he couldn't catch up.

Star Dust, substantially unchanged, has had only four owners: the Sawyers from Marblehead, Dorothy Quartrop from Glen Cove, New York, Edward

The Concordia Twenty-five *Lauan* was originally owned by Dr. Harry Forbes and is shown here at her home port in Hadley Harbor. She still looks good after nine owners and 44 years; she still sails well and is still much loved by her present owners, Mr. and Mrs. Richard Hawes.

Wood of Mattapoisett, Massachusetts, and now Jackson Sumner of Windham, Connecticut.

Lauan, following some cabin changes made along the way, has now been converted back to an arrangement quite close to the original. She has had nine owners, the second two in Rhode Island, the next five on Long Island Sound. Her owner since 1968, Richard K. Hawes, calls Westport, Massachusetts, his home port and cruises extensively along the northeast coast. Although the boat has had several names, including *Jolly Tar* and *Elizabeth*, she is now *Salt Wind*.

iii

The autumn of 1938 was a busy one for Concordia. One of the main excitements was a design opportunity from my contemporary and friend Dick Perkins, son of James H. Perkins for whom Concordia had designed *Weepecket*. Dick requested plans for a little motorsailer that could actually sail. She was to be named *Hurricane* in awed recognition of the storm that had just devastated the New England coast with so vast a loss in lives and property. The commission was a new and interesting challenge for us. True, Bill Harris had recently completed a motorsailer for a customer of Charlie Furnans's Yacht Agency. But excellent as she proved to be, she was much too big for Dick and had only a snug Hand-type auxiliary sailing rig. Major Smyth, whom we hoped would build *Hurricane*, suggested we give some serious study to a very successful fishing boat named *Dauntless*. This we did, and then Bill went to work on a short-ended 40-footer with fairly deep sailboat sections and a suitably fine stern to balance a motorsailer bow.

Conventional sailboats with overhanging spoon bows hate to be pushed dead to windward under power. Especially in rough conditions they get to their destination far quicker by carrying a little sail sheeted flat, and proceeding very close-hauled, first on one tack, then on the other. A good powerboat bow, with a narrow but deeper entrance, on the other hand, will tolerate punching directly into wind and wave. Motorsailers are perforce a compromise and are best designed with a compromise bow and a nice clean run to match.

Keeping in mind good appearance and sailing qualities, we held the freeboard of *Hurricane* on the low side, just enough to allow for full headroom under a well-proportioned deck and cabin house. To keep the cost down, the Major suggested inside iron ballast and a work boat-type helmsman's shelter with two top-hinged opening windows forward, but only curtains for sides and aft. Until you have tried it, you cannot appreciate how much money can go into constructing a fancy deckhouse. All those slanting front windows, opening side windows, and streamlining and rounded corners on the rooftop add to the complications and cost. If not planned and built properly, deckhouses also result in many problems and expenses in later years.

Our first sketches and specifications did not entirely fit with what Dick had in mind. The general effect with vertical windshield, low cockpit coamings, flat transom, etc., was, for him, too commercial in appearance. So Bill proceeded to spruce up the superstructure and add a double-planked rounded transom for what became the final plans. It was at this point that the directors of Peirce and Kilburn decided that the yard staff's estimate was too low and that custom boatbuilding did not fit in with their operation. *

Peirce and Kilburn's decision not to build *Hurricane* came as a great blow to us. In fact it made me damned angry. However, we were still welcome at

The Casey yard at Fairhaven built *Hurricane* in 1939 for $8,000. She was given a lean powerboat type of bow for efficient powering into a head sea; and her shape elsewhere generally made for an easy motion, seaworthiness, and decent performance under sail.

* About this time Peirce and Kilburn did build on speculation two Novi schooners advertised as Blue-nose Juniors. They were nice little vessels designed by the great William Roué. To me a scaled-down fisherman does not make an ideal type. However, the boats were well built, had a salty charm about them, and did sell. (Joe Plumb, Jr., bought one of them, as a matter of fact.) Then I lost track of Peirce and Kilburn operations for a while. In due course, their able second-in-command, Bill McDougall, moved to Falmouth and set up a very successful yard of his own that employed several of his sons and a brother. Major Smyth also made a change, acquiring an interest in the Mystic Shipyard, West Mystic, Connecticut. There his many devoted customers followed him and received the best of storage and repair service until he retired in the early 1970s.

Hurricane's spacious, natural-finish pine interior, with its special Concordia seat backs and cabin heater, made below decks a restful and friendly place to be.

Casey's. Having drawn up some new specifications to conform to Casey's methods and Dick Perkins's wishes, we settled on a price of $8,000, a figure slightly higher than the Peirce and Kilburn price. The final results were really excellent. There is no doubt that the yachtlike features Dick had insisted on added materially to his pride of ownership and to *Hurricane*'s resale value.

Conditions for many of us—for all of us, really—changed in 1940. *Hurricane* was put on the market and promptly sold herself. In 1943 she was taken over by the Coast Guard. Since World War II she has won the admiration of several fine owners, and her resale value has continued to rise. My friend Jack Adie owned her for many years, calling York Harbor, Maine, her home port. Later Richard Preston bought and sailed her very actively out of Manchester, Massachusetts, as he continues to do as of this writing. In the 1960s, when I visited Long Beach, California, I was delighted to see a sistership of *Hurricane* that had been built on the West Coast. She appeared to be in beautiful shape.

I suppose it can be said that a small motorsailer is neither hay nor grass. Yet I feel that *Hurricane* fills a real need. She has most of the good qualities of a cruising sailboat and of a displacement powerboat. In general, she has the easy motion, the seaworthiness, and much of the sailing ability of the former. At the same time she has the lesser draft, the larger accommodations, and the greater powering efficiency of the latter. For certain requirements *Hurricane* is a complete and first-class unit. She is one of my favorites.

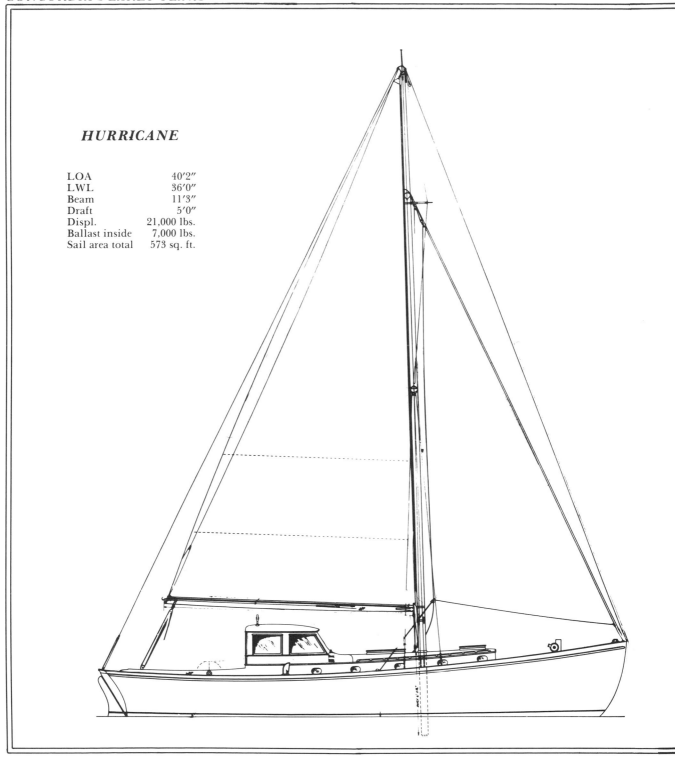

HURRICANE

LOA	40′2″
LWL	36′0″
Beam	11′3″
Draft	5′0″
Displ.	21,000 lbs.
Ballast inside	7,000 lbs.
Sail area total	573 sq. ft.

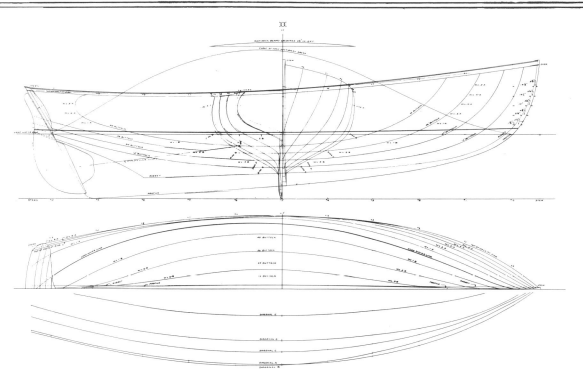

As built, *Hurricane* had the usual oak backbone and steam-bent frames, Philippine mahogany planking, and bronze screw fastenings. She was sheathed throughout the living quarters with ⁵/₈″ pine in narrow widths that was fastened by galvanized nails.

There are, as in so many other boat matters, differences of opinion on the use of sheathing (or ceiling, as it is also known). In a commercial hull, this inner skin is usually considered essential. For the sake of strength, it is often somewhat heavier than the actual planking, since it has to form the secure container for heavy cargo. In a pleasure boat, sheathing is more a matter of option—and ventilation. I had quite a lengthy discussion on this subject with designer Frederic "Fritz" Fenger. He felt that for small yachts no sheathing at all or simply slats spaced well apart for the passage of air between them made the best system. For my part, I claimed that close-fitted strips extending from the cabin sole up to within

a few inches of the structural clamp at the sheer were best. Installed in this way sheathing creates a circulation of air by its chimney effect between each frame. It also keeps living quarters, clothes, blankets, and cushions well insulated from the hull, prevents dust or small articles from falling into the bilge, and makes the cabin easier to keep clean. Fritz granted that my theory had some merit, but concluded that his arrangement was still the best. I stood by my theory.

For cabin finish the Peirce and Kilburn specs had called for painted plywood with mahogany trim. In those early years I was reasonably open-minded, and went along with plywood, but I never really liked it, especially for boat use. Big, one-piece bulkheads can be hard and clumsy to fit and install. The material has its structural merits but is hard and metallic in some respects, noisy like a drum, sweats under some conditions, and relies on a nice finish and trim to acquire any pleasing character. In later years I have found that even good plywood usually delaminates in damp areas. Be all this as it may, the Casey specs called for one of my favorite interiors; one built of white pine with hardwood trim, preferably locust. The tongue and groove bulkhead planking of random widths was to be fitted with a shallow V joint at its edges. Left bright and never stained, our native eastern pine imparts a sunny hue without being glary, and its pattern of grain is pleasing to the eye and a subtle decoration in itself.

There are several finishes that can be applied to pine interiors. Varnish can be good, especially when built up with many coats and then rubbed down with fine pumice and machine oil. The main objection to this procedure is that it takes time and skill. In the two McIntosh-built Concordia Thirty-ones we specified linseed oil applied in several coats. This makes for a rather primitive appearance but is quick to do and simple to maintain. On *Hurricane* we used a processed oil from Scandinavia. I never knew exactly what oil it had for a base, but it was labeled Oxan Oil and was said to be used extensively in its home country, both on the inside and outside of boats.

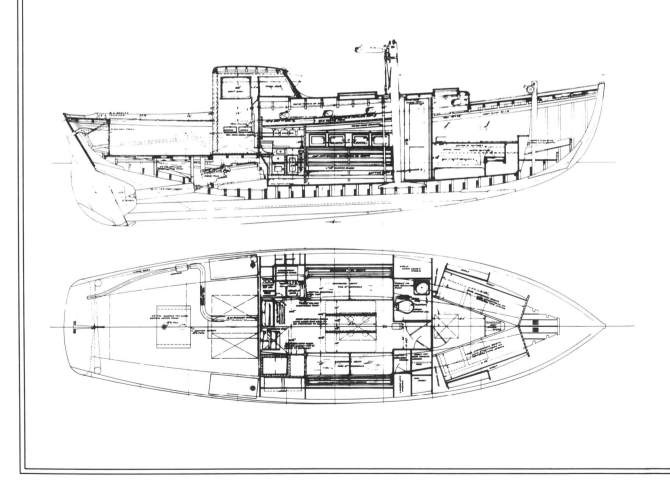

Concordia imported it as one of their special boat products. I imagine it was much like the Norwegian Deks Olje that has become popular today. A coat of Oxan Oil is on our home bedroom pine walls and after 40 years remains in good shape untouched and unchanged.

Hurricane was by plan a big enough boat to include comfortably a conventional and pleasingly symmetrical two-cabin four-berth arrangement. The shape of the hull forward was such as to make rectangular built-in berths with useful drawers under quite practical. The inboard face of the berths did not extend down to the cabin sole, but terminated some inches above to allow for extra toe room. This is the same idea as the faces under the main cabin seats that slope outward, allowing more floor space.

Working aft, a spacious toilet room squarely faced carefully designed locker and drawer space. The main cabin itself contained Concordia features that have since been duplicated many times: sloping seats of comfortable height and width and Concordia berths with lockers outboard and above the berth backs. By not having these lockers extend up to the deck, their useful top with its 2″ rail became a shelf, which is excellent for long articles such as flagstaffs, battens, etc. Also the design permits the eye to travel out beyond the locker tops to the skin of the boat, thus making the cabin seem more spacious and attractive. Our own Concordia Cabin Heater installed against the forward bulkhead added both useful and decorative features.

With an offset companionway the galley was as requested, very spacious, sink and lockers to port, big icebox and lockers to starboard, and stove amidships facing forward. The stove was an English-made Simpson Lawrence kerosene affair. Called a Clyde cooker, it had a cast-iron top and an oven in between the two removable Primus burners. For any boat that sails or powers mostly on her bottom and is not heeled over too much, a fixed athwartship stove works out well. When the ship rolls and the oven door is opened, neither the meat pie nor the potatoes roll out.

Hurricane's cockpit was watertight and substantially open. Its deck area under the house was raised slightly to prevent water from working forward to the flush hatches over the engine compartment. Sections of folding slatted seats were fitted on each side with locker openings in between. Aft was a wide locker door giving access to a special cable steering quadrant into which a tiller could be, and often was, inserted for handling the boat under sail. This special fitting involved two castings, male for the tiller and female for the rudder. The unit was somewhat complicated to make but simple to use. We sold a number of them in later years.

As to outside finish the Peirce and Kilburn specs called for a white hull with a black guardrail, main rail, and rail cap. Other outside trim was to be Oxan-oiled. Decks were to be canvas-covered and painted sandstone buff. This was all in line with simplicity, and would have given the boat a shipshape commercial look. The final Casey specs, however, were changed and called for bright, Oxan-oiled rails, which likewise accentuated the boat's lovely sheer. The decks were to be white rift sawn pine laid in narrow widths and swept with the sheer.

Hurricane's simple inboard jib and mainsail rig is balanced in appearance and, more important, balanced for sailing. Originally we showed the jib on a club, but then we eliminated the club to keep the foredeck clear for handling the anchor. The need to trim sheets when tacking is, to be sure, an added operation. But on a motorsailer, most maneuvering is done under power, while for straight sailing a loose-footed jib causes no real trouble and is very efficient. The permanent backstay was designed to be temporarily removable. (Dick was an ardent fisherman, and a backstay can get in the way of fishing rods or lines.)

Because of limitations of space under *Hurricane*'s cabin sole, it was impossible to pack in the specified 7,000 lbs. of iron ballast. This naturally resulted in the boat being on the tender side when sailing in a strong breeze. We corrected this problem by replacing some of the iron with lead.

13
1938:
Actaea,
a Hurricane,
and a New Yawl

i

In 1935 Percy Chubb introduced me to one of his partners at Chubb and Son Insurance Company, Walter Gherardi. Slightly older than me, Walter was head of the firm's marine division. From the beginning, and in more ways than one, he was of great help to me and to Concordia's yacht insurance department. Several official visits to Chubb and Son's New York office led to numerous social visits at the Gherardi home in Greenwich, Connecticut. Especially during weekends, there were—and I imagine still are—some grand parties among the Greenwich yachting fraternity. It was at one of these occasions that I first met Henry Sears, a descendant of the illustrious Boston merchant David Sears, a founder of the Eastern Yacht Club in Marblehead who, in the 1860s, had owned a yacht named *Actaea.* Harry's uncle Herbert Sears had owned the famous 134-foot schooner *Constellation*, aboard which Harry had often sailed as a boy, before he moved to the New York area in the early 1930s.

One friendly introduction led to many more, and soon I came to know Jack Dickerson, Cooch Maxwell, Swifty Swift, and Jack Keeshan. How or why Harry and these particular friends of his came to be dubbed "the towel boys" I do not know. I do know that for some years they had been racing with and

The first boat of what was to become the Concordia Yawl came out as a replacement for Father's beloved pilot-cutter *Escape*, after the great hurricane of 1938 smashed her beyond any hope of repair. At the time the new yawl was simply another (good, we hoped) design from our Concordia office. We never dreamed that in the years to follow over 100 of these boats would be built or that the design would become an all-time classic.

against each other and having a lot of fun doing it. I took it as a real compliment when they invited me to join them for the 1938 Bermuda Race aboard *Actaea*.

This *Actaea* was a lovely Sparkman and Stephens-designed Nevins-built sloop that had been commissioned by Harry to take the place of the Paine 36-footer *Actaea* in which he had won a Class B second in the 1936 race. The new boat was very much like the Chubbs' *Victoria* in size and general appearance, except that she had a very tall sloop rig and a secret new weapon in the form of a centerboard housed within her keel. Besides the "towel boys," Harry's crew included two slightly older sailing friends from Boston, John Yerxa and Oliver Ames. Then there was big Bob Meyer, whose name often appears in Seawanhaka Corinthian Yacht Club annals, especially in connection with International Six Meter racing. As a real luxury, the ship also carried three first-class professionals—the captain, a sailor, and the cook. The cook went by the name of Knute, and he was a wonder, one of the greats of his trade.

After a number of sail-practice spring weekends, each salted and peppered with work and pleasure, *Actaea* and her crew arrived in Newport to prepare for the June 21 start to Bermuda. Almost from the beginning the race insisted on being a hard windward thrash, so that the bigger sloops and yawls, most of them Sparkman and Stephens designs, took the honors in both Class A and Class B. Mr. Henry Taylor's great yawl *Baruna* was outstanding on this, her first ocean race, and Harry was mighty disappointed, as were all *Actaea*'s crew, to place no higher than sixth in Class A.

Nineteen thirty-eight marked the last Bermuda Race held until after World War II. It also proved to be my own ocean racing finale. War came. *Big Actaea*, as we called her, was eventually sold to Commodore Henry S. Morgan and became the well-known, well-raced, and well-traveled *Djinn*, home port Oyster Bay, Long Island.

After serving with distinction in the U. S. Navy and surviving a typhoon at sea, Harry continued his yachting career by ascending the ladder to become Commodore of the New York Yacht Club. It was he more than any other individual who was responsible for getting the *America*'s Cup competition going again, this time in Twelve Meter boats.

For Concordia Company in general and me in particular, *Actaea* and her skipper opened up a whole new world of opportunities, yachting and otherwise. Over a period of 25 years Harry included me on a goodly number of New York Yacht Club cruises, and he owned and raced during that period three different Concordia "yawls," each of which he sailed with sloop rigs. (Harry referred to our mizzens and their gear as "tank traps." This description has some merit. I long ago forgave him for making it.) Harry died in the late spring of 1982, after a long and courageous battle with cancer. He was a good friend.

In 1938, I sailed the Bermuda Race aboard the new 62′ Sparkman & Stephens sloop *Actaea*, owned by Henry Sears, a man to whom both Concordia and I owe a great deal.

ii

At 5:00 P.M. on the afternoon of September 21, 1938, I boarded my regular commuter train for the 60-mile run to New Bedford. It had been an oddly oppressive afternoon, airless and muggy, and I supposed we were in for some rain. But I don't recall having had any serious forebodings—or any forebodings at all. Even as the train gathered speed, however, the rain began, great whirling sheets of it that slashed down the windows of the coach. With the rain came wind, the force of which was obvious in the writhing shapes of trees along the tracks.

Our progress became endlessly slow, a succession of slow starts and sudden stops. Evening darkness took over from the unnatural cloud darkness. It must have been nearly nine before we reached the New Bedford depot, and when I stepped off the train I found myself in a nightmare of litter and confusion.

Without thinking I crossed the street and climbed into my Plymouth coupe. Then the magnitude of the storm began to hit me. I felt wet mud on the seat and the clammy dampness everywhere. Obviously the car had been under water. Salt water. A courageous taxi driver, following a devious tree-strewn route, finally delivered me within walking distance of my Padanaram home. I had a late cold supper by the light of a single candle.

Early next morning I walked down to Padanaram Harbor. The devastation there exceeded my worst fears. I found it hard even to recognize familiar objects. Boats and buildings littered the shore, pitifully displaying their broken frames and sodden innards. Our old pilot cutter *Escape* lay up against the bridge causeway, her starboard side completely gone. She was a total loss. In this sad condition she had plenty of company. Indeed, hardly a boat remained afloat in the harbor. The few that did showed costly evidence of their ordeal. Considering the huge loss of life and property along the entire New England coast, it was no doubt selfish to mourn the loss of a yacht. But perhaps the enormity of the storm would otherwise have been too great for me to grasp.

The loss of our dear *Escape* against the Padanaram breakwater in 1938 was tragic for the Howlands, especially for Father.

During the hurricane, Mother and Father had been in Petersham, where, from their cottage window, they had witnessed the destruction of the great pine forest that surrounded them. The sight of those lovely tall trees completely flattened had prepared Father for the loss of *Escape*. Back in Padanaram, he

took one look at her, turned away, and said, "I'll never sail again! Never!" There is no doubt he meant it. At the time. Later he reconsidered, and before long we were working together on plans for a new boat.

My own first tentative suggestion to Father was for an enlarged Concordia Twenty-five—one about 28 feet on the waterline. For this Bill Harris drew up several sketches to help us in our thinking. One of these sketches showed a hull with an outboard rudder. The other pictured the same boat with a short overhanging stern. These drawings were really tempting and some years later we used them in building several Concordia Twenty-eights (or Thirty-threes, as they were later called). However, they were not the type that Father had in mind. He sought to get away from bowsprits and short ends. Primarily, he visualized a boat that would perform well going to windward in Buzzards Bay—a point of sailing in which old *Escape* had thwarted him at times.

The Eight Meter *Balek* had certainly been a great sailer, especially on the wind, so we talked about her for a bit, and then got together with Ray Hunt. For rating purposes the meter boats had become very round in section in order to develop a maximum displacement with a minimum wetted surface. In our case we were not considering any constrictive racing rules. Just the same, Father was always competitive in spirit, and he hoped to take on some local racing in a cruising class governed by the Cruising Club Rule. He also had in the back of his mind the boat *Wonder How*, which, back in school days, he and Allan Forbes had built and successfully raced on Milton's Neponset River. Father had designed this little light displacement sloop and had given her a very hard bilge. In fact she was a good example of a hard chine boat. My own vague design thinking drifted back to *Java*, the 75-square-meter boat, which had fairly hard bilges, a midship section with straightish line from bilge to keel, and a modest displacement.

Ray was in sympathy with all of Father's thinking and drew up a beautiful set of lines, showing a profile with moderate ends, a lovely sheer, and moderate freeboard. The stern was narrow and relatively deep to balance a bow that was fine yet rounded and without hollows. The midship section above water was on the straight side, with a slight tumblehome giving the hull her greatest beam a few inches above the load waterline. Just below the waterline the bilge took a hard turn and went from there in a relatively direct line to a quick fairing in at the keel. This hull showed no bumps or fullness to obstruct the water from a flat and easy flow from bow to stern. In many ways the new hull looked much like *Victoria* but had the harder bilges that Father sought.

We all gave the rig a great deal of thought before Ray drew up the final basic sail plan. Our first idea was a cutter with the mast stepped well aft, so that with the mainsail set, the boat would lay quietly head to wind at her mooring. *Balek* had always wanted to get underway as soon as the main was hoisted, and that

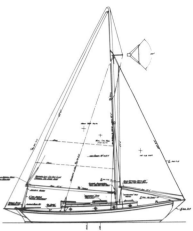

One proposal, as a replacement for Father's hurricane-smashed cutter *Escape*, was an enlarged Concordia Twenty-five; about 28′ on the waterline. This Bill Harris design was set aside in favor of what was to become the first Concordia Yawl, but was resurrected after the war to produce *Mitty*, the first Concordia Thirty-three. Several more like her have been built in recent years.

Father's new boat ended up as
a yawl, although other rigs
were first considered. She was
launched in 1939 as *Escape*,
since she was to be old
Escape's replacement, but
Father renamed her *Java* in 1944.
The new yawl's lines were
drawn by Ray Hunt to a
length and general form specified by father. Her construction and arrangement plans
were prepared by Bill Harris
and incorporated various features and details worked out
by me—ones that had proven
useful in earlier Concordia
designs.

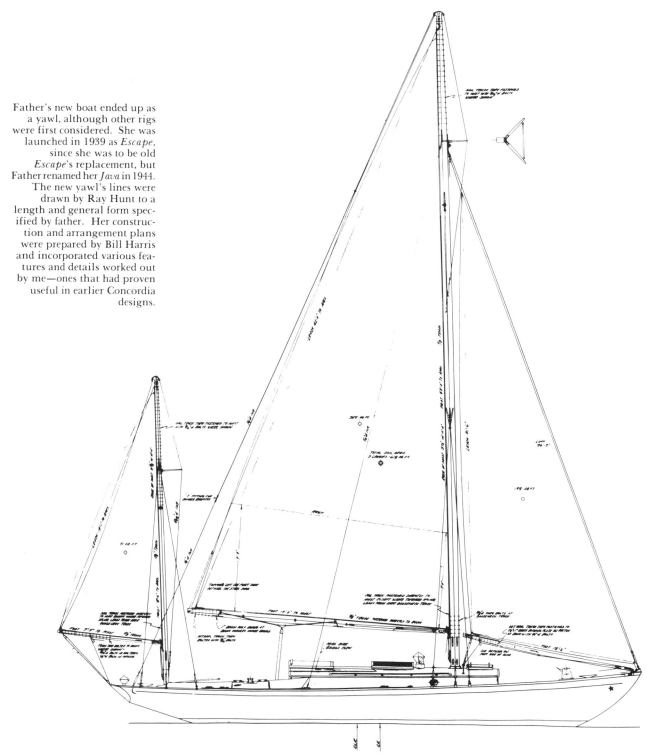

was a nuisance for day sailing or cruising. With a big foretriangle, a double headrig would be very efficient and have its good sides for shortening sail. However, when we got to figuring all the jibs and gear we would need, it became obvious that there wouldn't be room enough below to stow it all. The final decision was to move the mast forward, settle for a single seven-eighths-height headsail, and then add a mizzen to assure our head-to-wind feature. The decision was a good one. For general cruising and downwind sailing, a fair-sized mainsail has many advantages. With mast not too far aft a good sloop using only her main will maneuver like a catboat. Certainly on a small boat the single moderate-sized headsails are easier to handle than double or large ones. This is true for sailing or stowing, and such a rig is kinder on the pocketbook as well.

Not too much discussion time was needed for the cabin plan. Bill Harris and I had, on previous boats, developed a general Concordia arrangement and detail, with which Father was both familiar and satisfied. Our waterline length of 28 feet 6 inches was long enough to include comfortably a symmetrical arrangement of two Root berths forward, the toilet room with lockers opposite, then the main cabin with Concordia berths, and finally a very simple galley aft.

When we got to the cockpit we gave its arrangement a lot of extra consideration because that is where Father, with his planned daily sails, expected to spend most of his time. Our final conclusions brought about several changes from previous Concordia cockpit designs. We held to the Concordia Twenty-five bridge deck and full floor-width theory, but by the use of park-bench-type slats we contoured the side seats, and divided the fore and aft space into two sections, the aft two-thirds being fixed with stowage under. The forward third was left open with provision for a portable seat top when wanted. Especially for old folks, it is helpful to be able to walk all the way from one side of the cockpit to the other for the tending of sheets, without having to kneel on a seat or to stretch across one.

A bridge deck does require climbing over in order to get below, but for Father's use, the arrangement had more advantages than disadvantages. Structurally, it forms a simple fundamental feature of strength that ties the whole hull together. It provides an ideal base for the mainsheet blocks. With long bridles on the main boom, strains are distributed on that vital spar. Any slight bowing down of the boom tends to have a favorable flattening of the mainsail as the wind increases. A mainsheet at the end of a boom on the other hand tends to tighten the leech adversely and make the sail more baggy just when you don't want it that way. Finally, it is extremely handy to have the mainsheet in front of helmsman and crew rather than angling or whipping about over their heads.

Not being able to come to a firm decision on whether to set the jib loose-footed or on a club, we made provision to handle it either way. The use of a club makes it easy for single-handed tacking but does clutter up the foredeck.

Sailing efficiency suggests many reasons for keeping a boat's rig light and free from unnecessary windage, but Father quite rightly aimed at strength and reliability as a top priority. At his suggestion, we arranged a visit with our friend Bror Tamm at Lawley's, and ended up by commissioning this exceptional craftsman to design and furnish all our spars and rigging. In doing this for us Tammy kept dimensions on the large side. We couldn't have chosen a better or more up-to-date advisor. Along with Burgess and Francis Herreshoff, he was one of the very first to introduce and engineer box-section spars and bronze strap tang fittings for the purpose of attaching stays to a yacht mast. Previous standard procedure was to use wire eye splices around the mast and over shoulders to prevent them from slipping down.

The Howlands had owned but one boat with an engine in it. That was *Great Republic* and, as described earlier, her motor ran but once for us. As a result our power planning for the new boat was simple indeed: a small four-cylinder gas engine that could fit under the bridge deck. It was to be readily accessible, and for good ventilation it was to be covered only by a box with removable solid top and slatted sides. Essentially, it was out in the open where the engineer could comfortably tend to its needs.

The major design features having been settled on, Ray and Bill worked together on stability and weight calculations and the like, and then Bill took over to draw up final construction, cabin, and deck plans. Several features received special attention, one being visibility. For both pleasure and safety it is vitally important that the helmsman, and the crew to a lesser degree, have an unobstructed view. The deck and rails are fixed structures that can't be altered, but the cabinhouse can, and really should be designed so that it doesn't protrude up and out into the helmsman's vision. On Father's boat, house dimensions and shapes were very carefully worked out so that the sheer and height of the house sides blended in with the whole hull design. The width of the house was kept on the narrow side, and roughly paralleled the main rail in order to retain evenly wide decks. The line or profile of the house top was drawn to give the whole boat a pleasing appearance. Father was prepared to accept limitations, if any, in the cabin headroom. Achieving all these desired elements meant that each house beam had to have a different crown, and they progressed from shallow ones aft to more deeply curved ones forward. Extra work is involved, but being able to see where one is going does add immeasurably to sailing pleasure.

Another important decision was to provide for a long bronze track extending from main to mizzen rigging. This was to be mounted on, and to protect, the toe rail, and was to be through bolted and equipped with enough slides to handle all jib sheet leads, spinnaker gear, backstay runners, and boarding ladder fittings. It would thus avoid the need for deck fittings that so often cause leaks or damaged toes. The deck itself was to be canvas-covered with the canvas finishing outboard under the toe rail.

Planning a new boat is often as much fun as sailing one, and Bill's drawings were so beautifully done that I hung copies of several on my bedroom wall. As I reclined on my back observing the profile plan, the idea subconsciously came to me that the new ship should have a painted eye on her bow so that she could see where she was going, and enjoy all the lovely sights that would be ahead of her. I had seen pictures of such eyes on native boats in faraway places. Actually on our boat the eye didn't look too well as sketched in below Bill's cove stripe, but an emblem there did add something and gradually transformed itself into a five-pointed star. To balance this bow decoration a crescent moon suggested itself for the stern. This inspiration was unquestionably prompted by my mental picture of an autumn new moon hanging daintily beneath the bright evening star. The combination star and moon subsequently became a Concordia trademark.

Without shopping around, Father made a deal with George Brodeur to have the Casey yard build the new boat. Work commenced late that fall of 1938. Bill Harris was close by to supervise and furnish detail plans as needed. I had the

Taken in 1908, this shows Major Casey (second from right) and others in his early crew, several of whom were relatives.

fun and education of talking matters over with Father and relaying special requests. George was most cooperative, and during construction was always willing to make use of special materials such as locust and red cedar, or install secondhand equipment as we produced it. The salvaged Major Smyth-built skylight off old *Escape*, for example, fit in perfectly. Then from a salvage firm in Fall River we acquired enough of the great bark *Aloha*'s beautiful teak decking to resaw and use on our cockpit floor. Casey's had a little trouble in developing and fairing out the stern and transom, but on the whole the work progressed in good order and *Escape*, as Father first christened her, was ready in time for a spring launching.

For the next three summers Martin Jackson continued to work with Father. Together they reaped pleasure, satisfaction, and knowledge from testing out and modifying features of the new yawl.

Martin Jackson reminded me recently that in her first two years we raced *Escape* eight times and won six firsts. So right from the start the boat had a good local reputation. Ray Hunt came along on several occasions to evaluate his handiwork and spruce up our racing tactics. However, Father was our usual helmsman. He knew well how to coax the best out of *Escape*. Buzzards Bay, its tides and winds, he understood better than anyone else.

The full story of the Concordia Yawl, of which *Escape* was the first, I will tell at another time. For the purposes of this book, I would only add that *Escape* was badly damaged in the 1944 hurricane, extensively rebuilt by Bert Briggs and Captain Harold E. Hardy, renamed by Father *Java* (after a fortunate Howland whaling vessel and Father's no less fortunate square meter boat), and sailed by Father and Captain Hardy until Father's death in 1956 at the age of 80.

Escape had one prewar sistership. In the early spring of 1939 my college friend Phil Rhinelander ordered the yawl he named *Jobiska*. Frank Paine very easily persuaded us to let his Lawley yard build her. (At the time, Lawley was building the Sparkman and Stephens Week Ender Class.) These attractive sloops were a foot shorter on the waterline than the Concordia Yawls, but being short-ended they tolerated a bit more freeboard and higher house sides. In this way they gained full headroom and had space for the same general layout as our yawls. Paine's very reasonable contract price for Phil's *Jobiska* was predicated on the understanding that the construction, equipment, and general finish of the Week Ender would be followed insofar as possible. This accounted for *Jobiska*'s bright sheer strake, rectangular ports, small main hatch, conventional forehatch, Lawley fittings, and so forth. After World War II the boat was bought by Drayton Cochran and became *Ina*. Still later she was bought by Dan Strohmeier and renamed *Malay* in honor of his father-in-law's little Roué schooner of the same name.

As I write, Concordia Yawls No. 1 and No. 2 are still in active use.

Escape, later *Java*, at her Padanaram mooring, sails being bent on. It was Father's custom, when not actually using the boat, to completely remove her sails and drop them through the companionway hatch to the dry shelter of the cabin below. He rightly claimed that this took no more time than furling and that it greatly increased their useful life. Until his death in 1956 and with the able help of Captain Harold Hardy and Martin Jackson, Father got much use and very much enjoyment from this, his last, boat.

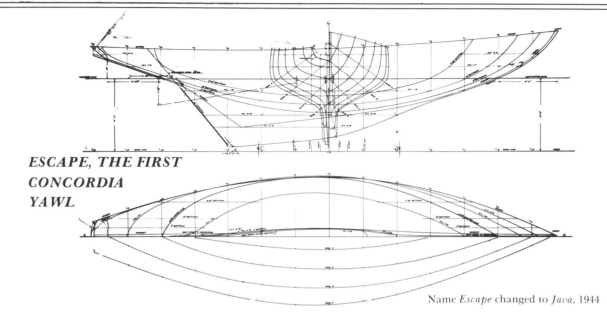

ESCAPE, THE FIRST CONCORDIA YAWL

Name *Escape* changed to *Java*, 1944

No major changes seemed necessary. Father spent long hours at the helm. On the wind in a breeze he could support his back against the sloping coaming and be securely braced across to the leeward seat. With sails properly trimmed there was seldom any strain on the tiller. In spite of his sitting slightly below deck level, he had a clear view forward with no interference from the house. Martin Jackson's favorite station was on the forward end of the leeward seat. Here, facing the bow, he could keep an eye on the jib and handle the sheets, both jib and main, without moving or getting in Father's way.

For some time they used the loose-footed jib on a club. It was handy when tacking, and as the club pivoted from a point somewhat aft of the

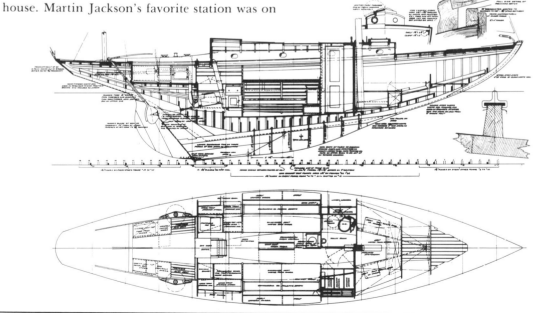

jibstay, it made for an efficient sail, automatically flattening itself as the sheet was hauled aft. In the end, however, the club was left ashore to make more room on the forward deck for handling the anchor or picking up the mooring. With our cockpit arrangement it was no trouble for the helmsman to handle double sheets if necessary.

For fall sailing Father designed a special mainsail for *Escape*. It was long on the foot, easily reaching the regular clew outhaul fitting. It was, however, short on the hoist, the head setting about as high as the jibstay. There was no roach to the sail. In fact the leech had a slight concave curve to it, so that no troublesome battens were needed. Winds in the fall do not necessarily blow with any greater velocity than in the summer, but the cooler air is heavier, and Father's small flat sail worked out well, and was easier to reef or furl than the full size one.

Escape's mizzen seemed small and by some was even called a rule cheater, but it served its purpose of holding the boat head to wind. Leaving an anchorage, the mizzen was hoisted, tacked down, and sheeted flat. Next the main was set, but the sheet was left slack so that the sail could flutter but not fill. This static condition allowed as much time as needed to up-anchor and get it well stowed. When all was shipshape and ready to sail, Father pushed the tiller hard over for the desired tack, tucked its end behind a mizzen lower shroud, and with both hands free slacked the mizzen and hauled in the main. *Escape* bore off obediently as Martin put the jib to her.

Below, arrangements worked out equally well. Ventilation was excellent with the big opening port in the forward end of the cockpit, big companionway hatch, opening skylight, and special forward hatch. There were also two opening ports in the forward end of the house plus one in the toilet room and one opposite. *Escape* had no additional side ports, however, in either the main or forward cabin. In days gone by, on another boat, a port had leaked onto Father's bunk, and he wasn't going to have any of that again.

An occasional cruise aboard *Escape* gave me a first-hand opportunity to experience Concordia

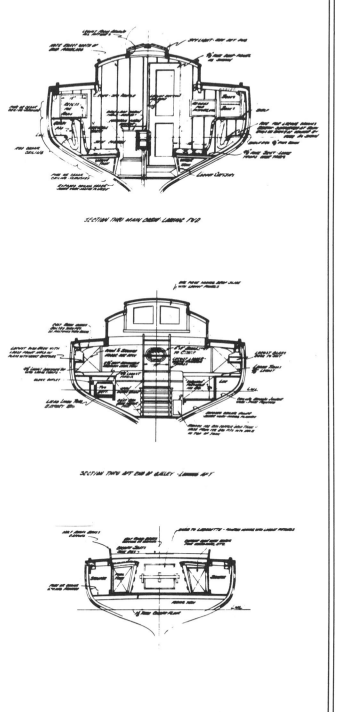

SECTION THRU MAIN CABIN-LOOKING FWD

SECTION THRU AFT END OF GALLEY-LOOKING AFT

cabin detail, and make notes for the future. The spare ground tackle stowage forward of the fo'c's'le locker seats worked out well. The anchor was low down, easy to get at, and not too hard to hand up through the forehatch. The Root berths were wide, comfortable, and long. They stowed out of the way and were dry when needed. My only complaint was that they were a little clumsy when one tried to set the single pipe in its sockets. The Concordia berths in the main cabin were really great; wide, long, and easy to operate. They just needed a little refinement here and there. The main cabin seats too with their slant outboard, their 18″ depth, and shaped backrests seemed about perfect.

The galley arrangement was perhaps too primitive, but it contained all the essentials that the Howlands needed. The Concordia Cooker with cast-iron top and its two Primus burners on either side of the oven boiled the water, fried the eggs, and baked the cornbread in good shape, even if it did require a little skill and patience to light. The Concordia Heater, fired up with a proper collection of driftwood, warmed the main cabin, dried out the towels in the head, and did a little auxiliary cooking on request.

A comfortable cockpit, a bridge deck for strength, a trunk cabin kept low so as not to obstruct forward visibility, and a yawl rig for convenience in cruising were some of the features we felt were important for *Escape*.

iii

In 1940, Concordia Company, as well as America at large, was feeling ever more strongly the sobering effects of European war conditions. For Concordia, these months were tough and perplexing. But we had no wish to give up the boat business, and we plugged on at various hit-or-miss experiments until the aftermath of Pearl Harbor.

During that summer Bill Harris designed a most attractive 25½-foot water-line sloop for Russ Genner of Elmhurst, Long Island. This boat was essentially a modification of the Concordia Twenty-five but had an inboard rudder and no bowsprit. In a way she represented our version of a Lawley Week Ender or a New Bedford Thirty-five. Contracts were drawn, and Bud McIntosh was all set to build her. However, at the last minute Mr. Genner decided that due to the recently passed draft law, he would be wise to cancel out.

We were all very upset to lose this order, but actually it was just one of many design disappointments that we were facing. Bill Harris was extremely versa-tile in his designing skills and drew up an impressive number of most tempting preliminary sketches including one for a big motorsailer. If only Hitler and his ilk had not started their operations, Concordia would now have many more finished plans in its files.

As it was, Concordia did sell at least three new designs during the year 1940. They varied greatly in size and type. For Mrs. Durand we worked out a 20-foot waterline version of a Concordia Twenty-five. She was a cute little ship, and did have enough cabin room below for afternoon nap seats and for workable toilet facilities. Although she was perforce of a somewhat boxy appearance, we partly disguised her relatively high freeboard by giving her a bright sheer strake. By using a neutral gray color for house sides and cockpit coamings, we also visually lowered these structures to some extent.

Carl Beetle, son of the whaleboat-building family and producer of the New Bedford Thirty-fives, signed the contract for building our new sloop, but during construction he became involved in a commercial enterprise, and his helpers Clark and Brazie finished up the work for us. They did a very good job of it, too. The boat was named *Jeanne* and happily proved most satisfactory for Mrs. Durand's day sailing excursions. For most owners, however, I always felt that the Concordia Twenty-five had much more to offer at comparatively little extra cost. Materials were less, but hours of labor were nearly the same for either boat.

Indeed, there definitely do seem to be good sizes and poor sizes for any particular design type. To explain this statement, I often cite the example of a common bed. One that is about six-and-a-half feet long is useful. A five-footer is pretty worthless except for children. An eight-footer is a wrong size for anyone under seven feet six inches tall. So it is with boats. There are a few certain lengths that, over the years, have worked out well for individual human needs or water conditions. For a limited accommodation four-person cruising auxiliary, a 25-foot waterline length has proved practical. For a good two-cabin auxiliary with enclosed head, a waterline length of 28 or 29 feet seems to work out well. As another example of size, an 18-foot bass boat is just too small for Buzzards Bay conditions, whereas a 22-footer copes in good shape.

iv

A second 1940 design that Concordia carried through from the planning stage to a completed boat was one for our early supporter James H. Perkins. Following a human age progression, he had switched his sights from sail to power. As Mr. Perkins explained his wants to me, I immediately thought of Captain Fuller's beautiful little Jonesport lobster boat. It was always a real pleasure just to watch this slim graceful hull quietly slipping through the water, leaving scarcely a trace of wake. On one recent occasion we had persuaded the captain to charter this boat to my brother and me for a picnic excursion to Cuttyhunk. Morgan Plummer,* a close friend of Mr. Perkins and ours, went along with us. Everything was working out just fine until, on the way home, the engine suddenly stopped and refused to start again. Fortunately the boat was a seagoing design and was fitted with a small mast, a riding sail on

This 30′ powerboat for James H. Perkins was drawn up in 1940 by Bill Harris using the Jonesport lobster boat model as a guide.

*Morgan was a son of Henry M. Plummer, the famous wood-carver and author of the classic book *The Boy, Me, and the Cat* (Rye, N.H., 1961). Morgan's brother, Henry Plummer, Jr., was "the boy" in this grand narrative.

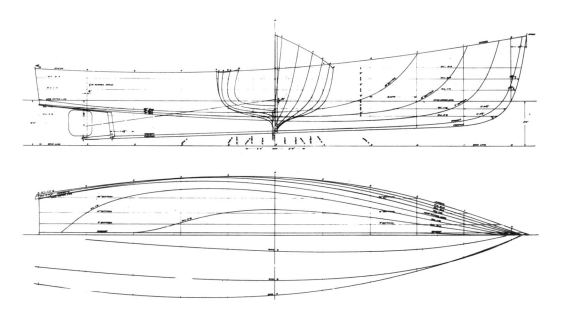

The Perkins boat was built by Casey's yard in Fairhaven, Massachusetts.

an all-purpose boom, and a long footed jib that tacked to her high stem. Not knowing what else to do, we set these sails and headed toward Mishaum Point, which was the nearest land. To our great satisfaction and somewhat to our surprise, the Jonesport responded to sheet and helm, and reached back slowly but surely into the lee of Mishaum Ledge. She was a good boat for her intended work, and we used her as a model to modify for Mr. Perkins.

To accommodate a forward toilet, two full-length transom seats, a small deckhouse, and a good cockpit, Bill Harris and I chose a waterline length of 30 feet. Casey built the boat. She looked and performed as she should, but unfortunately Mr. Perkins didn't live to enjoy her for more than a few weeks. Looking back now I guiltily suspect that my own personal admiration for Captain Fuller's Jonesport may have prompted me to build the wrong boat for Mr. Perkins. Not that he ever said anything about it, but a wider and shorter craft might well have been better fitted for his family day boat needs.

Over the years I have learned that the hardest thing about acquiring a new boat is to choose one of the right size and type, one that you, yourself, can actually use and derive pleasure from. The correct selection requires serious practical thinking, rather than the following of popular trends or fanciful theories. I have seen the owner who has jumped to a craft that was first-class in its own way, but for him soon became more of a burden than a joy. Then I've seen the man who took so long with his planning and figuring that his choice became out of date with his later abilities and needs. Sometimes the charter of several different boats can help to clarify one's decisions.

One example from my own experience. Thinking to use her for day sailing, I brought one of our *Plover* frostbite dinghies to Padanaram. Unquestionably she was a good two-man racing and sport sailing boat, but I found she had her drawbacks for my intended use. She was too fancy and fragile to keep alongside a float—and too big to haul out easily on one. Her mast interfered with a stake and outhaul arrangement. It was awkward to keep her on a mooring, in that this required another small boat for getting off to her. More important, she was not basically suitable for fishing, beach parties, or even for a leisurely evening sail. I just ended up by not using her very much. Light displacement has its place, but for me a sailing skiff or a small catboat would have been much more satisfactory.

One substantial 1940 design came our way when Mr. Taylor of the Duxbury Boat Yard asked us for plans of a schooner similar to *Victoria* but somewhat smaller, or 35 feet on the waterline. His proposition was that he buy the plans and then take over from there. He would build the boat and do his own supervising for his customer Dr. H. C. Bumpus of Duxbury. Ray Hunt drew up the lines and sail plan and then he and Bill Harris cooperated with accommodation and construction drawings.

The Duxbury Yard made a special effort to do a top job and create a fine-quality, long-lived boat. In doing so they increased some of the scantlings, which may have added to the strength of the boat, but also brought her down somewhat below her lines. This in turn added slightly to her displacement and gave her less freeboard than planned. Fortunately the changes did not seem to affect the good sailing qualities of the boat. In profile she looks very much like a Concordia Yawl, and her sections likewise are quite similar, although the turn of her bilge is not quite as hard.

Mya, as Dr. Bumpus called his new schooner, has, I believe, had just three other owners.* She has kept her original name and has always called Duxbury her home port. Such continuity is usually a good sign and certainly *Mya* has won her share of races and seems to have stood the test of time in all respects.

v

The last prewar plan that I now find in Concordia files is incomplete and labeled "Concordia 30 Footer, designed by C. R. Hunt and Waldo Howland, 50 State Street, Boston, Mass., December 5, 1941." This boat was built, but although I sailed her once or twice I never really got the chance to use her. Ray was at the time much engrossed in the production of his so-called 110s and larger 210s. After some discussions between us, he drew up for me a somewhat conventional-looking sloop with rounded bow and rather deep overhanging

*Eugene Danaher, Jeffrey Hugret, and Matthew Stackpole.

The 50′ schooner *Mya* came out in 1940 to Concordia plans. Much like a big Concordia Yawl, she has proven fast and is still going strong today.

stern. Although this design had round bilges, they were still very hard, and the bottom was shallow and flat. To gain the sitting headroom that was needed for minimum two-person cruising accommodation, it was necessary to go to a raised deck, which had the disadvantage of making an already high freeboard appear even higher. The cockpit was open, with sloping slat seats and conventional angled coamings to lean back against.

In some respects this little, light displacement sloop, with her spade rudder and fin keel, was a forerunner of the so-called modern boats of the early 1980s, ones that I now find myself somewhat critical of. Ray furnished me with one of his 210-type cast-iron keels, and Mr. E. L. Goodwin at Cape Cod Shipbuilding

Company in Wareham built the boat. She had conventional steam-bent oak frames and cedar planking; but in the hopes of saving labor, we persuaded ourselves, with the help of the salesman, to use the round Monel Anchorfast nails in place of screws for plank fastenings. The boat's bilges were too hard for them to hold, however, and the nails eventually had to be backed up by screws.

At about this time Dr. Harry Forbes paid me a visit to explain that his children had all grown up and left home, and that *Lauan* was becoming rather too big for his needs. My new boat, on the other hand—with only 380 square feet of sail to handle, with an adequate two-berth cabin and a comfortable cockpit—appealed to him as being about right, so he bought her and named her *Koala*.

Dr. Forbes found that *Koala* sailed well and easily and was a handy size for him, but that if she had a cup of water in her shallow, flat bottom, it sloshed over all his cruising cushions and gear. After the war, he asked us to work out a new boat for him that would retain *Koala*'s rig and accommodations but have a conventional hull, which would allow some depth beneath the cabin sole. For this design I called again on Ray Hunt, who now had his own independent design office in Boston. Ray drew up a beautiful small, shoal draft version of a

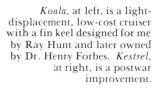

Koala, at left, is a light-displacement, low-cost cruiser with a fin keel designed for me by Ray Hunt and later owned by Dr. Henry Forbes. *Kestrel*, at right, is a postwar improvement.

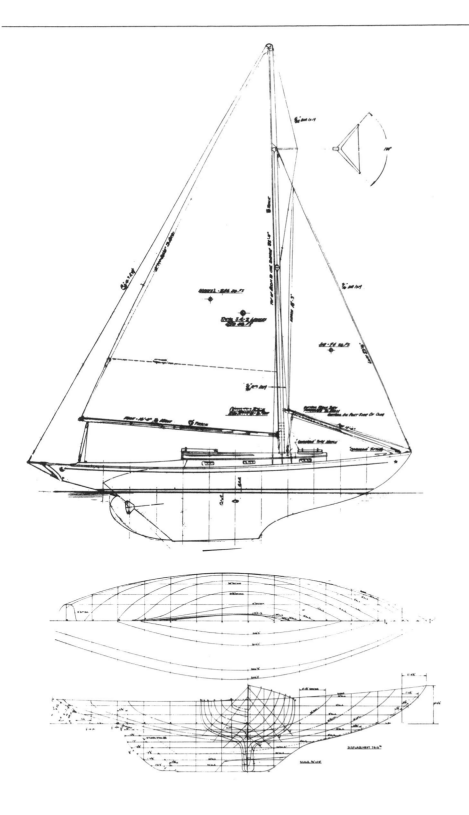

Kestrel's lines are by Ray Hunt whereas her other drawings were prepared by H. Miller Nichols, then of Concordia.

Concordia Yawl. Miller Nichols was doing Concordia's drafting work at the time, and he completed a sail, arrangement, and construction plan. Bud McIntosh built the boat and otherwise helped us with the construction detail for a special raised deck amidships, to take the place of a conventional cabin house. This feature was necessary to allow for good deck space and still maintain adequate sitting headroom below.

Kestrel, as Dr. Forbes named her, was to my mind one of the best little boats Concordia ever produced. She seemed bigger than her dimensions indicated; she was very handy to sail, but still deliberate and solid feeling in her motion, very different from *Koala*. In spite of her modest draft she performed exceptionally well on the wind and in the choppy waters of Buzzards Bay. The raised deck, which extended forward of the mast, not only made the cabin seem large, but also made it easy for one to get forward and work around the mast, tend halyards, or furl sails. The fact that the house sides sloped inboard as they came up prevented any boxy appearance or interference with the helmsman's view. I realize that many folks would feel restricted by the lack of standing headroom below; but for a 21-foot 6-inch waterline boat, *Kestrel* always appealed to me as "finest kind" for day sailing or overnight cruising. When she had served her time with Dr. Forbes, she was taken over by younger Forbes cousins, and for many more years (painted blue) remained in Hadley Harbor, snugly moored off the west end of Nonamesset Island.

Kestrel was built by Bud McIntosh and proved to be an outstanding boat—one of the best small boats that Concordia ever had a hand in creating.

271

Part IV:

THE CALM BEFORE THE STORM

South Wharf in 1942 as it looked when Concordia bought it from Colonel Green's estate.

14
Prospector

One episode in Concordia's early history unfolded over a period of years and was to influence very deeply the shape of my own life in all the years to follow.

I have mentioned that Ray Hunt and I in 1936 set up our own business at 50 State Street, Boston. This location was in the financial district, and the headquarters of the State Street Trust Company was just across the street. More important to me, Hutchins & Parkinson and A. L. Albee, both specialists in Canadian gold mine stocks, were close by. A Mr. Davis came out of the blue to see me one day and allowed as how he would find me a gold mine if I would invest $250. I did, and things moved pretty fast after that. I received some beautiful-looking certificates indicating that I had thousands of shares of vendors stock in Pan Canadian gold mines. I was a major stockholder and accepted an official position in the company and an invitation to visit the property in question. It was not clear to me what it was all about, but I took a night train to Montreal and changed there to take a train going west toward Winnipeg. I got off at the town of Amos, which is in the western part of Quebec Province some 150 miles south of James Bay.

I was surprised that there were no roads to Amos. There were some that fanned out from there a few miles, but train was the only way to get there from outside. Mr. Davis met me, and we drove south for a spell and then switched over to canoe, which in an hour or so brought us to a small camp where several

This photo shows *Prospector* alongside Dooley's covered shed up Ft. Lauderdale's New River in late 1940. She was a special boat and a good one. Although conceived in 1936, four years passed before her owner, Jack Harper, got his boat. The events that surround *Prospector* make a tale worth telling.

275

prospectors were staying. They had a cook but he was not feeling very well, because the day before, bothered by a toothache, he had gone into town and had all his teeth pulled.

As I remember things, I spent the next few weeks walking with Mr. Davis over some pretty barren land, in company with many flies. At intervals we drove stakes and attached aluminum tags to them. In general, I learned that the government owned the land, sold the prospector a license to stake out certain claims, and gave him a right to explore their possibilities. To keep a claim the prospector or his company had to do a certain amount of prospecting or development work each year.

I found the daytime walking and staking pretty heavy duty and the evening drinking likewise. Every few days we went back into town and stayed at the hotel, which belonged to the mayor, who was French. This hotel was a social center, and here I became acquainted with a young American from Philadelphia, Jack Harper. Jack was an engineer and prospector, but he always ended up talking boats with me. Before leaving Amos I had gotten fairly well into the ideas for a boat that Jack could sail to Central America and live aboard while he did further prospecting in that area.

After my return to Boston my gold-mining ventures had their ups and downs. Pan Canadian looked pretty promising; free shares sold at figures that made my holdings look very good; but the law would not allow me to sell if I wanted to. I bought 10,000 shares of Little Long Lac for $0.0125 per share. Then I told my father that I was making another trip to Nassau (I had made similar previous vacation visits with the Spencer Bordens), but received in return a bit of parental advice followed by a command to stay home and tend to business. This I did. Little Long Lac jumped to over $1.00. Unfortunately, I was at home and so able to sell it, whereat the stock went considerably higher. I bought 10,000 shares of something else, the name of which I am glad to forget because it went from $1.00 to about $0.01.

And so my gold ventures up to this time were educational and exciting but not profitable, and my time and energies went back full-time into the boat business. One of the projects that developed involved me again with my Amos friend, Jack Harper. Distance now prevented us from spending the evenings together talking and eating live oysters out of a barrel of corn meal and sipping rum; but we got into a large volume of correspondence, which lasted over a period of several years. I have recently reviewed these letters, and I hope they will give you a fair idea of what a would-be yacht broker's life was like in the years just before World War II. They also reveal the birth pangs of a special boat.

To simplify the writing I am marking Jack's letters with a *J* and my letters with a *W*. The date of each letter is also noted.

J.—Dec. 30 '36

I am taking up the search for a boat again and hope you will be able to help me....If we are unable to locate something in this country, the thought came to mind that a used boat may be found in Sweden or England....Last year I had a letter from Reimers and he had a couple of very attractive Colin Archer ketches to offer around $4000. (Shipping cost about $315.)

W.—Jan. 4 '37

After buying *Escape* I became enthusiastic about bringing more boats over from abroad, and I wrote to David Robertson, previous owner of *Escape*, for information. He told me that he had spent two years of serious effort looking for a boat like *Escape*, and that she was the only one of her type that seemed like a good buy. He said that if you were fortunate enough to strike a nice design, the chances are that this boat would not be in too good condition. He suggested building, and I followed this idea down. In the end I came to the conclusion that a good Colin Archer design could be built in Norway of good quality and at less cost than over here. However, this could involve considerable extra planning and work, and that with a duty of 30% on boats built after 1929, the project would not be practical.

W.—Jan. 7 '37

I now believe it would be possible to build a boat some 45' O.A. with a long keel, short rig, about half inside ballast, a good sturdy job but nothing fancy for around $8,000. The engine would be additional, although I think a very good installation could be made for around $700, if a gasoline engine were used.

J.—Jan. 9 '37

Five thousand is about all that I can see my way clear to spend at present but with the number of things I am interested in up here, this may easily change overnight and $12,000 would not be difficult. I have written several brokers for listings and will write others.

W.—Jan. 13 '37

If you get any other listings that seem interesting to you just let me know and Major Smyth and I can look them up....In about six weeks' time I'm going to send you some fairly complete sketches as to what my idea of a proper boat for you would be, and I believe that such a boat can be built to advantage within your price range.

W.—Jan. 23 '37

In taking up these [designer deleted] jib headed yawls and ketches—they are built at a price and are a combination of a rough job and a yacht, not really being either. They are inclined to be on the light side, although for knocking around the shore in the summer they are very good. The design would not be ideal for your purposes....Of all the listings *Old Glory* interests me most. Mr. George Bonnell who owned her for many years is a real sailorman as well as a nice gentleman and unless the boat was good he would not have kept her as long as he has. She might be made into something that would be very useful to you, but I should think that to do so might cost several thousand dollars....

W.—Feb. 1 '37

I have at last got out a very simple sketch of a boat that embodies most of the essentials for your vacation. (Sketch and Comments enclosed.)

J.—Feb. 5 '37

I am getting quite interested in the little sketch you sent me and the more I study it the more I like the boat in general.

W.—Feb. 9 '37

Before answering the various questions you bring up I would like to make one general comment. I know from personal experience that it is far more fun and more educational to build your own boat than to buy a second hand one, and although I'm fully aware that it generally costs more in the end, I doubt if the difference would be very serious in this particular case. I am not absolutely sure that we can build the boat you want within your price limit, but I think it will do no harm to follow the idea of building to a conclusion, to get bids and so forth, and then either plan to build next summer, or dismiss the idea and work on second hand boats.

W.—Feb. 15 '37

We now have sufficient bids for building your ketch to come to some conclusions. I would not be able to properly supervise or guarantee the job we might get, either way Down East, or in Florida, where prices are definitely the lowest. Gamage in Maine gave us a price of $6,500 without sails and engine. Post's yard in Mystic, which has built a great many small fishermen and built them well, has given us a price of approximately $8,000 without sails and engine. Reid here in Boston about the same. Peirce and Kilburn in Fairhaven have not given me a definite figure but I think they could do the whole job with engine and sails for $9,000....Unquestionably we are getting in this design more accommodation and ability to go places, at less cost, than in other types of hull.

J.—March 17 '37

The prospects of building at present don't look so very bright. As you know, I have set aside only about $6,500. It would be foolish to spend most of the ready cash on a boat and then have nothing left to run it on.

J.—April 6 '37

The sketch of the boat which I think I would call "Prospector" for want of a better name, which was enclosed, is to my mind getting very close to perfect.

J.—April 13 '37

I'd like very much to get your thoughts on the economic situation both in the States and abroad, and what they think in your part of the world on the probable future price of gold. There have been repeated rumors of Roosevelt lowering the price of gold but he apparently denied this. It certainly has had a decided effect on the market here.

W.—April 21 '37

Palmer Scott has rented at low cost the Fairhaven boat building shop belonging to Mr. Bill Hand and has built three boats there recently. He is anxious to get a good job for the latter part of this summer. I believe his work would be very satisfactory and he has agreed to build a boat according to the general specifications for $6,200. This to include 7,000 lbs. iron on the keel, 10,000 lbs. inside iron ballast. White oak backbone, frames, etc., 1½'' mahogany planking, rift sawn fir decks, galvanized nail fastenings, etc. The figure includes sails, engine, and equipment as written into the specifications. This assumes that you are willing to put up with simple accommodations and plain finish.

W.—April 29 '37

...I am extremely pleased that you have decided to build this *Prospector*....

W.—May 6 '37

This brings the contract prices including sails, engine, mattresses, in fact the complete boat with the exception of the dinghy, personal gear, navigation equipment and topsail to $6,500. But we are going to make some savings on second hand spars, chainplates, windlass, etc., that will offset this raise.

J.—May 12 '37

[Much discussion of details]....If the mining market does not improve we will probably sell the boat and spend the winter cutting logs in the Abitibi instead of sailing in the West Indies.

W.—May 14 '37

Please find enclosed contract....Total Builders' Risk Insurance approximately $75.

Letter from Palmer Scott—May 26 '37

This is to acknowledge receipt of check for $500 as a binder on 40' ketch for Harper. This will cover the following list of materials:

600 ft Dry oak for floors	@ 9¢ per ft	$ 54.00		
800 Butt stock for frames	@ 7¢ per ft	56.00		
500 ft Pine for molds	@ 5¢ per ft	25.00		
1000 ft Oak for keel, deadwood, and stem		80.00		
100 lbs Galv iron rod for keel bolts	@ 9¢ per lb	9.00		
7000 lbs Keel casting	@ 4¢ per lb	280.00	=	$504.00

J.—July 31 '37

Under separate cover I am sending a map of the Malartic area. You will note the location of National Malartic in which I am a shareholder, and in which you will be shortly.

W.—Aug. 4 '37

I'm glad the blueprint of the lines arrived in good order. Undoubtedly we will all have doubts about different matters as the boat progresses. However, we have all put a good deal of thought into this boat, and although I don't expect she is going to be much of a speed demon, I can't see how she can fail to be reasonably satisfactory at least as to design.

J.—Aug. 28 '37

I note that Scott is coming along slowly with the construction which is quite satisfactory and if the boat is finished by early spring I will be satisfied, as I do not see any possibility of using her until that time....

W.—Sept. 30 '37

Actually the boat has been entirely framed. There are three strakes of planking starting at the rail going down, and the garboard and one strake coming up. The cabin houses have been built as well as most of the hatches. In regard to the sails we had a price of $180 for the four lowers to be made out of commercial duck which costs about 30¢ a yard. I have taken the liberty to order for you some Wamsutta yacht duck seconds, which ordinarily would cost about 70¢ a yard but due to defects can be acquired for 35¢. This means your sails may cost about $200 instead of $180 but the difference I know will be tremendous....So far the work looks good; although it is not first class yacht finish it is good sound construction.

J.—Oct. 22 '37

Of late I have given the painting of the boat some thought and believe that the proper selection of colors both inside and out will make or break the boat as far as appearances go. Flat white hull and the proper use of some trim should make an exceptionally smart job.

W.—Oct. 27 '37

Regarding paint I feel in general that it is poor to mix too many artistic colors inside a boat, in that the result is often sickish, although the colors themselves may be well chosen. My recommendation would be to use flat white throughout with either brown, black, or gray trim wherever dirty hands or kicking feet might come in contact with the paint. Any elaborate color scheme would be considerably more expensive due to the fussiness of preparing the paint and getting it on in the right place.

J.—Nov. 1 '37

I gather Scott is going right ahead with the completion of the boat including rigging, etc., and will deliver same this fall. What will we do with the boat after she is delivered?

J.—Nov. 6 '37

Yours of the 28th received also the circular on Bahama Harbours, which to say the least is a hell of a thing to send a chap in the north country, especially in my predicament, and at this time of year.

W.—Dec. 8 '37

I shall save next Saturday, Dec. 11, for your visit.

J.—Dec. 29 '37

I think you have made a lovely job of *Prospector*. [She] is away beyond my fondest expectations. If this boat does not cause a great deal of favorable comment among the boating fraternity, there must be something drastically wrong with the fraternity. She appears to have a great deal of room for her size, and her deck room is more like that which will be found on an 80 foot boat....There are several little details....

W.—Jan. 4 '38

I am very glad that you were pleased with the *Prospector* because it is hard to obtain the results that we all want when we have to keep cost in mind at every turn....If my memory is right the cabin table has already been finished in paint, as any other finish outside of a coat of linseed oil was going to cost extra. This is one point that Scott has adhered to and quite justly so. It is a very different matter finishing a piece of wood that is going to be left bright than one that is going to be painted, and he lost a lot of money on a boat built just previously to yours due to the fact that he thought one type of finish could be done at more or less the same cost as the other.

W.—Telegram, Jan. 11 '38*

Scott Boat Yard including *Prospector* is a total loss through fire last night. Stop. *Prospector* was fully covered by insurance.

J.—Jan. 11 '38

We seem to be having one hell of a job to get a boat, but hope we will be able to work out something.

J.—Jan. 14 '38

For the time being I think you had best keep the insurance money until we decide what we are going to do....I don't think that I shall ever be satisfied until we build another *Prospector*.

And so at the end of some 14 months Harper had some fairly well-organized ideas for the boat he wanted, he had the plans for same, and he had his money—but he still had no boat.

As for me, I had another year's experience in the boat business and a few shares of exciting gold mine stocks of questionable value.

ii

For Jack Harper, the days between January 1938 and May 1939 were ones of indecision as far as boats were concerned. We considered *Mobjack*, a beautiful, fairly shoal draft 45-foot Francis Herreshoff ketch; but at $8,500 she was too expensive. The 35-foot Alden ketch *Maya* built by Casey Boat Company in 1929 was interesting but too small. We advised Scott we were not going to rebuild in 1938, and by March Jack's letters were coming from Fort Lauderdale, Florida, rather than from Amos, Quebec. By August he had bought property there, and

---

*Mrs. Palmer Scott tells me that in the middle of the night of January 10, 1938, she and her husband were rudely awakened by a telephone call from a stranger advising them that the Scott boatbuilding shop in Fairhaven was in flames. Hurriedly slipping on some clothes, they raced from their Padanaram home to the Fairhaven bridge—in the center of which they stopped to witness the tragic sight. The shed was gone, but *Prospector* was a veritable Fourth of July display, each of her frames a towering torch of flame. All that Palmer could say was an anguished "there goes everything I own."

By morning all Palmer's tools and equipment were gone. Of the proud new boat completely ready for launching nothing remained but an iron keel and a few little puddles of molten bronze. No cause for the fire was ever determined.

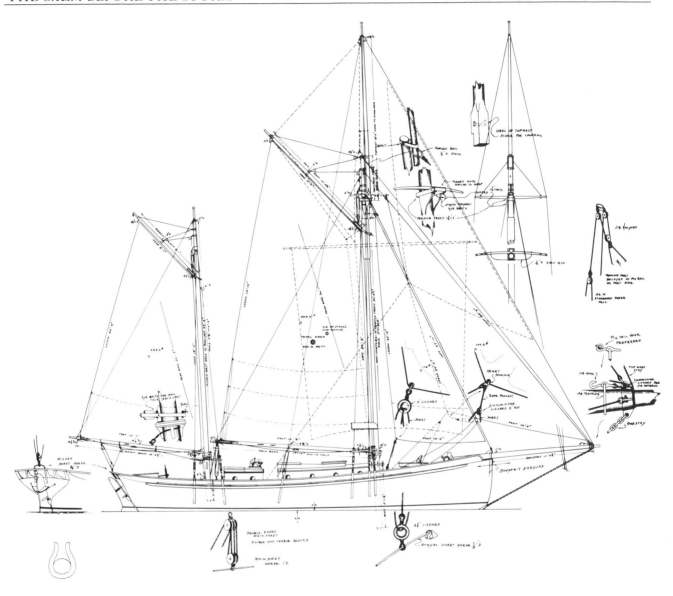

As originally designed, *Prospector*'s mizzen was gaff-rigged and she had no doghouse. Both features were altered as thinking progressed and the boat finally materialized.

by January 1939 he had built a house and a shop on the banks of the New River, and plans were under way for producing handmade furniture and other odds and ends.

All the while letters passed back and forth about small used and new boats. There seemed to be no suitable small boatbuilding yards on the Florida East Coast—or many interesting work boats—so most of the ideas were coming down from Boston. If I had known that the decision to build or not to build *Prospector* was to have an everlasting and momentous effect on my life, I would have been in a state of complete panic about the daily changes in plans. However, I did not know, and just kept up the stream of correspondence. On May 6, 1939, Jack had some good mining news and made the decision to rebuild *Prospector* himself at his own shop. Once more I will let our correspondence tell the story.

J.—June 17 '39

There is a chance that I might also build my boat at Grand Cayman Island, if I think it is going to be too difficult to get the right materials here. The labor down there is quite cheap and they have good wood for frames, etc. I think their labor costs run about $2.00 per day. They figure about $100 per ton for commercial boats and $125 for fancy boats without engine, etc. I think it would be necessary to take down quite a lot of your own equipment....I also understand that the duty on boats from the British Empire is now only 15%.

J.—June 18 '39

...What do you think the best paint to put on the bottom? We have putty bugs or gribble down here in most of these rivers and I don't know anything that will keep them off your boat. They are not as bad as teredos; they bore straight in the plank. They certainly raise hell with most of the boats down here....Do you know of a good re-built Lathrop or other heavy duty engine? Would rather have a used Lathrop than a new Gray. I would like a heavy engine that will swing a large wheel.

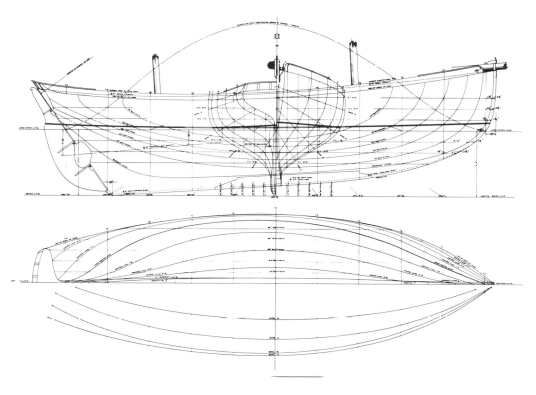

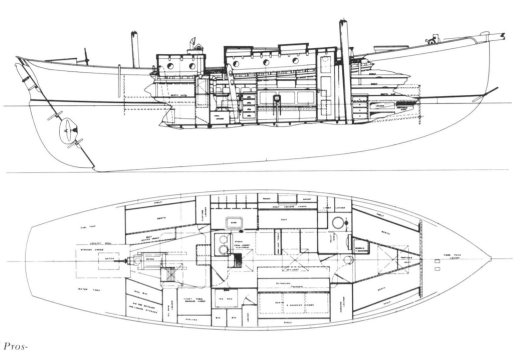

Bill Harris drew all of *Prospector*'s plans with the same care and attention to detail that he put into all his work.

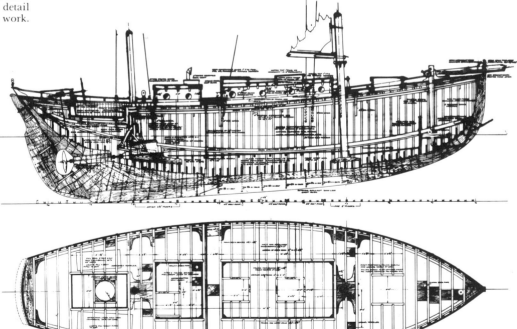

J.—August 16 '39 (from Jakoba, Oriente Province, Cuba)

...You probably wonder what has happened to me as I seldom give you this long a rest without bothering you with letters. I think I told you I was coming down here to look at some gold properties for some friends. Well here I am in rural Cuba...I rather think that some very interesting things can be developed here with a little work. We may take a "crack" in a small way at one of two properties we are examining....I wish I had some of the timber back in Florida that you see used here in gates, fence posts, and sheds. I saw a storage shed the other day made out of the most beautiful mahogany you have ever seen. The rough table I am writing on is made out of a wood that would make the most wonderful frames....I expect to be back in Florida in a couple of weeks.

J.—Sept. 15 '39

I think building in the islands would be out of the question although Cuba might be a possibility as they build some nice boats there, beautiful woods and workmanship but the designs are not so good....

J.—Dec. 10 '39

As yet I have not sold the house, but I think I will be able to get enough money out of Canada after January 15 to start work on *Prospector*....

At this point there were many letters concerning real modifications in *Prospector*'s design and arrangement. We considered lighter displacement, less draft, jib-headed rig, modern gas engine, and other ideas. However, the current purpose for the boat was to live on board all year around and use her as a base for gold prospecting in Central America; so we pretty much came back to the original boat with only modest changes.

J.—Dec. 21 '39

Everyone says she has so much character and it is very seldom today that one sees anything other than just another boat....I still think the rig could be improved by using a jib-headed mizzen. As to the engine I rather agree with you and have decided to use a Gray 4-56 with as large a wheel, 2 blade, as possible....I think the cabin trunks could be a bit wider....If we can't get a better price bid than $5,000 for the hull I will get a big band saw and a few heavy tools and start the boat at our little shop. We have most of the light tools....I think I may have located enough madera for stem, backbone, floors, etc.

W.—Jan. 20 '40

I would like to see the mainmast a little further aft. This would keep the weight more where it belongs. The stays would come down at the widest part of the boat where they get the best leverage. It would allow for a more efficient staysail of proper proportions of width to height. I would also like to see the mizzen further aft as this would allow a better shaped mainsail with a little more area....These slight changes would divide the sail up in a way very similar to that on all those Brixham trawlers and their proportions were evolved from actual practice....One more thing, Scott still has your old iron keel. He says it is in good shape and that he will sell it to you for $100.

J.—Feb. 5 '40

I have not exhausted the possibilities of getting the wood from Cuba including Majagua (pronounced Mahagua) for steam-bent frames.... I realize I would be a fool to sell my "National" stock @ .15 but I'm anxious to get started on the boat and get her in the water before the hot weather starts.

W.—Feb. 7 '40

Enclosed is a list of gear, most of which came off old *Escape*. If you will check the items which you want, I don't doubt but what Father will be willing to take payment in National Malartic stock in accordance with previous correspondence.

Gaff—new hollow with bands for blocks and sheave for topsail	$10.00
Gaff saddle complete	10.00
Trysail Boom—2 bands & jaws to fit saddle Blocks mostly 6" ash	5.00
Main Sheet blocks	
1 Triple with strop for boom	5.00
1 Double with swivel for traveller	4.00
2 Singles for quarter blocks @ $3.	6.00
1 Windlass	10.00
1 Old Mainsail	20.00
1 New Flax trysail	40.00
2 Bronze rail chocks	4.00
1 Outer fitting for bowsprit	2.00
Ring & hook for sliding jib	2.00
1 Jib sheet pennant with sister hook & bullet blocks	2.00

J.—Feb. 29 '40

Do you know where we can get some Swedish Iron hatch nails for planking, ceiling, and decking, or some *good* quality square boat nails that are really galvanized? Do the Atlas Tack people in Fairhaven, Mass., make those nails?...Have most of the material lined up for the boat.

W.—Feb. 29 '40

...I can send you all the Oxan Oil you will need for $3.00 per gal. It is hard stuff to get looking like yacht varnish but I think it is great and very durable. I would use it on deck, and rails, and rubbing strake.... I have had very good experience with Coperoyd bottom paint on our own boat. I recommend for you, however, that you use that black "Everjet" tar paint covered by any good copper paint that can most easily be bought.... 3" x 3" frames are difficult ones to bend. I advise not going over 2½" x 2½". I believe these are amply heavy.

J.—March 21 '40

The shed is finished. Have ordered the iron-wood keel from Cuba.... As it may take three months to get the spars from the west coast we would like the sail plan or at least the spar list as soon as possible.

W.—March 25 '40

Your keel went out today by truck and should arrive inside forty-eight hours. The

The Howlands' old cutter *Escape* was the design base for much of *Prospector*. And gear salvaged from *Escape* became part of the new boat's outfit.

shipping cost to be $75 and you should pay the truckman. Mr. Scott arranged that without my knowing it but it sounds all right to me.

J.—April 2 '40

I note that spruce is specified for the gaff, topmast and yard but these will have to be fir (selected) as it is too difficult to get good spruce down here at anything near a fair price.... I think we can get the spar fittings made up down here. We can do most of it ourselves and there is a blacksmith who does good work and who can make what we can't. Galvanizing we can get done for 7½¢ per lb. for large pieces and 10¢ for small pieces.

W.—April 11 '40

Yesterday by express collect I sent out one wooden crate full of rigging gear off the old *Escape*.

J.—May 8 '40

Have ordered live oak stock for the frames but it has not as yet arrived. The keel is a lovely stick 10'' x 12'' of Acana, a deep red Cuban hardwood, which weighs about 2,250 lbs. The balance of the backbone is Florida mahogany, called madera down here, which is the finest mahogany known and I guess the hardest. It is harder than oak and a little heavier. It has been in the log since the 1926 Hurricane so it is fairly well seasoned. All beams, mast steps, cabin beams, carlins, knees, and floors will be of the same mahogany. The planking will be yellow pine and the deck, teak. There was a chap up yesterday who said you only see a boat built like this, and out of such material, once in a lifetime....

J.—May 20 '40

Due to the service this boat is to be put, we have decided to use 2½'' x 2½'' finished live oak frames, instead of 2'' x 2.''

J.—June 4 '40

We had a bit of trouble getting 2½'' x 2½'' frame stock that would take the bends so we have had to use 1½'' x 3'' double bent making 3'' x 3'' from Station 3 aft to Station 7, and 1¼'' x 3'' double bent making 3'' x 2½'' forward and aft of Station 3 and 7. We are treating the frames with Selcure before steaming and then treating them several times after they are bent. The nails are going to be long enough to go through into the second frame and there will be about four 5/16'' bolts holding the second frame to the first.

J.—June 6 '40

The backbone is all finished and we have got about one-quarter of the frames bent, about two-thirds of the floors ready to fasten in place and the rabbet all cut and finished, also the sockets all cut for the frames.

W.—June 6 '40

I have now got costs for the various sails itemized as follows:

Mainsail	$220.00	
Forestaysail	75.00	
Mizzen	52.00	4 lowers
Jib (wire luff)	80.00	

| Jib topsail | 63.00 |
| Gaff topsail | 57.00 |

You will remember that the suite that was built for you before we figured at $342.00 for the four lowers and that this suite figures $427. Two things account for this: 1. that although we got Wamsutta duck seconds [before, these sails will be of] better material. 2. I spoke to [Ralph] Silsby about special reinforcement in the clew of the mainsail which I believe very advisable after our experience with the old *Escape*'s loose-footed mainsail. I know nobody can get good sail duck any cheaper than we have supplied it to Silsby, and I don't think that anybody could build the sails properly in any less time than he has figured.

J.—June 8 '40

Received your letter on the sails but I'm afraid that the price is out of the question....We have a quotation from the sail maker in Miami as follows made of the best Army duck. Four lowers $275.00, flying jib $55.00, topsail $30.00 all sails 10 oz.

J.—June 11 '40

We have to pay about 35¢ per lb for manganese bronze casting and this is going to run the price of the rudder yoke up pretty high. I am wondering if a mild steel forging well galvanized would not be cheaper.

J.—June 20 '40

By Friday we should start planking and after that things should go faster. We also have made all the cleats of dogwood and scraped the blocks and oiled them.

W.—Aug. 16 '40 (to Foreign Exchange Control Board, Ottawa, Canada)

Gentlemen: From the Canadian Bank of Amos, I am advised to write you to obtain a permit to have 3,900 shares of Diproc Mines Ltd., which are registered in my name sent to me here in Boston. The stock was given to me in payment for services rendered to John Harper formerly of Amos. The work rendered was the design of a boat and covered a period from 1936 through 1939.

J.—Oct. 26 '40

It has been such a long time since I last heard from you that I have been wondering if there is anything wrong.... *Prospector* is in the water having been launched September 25, and I have been living on her since October 1 although she is not yet finished inside. The boat has leaked about eight buckets. We pumped her for the first time yesterday. We have about two more months before everything will be completed and then we can try her out. Why don't you come down and stay with me? I certainly would like to have you here when we tune her up. The boat is now at Dooley's Basin, Fort Lauderdale.

J.—Nov. 15 '40

Was terribly sorry to hear of your mother's death and I would like to take this opportunity of extending my sympathies.... Glad to hear that there might be a chance of your getting here around Christmas time.... You certainly would be a great help in ironing out some of the rigging details....

W.—Nov. 25 '40

I am hoping very much to get away for a week or ten days, possibly including Christmas and up to New Years. I don't know if my being down there would be inconvenient to you over Christmas but I have no family plans up here and it would be a very good time as far as my business is concerned.

J.—Dec. 8 '40

...Am working like hell to try to have things looking fairly well when you get here and think I can get most things finished....

W.—Dec. 10 '40

I am planning to take a super deluxe day coach special called the Silver Meteor from New York on the afternoon of Dec. 16, and am told I will arrive in Fort Lauderdale on the 17th at 3:42 P.M.....

This concludes the building correspondence with Jack, and I will therefore have to give my memory a chance to piece together the end of *Prospector*'s story.

When I stepped off the Silver Meteor in Fort Lauderdale, I was met by Jack and driven to Dooley's boatyard some four or five miles up the New River. My first sight of this yard convinced me that it would be the pattern for my own boatyard, when and if my dream of owning one should ever come true. There was deep quiet water along the river front, with lift dock at one end and high covered storage at the other. On the shoreward boundary were clean high storage buildings. In between was a level mowed lawn, with transfer tracks to move the boats quietly and safely in any direction. What a fine place in which to varnish or paint. No dust. An area largely protected from wind. No muddy or greasy feet to track dirt on deck. An ideal atmosphere for a good workman to do his best. Although I never achieved the Dooley ideal at our Concordia yard in the years to come, I worked at it.

Prospector herself was a thrilling sight for me, as in her new coat of paint she floated happily and proudly in one of the covered slips. When I stepped aboard with my duffel bag, I was greeted by one of the workers in paint-stained jeans and jersey. There were several others there too, but this particular one was a girl. As well as being odd-job specialist, she apparently was errand girl and secretary. Many of Jack's letters that I had been reading during the past few months had, I learned, been typed by this young lady. Jack Collison was also working aboard. He had among other jobs been designing and making bamboo furniture to sell, before he joined the *Prospector* project. He and his wife, Marie, lived aboard their little boat, which was moored up the river a short way. Marie was always generously ready to feed any hungry visitor that passed their way. In Jack's crew, there were no experienced boatbuilders as such, just a small community of free-lancers with ability and a desire to build a boat.

The daily routine for the next several weeks was wonderfully pleasant for me. Jack and I lived aboard and cooked our bacon and eggs in the uncompleted galley. This gave us some first-hand experience about how to arrange the final galley details. Lunch was a sociable affair, on deck in the shade. Everyone brought his own sandwiches, including visitors, regular and occasional. Everyone except myself went to the little nearby canteen to get a beverage—orange juice, milk, coffee, or Coke. Miraculously, my milk always appeared by itself via the errand girl. After working hours, the crew went their several ways. At the end of the row of storage sheds there was a small building simply equipped with shower and other facilities. A few chips of scrap wood under the boiler supplied a bit of hot water when wanted. After a constructive day's work on a boat with pleasant companions, some good food and a nice shower, and then a quiet stroll around a lawn-covered boatyard—what more could a reasonable man want? This is the way a yacht broker's life should be, but seldom is.

By this time the small spars were on hand, having been shipped from the West Coast in their finished form. They had only to be varnished. What was to be the mast arrived while I was there, in the form of a square balk of fir. It had been sent by water freight as part of another shipment of lumber from the state of Washington. Although it was nearly 10 inches square there was no sign of the center of the tree from which it came, so the tree must have been a fairly large one. I have heard it said that a good man with an axe can go out in the woods and shortly come back with a plank, but I was still impressed to see how quickly Jack with an axe and adze turned that balk into a round and tapered spar.

After work we often went down into town for supper, and usually patronized a special little restaurant over on the ocean beach at the foot of Las Olas Boulevard. We had the best of service here, because *Prospector*'s errand girl waited on tables in the evenings.

In 1940 Fort Lauderdale was just a small, quiet town. But then as now the Inland Waterway ran more or less north and south by its eastern edge. The narrow barrier beach with very little building on it was on the outside and accessible by a couple of bridges. There were several bridges across New River; and a short distance up from the Waterway, between two of the bridges, was an area known as the City Docks. Here a visiting yacht or a local boat could tie up along the bulkhead that formed the banks. It was our pleasant evening custom to park the car in this area and take a bit of a walk along the bordering paths. It was quiet and cool, and there was always a faint pleasant smell of hard pine smoke in the air. Sometimes we crossed over one of the drawbridges and went a block or two downtown to do a bit of shopping. At other times we chatted with some of the boat owners. More than once we went aboard the 43-foot Alden schooner *Blue Moon* and spent a happy hour with the skipper and his wife, Charlie and Ing Mayo. I learned that they were one of the half dozen or so charter boats that came down from the North each fall to take out parties who wished to cruise in the Bahamas. Their crew was a friendly black spaniel whose most intriguing duty was to keep the ashtrays clean by licking them out with his tongue. Tied up to the bulkhead a few steps away was the ketch *Spray*, a replica of Slocum's boat. Aboard her were her owners Pete and Toni Culler. I learned that they, too, had since 1938 been chartering winters in Florida and the Bahamas, and then in the spring went back to Cape Cod for the summer season. Pete, like Jack, had built his own boat, but in Oxford, Maryland, in 1929. And so there was plenty to talk about and questions to ask.

A Sunday excursion by small boat down the New River left me with the impression of a quiet little stream with green banks and a few scattered groups of small houses. As we got into the Waterway and turned north we tied up for a spell at an old broken-down dock on the east side. This was an isolated and deserted-looking area, which I was told was the old Coast Guard dock. It looked very little then like the big Bahia Mar marina, which it has now become. Turning back from the Coast Guard dock and going south on the Waterway for a bit, we passed the ocean inlet on our port hand and proceeded into an area of wider water. In my wildest dreams I could never believe that this quiet backwater was going to become Port Everglades, a major harbor for ocean going ships.

Just before New Year's Day we got off for the long-awaited trial run. Our doubts and hopes and questions would be, at least partially, answered this day. Going down the sometimes narrow and twisting New River we wondered what that long keel would be like in an emergency maneuver. Actually *Prospector* minded her helm much quicker than I expected, quicker than the old *Escape* would have. With her 56 h.p. Gray, she moved along so well and with so little disturbance that one of the guests suggested that if she wouldn't sail we could turn her into a motorsailer. As we went out into the chop of the Gulf Stream our little engine did not push us quite as fast, but we plugged on in surprising fashion. We surely would have gone farther to windward by the end of the day than many a fast little motorboat which would surely have been overpowered by the conditions.

As the sails went up one by one, mizzen first, then main, then jib set flying and hauled out on the ring, and last the fore-staysail, we realized for certain that *Prospector* was a very easily driven boat, and that no great press of canvas would be needed. This did away with any doubts we had about having too snug a rig. Every minute I had the thought that, as with all new boats, something must go wrong, some rigging must be altered to avoid chafe and such like. But no, everything seemed to go well. A loose-footed main on a marconi rig may not be the best, but on the gaff rigs of *Prospector* and *Escape* it seemed to set well. And

After she was built by her owner and launched late in 1940, I traveled to Ft. Lauderdale to help in the rigging of *Prospector.* Jack Harper and his crew had done a fine job, as these photos indicate, and I found that being involved in the final stages proved most rewarding.

so after a good sail we proceeded back up the river to Dooley's and I thought to myself as we slipped along, "Bill Harris, you drew a great plan," and "Jack Harper, you knew what you wanted and worked hard and well for it." *Prospector* was a special boat and a good one.

Much as I hated to leave, it was now time for me to go back home. The

EPILOGUE

No doubt this would be a good place to end the yarn, but the proof of the pudding is in the eating, and I think it is only fair to the little ship *Prospector* to bring her unfinished career up to date.

In January, Jack made a cruise to Nassau and wrote to me about it:

We really had a wonderful trip. Both crossings of the Stream were made after the wind had been from the North or Northeast for several days and I don't have to tell you what that means. Everyone was surprised at how well the boat behaved. We did 6½ knots on the trip over and 6 on the trip back which was not nearly so rough but the seas were disturbed. I think that speed quite good considering the very rough water. Crossing the banks she did 7½ and 8 knots as we checked her log every hour and we had a nice breeze. In all the rough water there was no time that you could not cook a meal if necessary and the decks hardly were ever wet. *Prospector* really is a remarkable boat, at least that is what everyone who has sailed her has told me. Also she sails beautifully on the wind. The other day we sailed her six miles to windward and made our mark without ever touching the wheel and she was buttoned down as close as she would go with a strong breeze and the rub rail just awash, coming back across the Banks. We sailed her about half a day to windward and even the native we had with us was impressed by the way she went. We ran her under power alone from Northwest light to Nassau and averaged 7½ knots @ 1400 r.p.m. which I would say is very satisfactory.

And so Jack was pleased with his boat and that made me happy.

As many people will remember, world conditions were becoming very unsettled in 1941. Jack could not get his money out of Canada and he had

reasons to move to California. Sadly, he put *Prospector* on the market. An associate of mine in the boat business, Alexander "Zan" Cochran, sold *Prospector* to Mr. Neil Rice, who sailed her out of Marblehead, Massachusetts, for several years. Then once more she was put on the market, and this time Zan bought her himself. He sailed her for over 30 years, first out of Manchester, Massachusetts, and then for the last few years out of English Harbor, Antigua. Quite by chance I saw *Prospector* there in 1970. It was early morning and I had been visiting John Barden, skipper aboard *Baruna*, and was walking through Nelson's dockyard to meet a taxi. I couldn't believe my eyes. I had no idea she would be there. She was beautiful. She looked like a brand-new boat, and she made me proud and glad to have had a small part in producing her.

Prospector has from the beginning remained in good shape. Over the years she received a new engine and some new rigging and sails. Some repairs were made to several of the hatches. Original hull, frames, planking, decks, fastenings, all were in fine shape. No electrolysis, no serious problems after 35 years. This good news is what prompted me to go into such detail about *Prospector*'s planning, her design, and her construction. I hope this chapter may be of interest to at least those happy dreamers who want to put their all into the building of a little ship. It's never easy but it can be worth it.

In the winter of 1982, while on a visit to the Percy Chubbs on Peter Island, B.V.I., I received a call from Mr. D. R. More, who told me he had just bought *Prospector* and was currently at St. Thomas. Since then I have heard again from him that *Prospector*, rigged with a square sail, was about to set sail for Spain.

errand girl, whose name was Katherine Kinnaird, drove me slowly in to the railroad station. Before boarding the northbound train I was prompted to suggest that if in six weeks she had the inclination to do so, she herself might come north, too, and we could get married. This she did, and thus my prospecting paid off as the best deal I have ever made.

15
To War

During the summer of 1940, war conditions prompted me to visit Boston's Naval Officer Procurement headquarters and there offer my services. I was interviewed by Sandy Moffat, a Navy commander whom I already knew and liked well as an influential member of the Cruising Club. He is about six feet three inches tall, which really has nothing to do with the story; but the end result of our conversation was that my knowledge of celestial navigation was too limited for special consideration, and that by regulation I was, in any case, too short in height for officer material.

Annoyed—really angry is a better description—I returned home thinking "to hell with the Navy." As events turned out, however, the commander's adverse decision was all to my advantage. It granted me time that became very precious.

During the fall of 1940 my mother's passing unraveled forever a major portion of my former cherished family life. Thereafter there was no valid purpose for the big brick Brookline house on Upland Road. Accustomed links with city living, the Boston Symphony Orchestra, the theaters, the famous old stores, and, most of all, the kind friends and relatives, suddenly became altered. National uncertainties had reduced basic property values, and our well-located and substantial family winter home on Pill Hill* was sold for a pittance, some $6,500. Familiar groupings of furniture and belongings were divided away to

*Doctors owned a great majority of the homes on our little circular Upland Road.

1942—a time of speculation and empty chairs as Katy waits out the war at home.

297

sister, brother, and myself. Father changed his pattern of life and moved for good to Padanaram, where he winterized his big summer house and modified it to make room for Grandmother Howland. All in due course, brother Louie's family came to Padanaram from Marblehead, and sister Priscilla and her family left Brookline for a new home in nearby Westport, Massachusetts.

Katherine—Katy—Kinnaird and I were married in February 1941 and forthwith decided that, come what might, we would establish our new home in old *Escape*'s uncompleted boathouse in Padanaram.

During the fall of 1941 another event with long-range consequences commenced to take shape. From boyhood days I had dreamed of owning Padanaram's old South Wharf. This great granite dock boasted a long and interesting history of salt grinding, shipbuilding, and other forms of commercial enterprise. At the time of World War I it had been acquired by my distant —very distant—and rich—very rich—cousin Edward Howland Robinson Green, son of the "Witch of Wall Street," Hetty Howland Green. By dredging, building a big machine shop, and installing a substantial marine railway, this eccentric gentleman had transformed the property into a hobby yard for his fleet of pleasure yachts and work boats. By 1938 he had been dead for some years and South Wharf and its buildings had been ravaged by the Great Hurricane. Several local interests tried unsuccessfully to acquire the property. Taking the long chance, and guided by my real estate brother, I approached the New York manager of the Green empire and miraculously came away with a deal. With no money left in my bank account, with my Fairhaven house sold, with yachtsmen suffering the wartime jitters, and with yacht yards planning toward government work, my own visionary boatyard aspirations hung precariously in mid-air.

Then came December 7, 1941. Katy and I were relaxing comfortably in front of our cheerful little fireplace discussing plans for the future when all of a sudden the radio blasted out the devastating news of the Japanese attack on Pearl Harbor.

God willing, I hope in another book to tell my own version of the Concordia Company's boatyard story, but for now let me tie a few loose ends together. Martin Jackson and my brother generously took over operations at South Wharf, repaired essential facilities, and made arrangements with storage and repair customers. Draft board pressures prompted me to leave our "first baby," as Katy called the Wharf, and I soon found myself working as a civil servant in Washington, D.C. There, in due course, my friend and benefactor John West, by now a Navy lieutenant, introduced me to the powers that be in the Washington Naval Officer Procurement headquarters. Times had changed during the past two years, needs were far more pressing, and entrance requirements were lowered. On October 12, 1942, I was duly appointed a Lieutenant (j.g.) in the

Naval Reserve. After 12 months of training in various naval schools my orders directed me to New York. There, one memorable dreary dark night and accompanied by 17,000 other bodies, I shuffled aboard the great converted ocean liner *Queen Mary*. I was 34 years old. Our present destination and the world's future were quite unknown to me, but a sober realization persisted within me, that I had seen the end of a unique and glorious era of our country's expansion, of special individuals, stately mansions, and glorious great yachts.

Credits

Kotic, a fixture in Padanaram Harbor for 40 years.

Designed by Arthur Binney and built by George Lawley & Son in 1899, *Kotic* (39′ x 25′ x 10′ x 6′) was the waterborne platform from which Dr. Prescott took so many thousand boating photographs and aboard which he charted almost every rock and passage in Buzzards Bay.

Many a Padanaram friend, young and old, experienced aboard *Kotic* day-sailing as it was done in the good old days, and had their picture taken in an atmosphere of bright varnish, well-shined brass, and turkey red cushions.

Although she was maintained in perfect condition by "Captain Charlie the Finn" and, later, Captain Freddy Welch, *Kotic* was broken up in 1943 by the Prescotts, who felt that their sailing days were over and that their beloved boat should never fall into careless hands. Much of her beautiful joiner work was converted into ingenious household furniture by the celebrated Rochester clockmaker Sherman T. Fearing.

Photographs play such an integral and important part in this book that a brief word about the principal photographers represented is surely in order.

First comes Dr. Harry Prescott. A classmate of Father's at Milton Academy, Dr. Prescott earned his medical degree from Harvard, but practiced only briefly. He married into the Swift family, an old Dartmouth clan, and became a close Padanaram neighbor of ours.

Partially hidden behind a great beard and often to be seen on his open porch target-shooting with his .22 pistol or peering silently out over Buzzards Bay through his powerful telescope, Dr. Prescott had to us children a definite air of mystery about him. Yet we soon learned that he was a kind and thoughtful person, and we treasured the photographs he gave us at Christmastime.

Dr. Prescott lived a very secluded and ordered life with his wife (whom we knew and loved as Aunt Hester). But his methodical practice of photography resulted in a succession of yearly albums that form a priceless addition to the topographical, social, and maritime history of the region. Family. Friends. Local folks. Village houses and scenes. The Prescotts' Scotty dogs. And above all local boats and boating. Each picture is carefully mounted, labeled, and dated in chronological order.

Through the kindness of Mr. and Mrs. William Swift (Mr. Swift is Dr. Prescott's nephew), I was, several years ago, permitted to study at leisure all the Prescott albums. (By error, the negatives of photographs taken after 1923 had earlier been destroyed.) This delightful look into a mostly familiar past prompted me to suggest that the albums be placed in the safe-keeping of New Bedford's Old Dartmouth Historical Society (sometimes known as the New Bedford Whaling Museum). There a recently hired young photography enthusiast and Melville admirer, Nicholas Whitman, took charge of the Henry Prescott collection.

As I write these notes four years later, Nick Whitman presides over a much expanded facility in the new library building of the Old Dartmouth Historical Society that has been specifically designed to restore, preserve, catalog, and make available an ever growing collection of photographs. It is Nick who, with the blessing of Richard Kugler, Director, and Elton Hall, Curator, of the Old Dartmouth Historical Society, has personally and most professionally processed a majority of the early images reproduced in this book.

Among the various negatives and prints that I checked through at the Old Dartmouth were many taken by New Bedford's Albert Cook Church. Although Church's greatest fame derives from his images of whaleships and fishing schooners, he also photographed several decades of local yachting activity. I am deeply grateful for the opportunity to study Church's images and pick and choose among them for this book.

"Bert," as everyone called Albert Cook Church, was an interesting and likeable character. Of average height, on the lean side, he invariably wore a small visor cap, droopy old jacket, and trousers with more wrinkles than press. He was a familiar sight, walking (always at a fast pace) back or forth over the Fairhaven Bridge, which connected his everyday New Bedford routine with his Fairhaven office. Church's office was a big garret room atop Peirce and Kilburn's main shipyard building. With its spectacular harbor view and grand display of famous Church photographs, this room inevitably became a club for old sailors in the vicinity. For rent I am told that Cliff Kilburn charged Bert 25 cents a month.

Bert had an uncanny knack of being in the right place at the right time for interesting boat action, and he knew with an artist's eye just when to catch his subject. Unquestionably a fine photographer, Bert was, however, not always a very good businessman. I remember being on *Java* one day, all polished up and sailing along with sheets correctly trimmed, when Bert, by appointment with Father, approached in the NBYC launch. He positioned himself perfectly off our leeward quarter, aimed his camera, and then announced, "I forgot my film." Some years later I met Bert by chance and asked him how he was. He promptly answered, "Just terrible." Then he paused. "At first I thought it was old age getting me," he went on after some deliberation, "but then I remembered I'd been old for a long time, so it couldn't be that."

Many of Church's negatives were lost. Others were scattered at random. One box of glass plates was found after his death, dumped and damaged in an old shed. Tragedies such as this show the value of facilities such as the Old Dartmouth Historical Society has created to save strayed or homeless photographs of our fast-receding past.

No boating book seems complete without a selection of "Photographs by Rosenfeld." Father Morris Rosenfeld's presence aboard his 33-foot powerboat *Foto* was as predictable a part of the start of any major American ocean race or regatta as the race committee boat itself. Even now I keep expecting to see *Foto* hustling up to the line, with "Rosie" at the ready.

In 1978 I made a pilgrimage to the long-time New York studios of Morris Rosenfeld and Sons on West 23rd Street, where by appointment I was to meet son Stanley. The building was unexpectedly small and narrow; the entryway and elevator were almost frighteningly diminutive; the locked door to the office had a package slot with cover that, when pushed back, revealed only darkness within.

Returning to the street I waited on the sidewalk until a man with a big folder under his arm appeared, introduced himself as Stan Rosenfeld, and ushered me back into his elevator. Even with the lights turned on, his office showed up long, narrow, and sombre. Endless shelves covered the side walls. Tables were arranged down the center of the room. Everywhere there were labeled cardboard boxes. The boxes contained the finest collection of yachting negatives in America, if not the world.

My list of some 20 requests puzzled Stan by its diversity. When I explained they were boats I had sailed on, he replied, "We'll see about that." From his files he quickly located the English-owned *Lexia*, including a crew shot with me in it. He found all my other requests just as easily—among them several views of the famous great Herreshoff schooner *Ingomar* taken in the first years of the century.

I am not alone in hoping that the Rosenfeld Collection will ultimately end up in the hands of an institution or individual that is in a position, financially and otherwise, to save it from the ravages of time, and to catalog and store the photos for the enjoyment and study of future generations. Otherwise yachting history will sustain an incalculable loss.

The marine photographer whom I know best is Norman Fortier, a neighbor and good friend for nearly 40 years. Born and brought up here in New Bedford, he became a tenant of Concordia Company shortly after his release from the World War II Navy, in which he served as a naval air photographer. Realizing that a boat business benefits greatly from good photographic service, Concordia built for Norman a small shed studio, later slightly enlarged, right on our property. We also assigned him a space in our basin for a Palmer Scott-built 23-foot motor boat named—aptly—*Norman Fortier*. Norman's long association with Concordia has been a happy one for all concerned. In addition to his photographic business, Norman has a flourishing career as a marine painter and watercolorist.

George Yater is a professional photographer I first came to know in Fort Lauderdale, when *Prospector* was being built there on the eve of World War II. George and his wife, Shirley, later moved to Truro on Cape Cod, where George continues to serve his friends and customers with first-rate photographs.

My brother, Louie, Uffa Fox, my neighbor Eliot Stetson's Uncle Ted, and others, known and unknown, have also contributed greatly to the photographic record of *A Life in Boats*. And as these pages suggest, even I have enjoyed trying to do a little picture taking of my own.

All photographs not listed above are from the author's collection.

Index to Illustrations

Index to Text

PROVIDENCE

N

FALL RIVER

MARION

BRISTOL

Acushnet River

MATTAPOI

Prudence
Island

NEW BEDFORD

FAIRHAVEN

DARTMOUTH
(see detail)

WEST
ISLAND

NARRAGANSETT BAY

Sakonnet River

Westport River

East Branch

NONQUITT

Sconticut
Neck

CONANICUT ISLAND

Round Hill Pt.

Dumpling
Rocks

BUZZARDS

NAUSHON
ISLAND

NEWPORT

LITTLE
COMPTON

Slocum's
Neck

Mishaum
Pt.

Barney's
Joy Pt.

Westport
Harbor

Gooseberry Neck

Penikese Island

Pasque
Island

Sakonnet Pt.

Nashawena Island

Quick's
Hole

Robinson's

Brenton
Pt.

CUTTYHUNK
ISLAND

*Canapitsit
Channel*

Brenton
Reef
Lightship

VINEYARD

Brenton
Reef
Lightship

APPONAGANSETT

SHIPYARD LANE
& CLEVELAND BOATYARD

PADANARAM

Little I.

BRIDGE

YACHT
CLUB

Rockland

Clark Cove

Gay Head

POINT JUDITH

N

SOUTH
WHARF

Our
House

BAY VIEW

Ricketson's Pt.

Squibnocket
Pond

BIRCHFIELD

BREAKWATER

P.O. WHARF

*Padanaram
Harbor*

NONQUITT

Nomans
Land

ROUND HILL

White Rock

Salter's
Pt.

Round Hill
Pt.

Dumpling Rocks

DARTMOUTH
(DETAIL)

Mishaum Pt.

Miles

0   ½   1